Angie.

Thanks for being there for me.

Just remember show your teeth and things will shine.. Keep out of trouble. A sister like you hurts to leave behind .

Nuff love

Bye

See you soon.

Love you

Simone

The ENCYCLOPEDIA of SECRET KNOWLEDGE

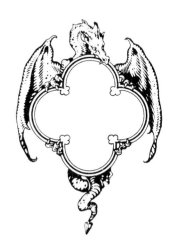

The ENCYCLOPEDIA of SECRET KNOWLEDGE

Charles Walker

ACKNOWLEDGEMENTS

All the photographs in this book were taken by Charles Walker and supplied
by the Charles Walker Collection Ltd. – an archive of arcane images marketed by
Images Colour Library, in London, and by Stock Montage, Chicago, IL, USA.

Charles Walker would like to thank all those who have permitted him to photograph, and use in
this book, arcane material from private and public collections. He would like to thank especially
Amiens Cathedral, Basilica of San Miniato (Florence), Cliffe Castle (Keighley), the Dar al Athar al
Islammiyyah (Kuwait), Dave Carson, David Murgatroyd, the Egyptian Museum (San José), Fay
Pomerance, Gordon Wain, Graham Fenn-Edwards, the Horniman Museum (London), Ray
Sherwin, the Sacra di San Michele (Val di Susa) and Dr. Wu Jing-Nuan.

This edition published by Limited Editions in 1995

First published in 1995 by Rider
an imprint of Ebury Press
Random House · 20 Vauxhall Bridge Road · London SW1V 2SA

Random House Australia (Pty) Limited
20 Alfred Street · Milsons Point · Sydney · New South Wales 2061 · Australia

Random House New Zealand Limited
18 Poland Road · Glenfield · Auckland 10 · New Zealand

Random House South Africa (Pty) Limited
PO Box 337 · Bergvlei · South Africa

Random House UK Limited Reg. No. 954009

Designed by Martin Lovelock
Edited by Alison Wormleighton

Printed in Italy by New Interlitho, S.p.a., Milan

A CIP catalogue record for this book is available from the British Library

ISBN 0 0918 1113 9

10 9 8 7 6 5 4 3 2 1

CONTENTS

INTRODUCTION:
THE LANGUAGE OF THE BIRDS

The key [to the Secret Archaic Doctrine] must be turned seven times before the whole system is divulged. We will give it but one turn, and thereby allow the profane one glimpse into the mystery.
(H.P. BLAVATSKY, *THE SECRET DOCTRINE*, 1888, VOL. I, P. XXXVIII)

he thirteenth-century occultist Michael Scot once insisted that honey falls from the air into flowers, whence it is collected by the bees. To us, the idea is fanciful, yet Scot was versed in the secret arts, and he knew that the bee is an ancient symbol for the human soul, while honey is the thing which feeds the soul. Scot was writing in what used to be called the LANGUAGE OF THE BIRDS – the secret speech of the occultists.

The Language of the Birds, sometimes called the GREEN LANGUAGE, was not one of

---

SYMBOL OF INITIATION

(*Left*)This fish with a golden key is one of the most enduring symbols of initation, expressed in fairytales. The fish is the initiate – a dweller on two planes – who swims in the sea (symbol of the spiritual world) and swallows the key that unlocks Wisdom of the material and spiritual planes. Having assimilated this Wisdom, he or she then returns the key to the earth.

NOURISHING THE SOUL

This engraving shows the symbol of the Rosicrucian rosy-cross, with its layers of seven-fold petals, tended by bees, symbolizing human souls. The Latin translates, "The Rose gives honey to the bees." The bees are taking nourishment from the rosy-cross, which symbolizes a renewed Christ impulse: the rose is Christ growing upon the painful, spiny cross. From Robert Fludd's *Clavis Philosophiae, et Alchymiae*, 1633.

mere arbitrary symbolism. The symbols it used were derived from cosmic truths: it was no accident that the bee was chosen to represent the soul. The occultists recognized that the temperature of the hive was always the same, and that, by a curious coincidence, this corresponded to the temperature of the human body. Since bees live in the hive, and human souls from time to time live in bodies, it was therefore cosmically appropriate to use the bee as symbol of the other "hive-dweller", the human soul.

Many occult systems adopted the Language of the Birds to express their secret teachings. For example, the Rosicrucians, a fraternity concerned with esoteric knowledge (that is, secret or forbidden knowledge), and especially with Christian esoteric thought, used the bees, hovering around the rose in the engraving (*left*) as symbol of the human soul. The hive in the stained glass (*right*) is a related early symbol. This hive represents not only the industry of the bees, but also the "body corporate" – the idea or impulse which unites human souls in one spiritual undertaking.

Although ordinary symbolism may explain the hive as representing the notion of work, or communal activity (for bees have a reputation for being good workers), the symbolism is actually ARCANE. It is an example of what alchemists call an "arcanum", or "great secret". In terms of the Language of the Birds, the arcane symbolism of the hive relates to the fact that when groups of people meet and work together with clearly defined and wholesome aims, they are bathed in the warmth of the spiritual world. The hive, like the human body, is a self-sustaining warmth-system, which is not hermetically sealed from the outer world, yet which is designed to afford a satisfactory habitation for those inside – the bees or the soul. In fact, what we call the "ordinary" symbolism is very ancient, and may be traced back to the Mystery Schools, for in the ancient Egyptian hieroglyphics, the image of a bee, besides denoting the creature, also meant "work".

We shall return to this word from the Language of the Birds on page 25, to examine its meaning on a deeper level; meanwhile, let us turn to what Scot had in mind when he wrote of the "dew-fall" of honey.

When Scot tells us that honey falls from the skies, his arcane theme is quite simple: he is saying that all things fall from the air, from the invisible realm of the spiritual. All things are the gift of the gods – man, woman, nature, ideas are loaned to the earth, yet have their origins on high. In Scot's view, the bees that collect the sky-given "honey" are the occultists, who try to make sense of this perpetual manna, in the hope that they can strengthen their wings, destined to carry them back into that invisible creative realm.

The spiritual realm is bountiful with its myriad forms, and a hundred arcane philosophies have been constructed to explain them. A bewildering number of different occult devices and philosophies are now available to serve the esotericist and those who would seek to understand the world through occult lore. This book examines the main trends of these devices and philosophies, in such a way as to confound the modern prejudice that occultism is concerned only with the realms of darkness. Most of the arts and sciences which will be discussed in this book are forbidden, or have been forbidden at one time or another. Generally, they are forbidden by orthodox viewpoints, by people who sense in the darkness of the occult arts a threat. Yet the darkness which is part – and only part – of the occult studies is interwoven into the lives of all. Without the light, there could be no shadows, and by studying the shadows one may estimate the direction and strength of its creative source. The forbidden arts have been called the occult arts, simply because the word "occult" meant "hidden". Yet occult things are hidden only from those who are not prepared to look into them, without fear or prejudice concerning what may be discovered beyond the familiar things of the world.

In the popular imagination – an imagination poisoned by the superficial media in modern times – occultism has become the domain of the dark forces. Aleister Crowley, and his meddlings with drugs and demons, seems far more famous as an occultist than the esotericist Rudolf Steiner, who did so much to redeem the modern world. The popular view of occultism is erroneous: the real esotericists are far more interested in the angels than in the demons, far more involved with leading the world forward into spiritual development, than carrying it back into atavistic psychicism.

However, it is also true that the occultist, being so finely attuned to the exigencies of the invisible world, does not make the dangerous mistake of the moderns in either denying the existence of the demons, or ignoring them. The true occultist is interested in the dark things because he or she recognizes that light is born from darkness. The French esotericist Fulcanelli (a true master of the Language of the Birds), writes, "It was from the darkness of Chaos that light was extracted and its radiation assembled."

Occultists maintain that every action, no matter how beneficial for humanity, casts its shadow, just as all light casts a

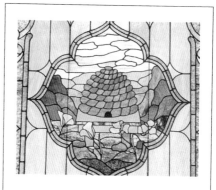

THE BEEHIVE

Stained glass in the Mormon Museum of Church History at Salt Lake City, a survival from the time when the Mormons had members who were in the Rosicrucian movement. Symbolism related to that of the previous illustration depicts the beehive as the place wherein the soul may grow. The nine levels of the hive almost certainly refer to the nine spiritual hierarchies which support the human realm.

shadow: they recognize that it is as necessary to work with the shadows as with the light. Only those ignorant of the secrets of the material world – such as the innocent Peter Pan – may think that light can exist without shadows. We may claim responsibility for the good deeds we do, yet we remain responsible for the shadows these good deeds leave behind. The occultist recognizes that every action in the light requires a corresponding action in the shadows. This is the main reason that occultists have been described as the "SHADOW WORKERS". The tragedy is that this appellation has been so fundamentally misunderstood.

The main branches of occultism, broadly represented in the four main sections of this book, are designed to reflect the dualities and mutual dependencies of Black and White. If the Black makes more hypnotic reading than the White, then perhaps this says something about our modern cast of mind, rather than about occultism. We are trained, partly by education and partly by natural indolence, not to play on the side of the angels – most of us prefer that easy slide downhill towards the dark streams of Hades, rather than the arduous climb towards the river of stars which is wisely called the Milky Way.

In the first section of the book, the nature of the OCCULT WORLD is examined in terms of world-systems and general philosophies. The traditional arts and sciences, such as alchemy, Rosicrucianism, the cabbala (the esoteric tradition of the Jews), and demonology, are examined first, followed by an assessment of some of the occult streams of the modern age, which by the very nature of modern consciousness are dominated by personalities. Thus, in these pages the irascible esotericist Gurdjieff and the wonder-struck journalistic Ouspensky rub shoulders with the scholarly Steiner and the verbosely syncretic Blavatsky – four unlikely bedfellows brought together by their interest in the occult image and destiny of man.

Next we examine WITCHCRAFT, and the

THE HAND OF DUALITY

The nineteenth-century occultist Eliphas Levi designed this curious wood engraving to illustrate the esoteric concern for the role of DUALISM in occultism. This was a hand raised in BENEDICTION towards Jehova. The shadow of the hand created upon the wall a shadow of a horned devil, the MALEDICTION. The hand and shadow cannot be separated; light and darkness are inextricably interwoven on the earth plane. Levi regarded this hand of duality as marking "Sacerdotal esotericism making the sign of excommunication ... the creation of the demon by mystery". From Eliphas Levi's *Dogme et Rituel de la Haute Magie*, 1862.

modern movement of wicca, which, for all the claims made to the contrary, has little to do with the demonism that lay at the roots of the ancient witchcraft. Traditional witchcraft had roots in heresy – in ideas which challenged the church – whereas modern wicca has its strongest roots in a romantic view of the past, and in New Age aspirations for a spiritually free future. The modern art of wicca is involved deeply with the search for satisfactory ritual, whereas there is little or no evidence that the witches of old practised any rituals at all.

Little effort is required to pass from witchcraft to MAGIC. In this section, we shall examine the white school of angel magic, as well as the dark school of demonic magic, observing that the followers of both tend to blur their definitions: one is never really sure whether the man or woman in the magic circle is conjuring angels of light or the more shadowy denizens of a murkier world. Curse magic, poppet magic – and even the powerful modern sigil magic – all too often conspire to misuse the gift of spirit for the purposes of self-aggrandisement. This is occultism gone awry, yet it is still part and parcel of the arcane realm.

Magic, which tends to the manipulation of occult forces for personal gain, often strays into the realm of predicting the future. This is understandable, for one who knows the future has power in his or her hands, and the lower reaches of magic were always dedicated to power-seeking.

However, this does mean that the section on DIVINATION follows easily upon that dealing with magic. Of necessity, divination proves to be the longest section in the book, for it explores in some depth half a dozen of the more popular forms of prediction, ranging from geomancy and the Chinese "I Ching", to palmistry and the Tarot. In a final general summary, it lists well over a hundred occult divinatory methods which appear to have stood the tests of time.

In this realm of divination, ASTROLOGY, which scarcely belongs to the forbidden arts in any real sense, dominates all the other occult sciences – indeed almost stands alone. It is the most cerebral of the occult sciences, and for centuries it has fed the other arcane sciences with its rich, closely defined terminology and its clear vision of the spiritual realms. However, astrology does not stand quite aloof: it is a philosophical machine, with some cogs enmeshed in occult philosophy, and others in the art of divination. In the section on astrology, we sketch something of the beauty of a philosophical schema, which is far removed from the superstitions of newspaper astrology.

The true astrology leads not towards the satisfaction of self-interest and the ego (an entity which can never be satiated), but towards the spiritual realms. In the past, it was taken for granted that an interest in history – ordinary, exoteric history (the knowledge of the profane, or non-secret) – was a good preparatory training for the approach to the esoteric. In former times, a historian, by virtue of his or her dedication to truth, could slip more easily through the guarded portals of the initiation schools. This is no longer the case, however, for the approach to history has all but lost its sense of the spiritual, and with it the ancient sense of wonder which was the historians' heritage.

Nowadays, the best modern training for someone who aspires to initiation is found in astrology. Flights of fancy offered by the esoteric branch of the science, tempered by the intense mental discipline required to practise the art of predictive techniques, make it a fertile ground for the growth of esoteric thought.

So much for the general divisions of the book, which reflect to some extent the divisions in the sciences of occultism. What, then, about the language of occultism, and that peculiar argot of the occultists, the Language of the Birds?

The word OCCULT is from a Latin word, *occultus*, meaning "hidden from sight". OCCULTISM is nothing other than the practice of, or belief in, knowledge which has been hidden from the sight of ordinary men and women. The work of the occultist is conducted in the secret darkness of the hive, wherein the temperature is especially adapted for spiritual work. Occultists study the hidden, or FORBIDDEN ARTS. These arts are forbidden not because they are evil but because they can be dangerous in the wrong hands. They are forbidden to all but a select few.

Occultists insist that only those who have earned the right to do so may study and learn their secrets. The occult wisdom cannot be dispensed to all and sundry, for there is a cosmic law ordaining that secret wisdom must be earned. There is nothing democratic about the OCCULT SCHOOLS which preserve the sacred lore – these schools are hieratic in structure, founded on the ancient practices of the mystery temples. Over the doors of these MYSTERY SCHOOLS was inscribed the injunction, "Learn, and keep silence."

INITIATES were forbidden, on pain of death, to proclaim an occult truth to anyone who had not been prepared to receive such truth. Training in the pre-initiation schools attached to the temples was arduous and could take many years: special moral faculties, and developed organs of perception, were required of those who wished to look with impunity on the sacred truths preserved in the mysteries. Silence about the forbidden knowledge was demanded not so much to protect the arcane lore and keep it in the hands of an elect, but to protect the uninitiated: there was a terrible danger confronting those on the pathway to occult knowledge.

In former times, the deeper truths of occultism could be reached only by way of INITIATION rituals, designed to open the inner eye of imagination, which the ancients called ENOICHIAN. All who sought to look into the higher and lower worlds, into what is now called the ASTRAL REALMS, had to be especially prepared, and led by degrees towards a vision of the higher worlds. To be permitted this experience, the person had to learn how to leave the physical body behind, and travel in the astral realm, to swim in the secret sea. This is why the initiates of certain mysteries were called DRAGONS or FISH: they could soar in the world of spirit, or dive into the universal ocean, yet keep contact with the earth. The legends of dragons as guardians of treasure in underground cells –

of fish that carried golden keys, or mysterious books, in their bodies – reveal a deep meaning in the light of these arcane terms.

Initiates were denizens of the TWO WORLDS of spirit and matter. Without the training which precedes initiation, the astrally free beginner might never find the way back from the spiritual realms to the physical body. He or she might well attain to a vision of the remarkable hidden world, yet would find it impossible to bring this knowledge back to earth. The unwilled artificial separation of the astral body from the physical eventually results in death; this was one of the dangers which the non-initiates would face in attempting to tamper with occult lore.

It is recorded in the occult books that the Roman Emperor, Nero, forced his way into the mysteries, commanding his priests (who were then the guardians of the occult lore) to initiate him. Threatened with death if they refused, the priests did allow this enforced initiation – almost certainly aware of its consequences. What Nero saw during his illegal sojourn in the invisible

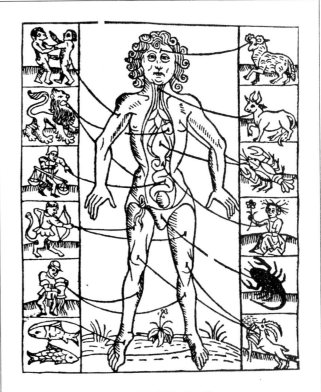

ZODIACAL MAN

The traditional astrological image of a man with twelve signs of the zodiac apportioned to his physical body. This image may be seen as a portrayal of the initiate – of the one who dwells in perfect unison with the spiritual realm. For example, since Pisces rules the feet, and is also the sign of Christ, the initiate is one who has learned to walk in the footsteps of the Son of God.

worlds drove him insane; this meddling with cosmic law is what brought the Emperor to incurable madness.

The first legitimate approach to the occult lore is by means of pictures. There are certain occult terms, with arcane and secret meanings, which are used in almost all the occult sciences, such as astrology, palmistry, alchemy and cabbala. While these arcane terms do tend to have specialist meanings within the particular disciplines, there is broad agreement as to what they mean in a general sense.

It is virtually impossible to understand even the most simple occult accounts of things without some knowledge of these basic terms. For this reason, before turning to the main divisions of occultism, we shall examine some of the arcane terms found in most of the occult disciplines. One instructive way of doing this is by glancing at a number of arcane images which portray these terms, either as personifications or in symbolic forms.

The first arcane image is alchemical, yet it illustrates many aspects of astrological, cabbalistic and magical lore.

It is the third plate (*left*) from the alchemical masterpiece of Steffan Michelspacher – the CABALA of 1616, which was sub-titled, "Cabala, Mirror of Art and Nature, in Alchemy". The image portrays the mountain of ALCHEMY, in which is a cave. In the cave is a magical room, reached by seven steps, each marked with one of the names of an alchemical process. Around the hill, like a splendid halo, is a circle marked with the twelve signs of the zodiac, and twelve alchemical SIGILS, or secret signs. On either side of the hill are terraces, on which stand personifications of the seven planets.

The four spaces which frame the halo of the zodiac are occupied by four small circles, marked with the words *Ignis*, *Aeris*, *Aquae* and *Terrae*. These are Latin terms for the ELEMENTS.

In occult lore, there are five elements, none of which is discernible by ordinary means of perception. The four elements (Fire, Air, Water and Earth) are held in union by the fifth element, or Quintessence, which is often called the AKASHYA, or Etheric, by modern occultists.

Some occultists claim that a person who could comprehend the workings of the five elements would have the key to all earthly knowledge. This is one reason why the circles are so prominently displayed in the Michelspacher plate: the experiments of the alchemists were directed towards investigating the secret realms of each and all of the elements. The guardian spirits of the elements, appropriately called the ELEMENTALS, have a variety of names, but in the Western tradition these are the GNOMES (Earth), SYLPHS (Air), UNDINES (Water) and SALAMANDERS (Fire).

The small circle marked IGNIS represents FIRE. This is regarded by occultists as the most spiritual of the four material elements. The term does not refer to the incandescent gases of flame with which we are familiar, but to a state of nature, in which materiality (the lower four elements), through COMBUSTION, seeks to rise to a higher spiritual level of being. It is a state of lightness, of spiritual warmth. In the human being, the Fire is seen in the CHOLERIC temperament. The warmth in the hive, and the warmth of the body are pertinent examples of this elemental Fire. We all know that if the temperatures of these are significantly disturbed, and the column of warmth which is the human body becomes very cold, or very hot, the soul flees this habitation, and the body is left suspended lifeless, in the state which ordinary people call death.

The small circle marked AERIS represents AIR. This is one of the five elements. The word does not refer to the mixture of gases we breathe. It refers to a condition of

THE ALCHEMICAL MOUNTAIN

(*Left*) The schema of alchemy, revealing the stages of perfection in attaining the philosophers' stone, the secret of life. Plate 3 from Steffan Michelspacher's CABALA, 1616.

nature, in which materiality is expressed as a gaseous, volatile and changeable nature. In the human being, the Air personality is called the SANGUINE. The combustion in the lungs, which keeps the physical body warm, is brought about by the air, for combustion in the inner caves of the lungs depends upon oxygen. Yet, it is also true that the column of warmth which is the living human body loses its heat to the air around it; warmth is conducted from the body by the same agency which creates warmth. "The inner becomes the outer" is one of the most important of the occult maxims. This is one reason why the occultist may say that life is death, and death is life: the life-process is also the death-process, and the altercation between Fire and Air marks this cycle of birth and death.

The small circle marked AQUAE represents WATER. The term does not refer merely to the liquid we use, but to a fluid condition of nature: in occultism, blood is water – yet to be serviceable, it must be warm water. Blood is a very special liquid warmed by the combustion of Air and Fire. In the human being, Water is seen in the PHLEGMATIC personality, which is somewhat lethargic, until galvanized into the service of others by the warmth of love. Water is the occult symbol for the inner unconscious realms, and for the outer spiritual realms. This is why there are rivers in mythological Hades, and why Lucifer sits immersed in a frozen lake at the centre of his hell. This is why the occultists created a mythology that named the myriad filaments of stars the MILKY WAY, or the SACRED RIVER.

The small circle marked TERRAE represents EARTH. The word does not refer to the materiality of rocks, soils and minerals which form the outer core of the planet earth. It refers to a quality of inert fixity in nature, to that which is solidified, non-fluid and heavy. Thus, at a certain low temperature, water becomes ice, and expresses the nature of Earth. According to the occult tradition, the mineral kingdom is light in a frozen state. In the human being, the Earth temperament is called the MELANCHOLIC. At its extreme, this becomes a paralysis of soul, in which the personality feels weighed down by oppression, by a sense of foreboding fate, or by the notion that the inertia of the body is too much to handle. The main fear or fears that we all carry are derived from the Earth element, which is interwoven into our being.

When the astrologer seeks to determine from our horoscope the motivating fear which permeates our outlook on life, they will look towards Saturn, for this is the heavy planet of earth. It is no accident that the ancients devised a symbol to represent the dark planet which combined the half-circle of soul being weighted down by the heavy cross of matter (the four arms of the cross representing the four elements).

Earth also refers to the planet upon which we dwell. Most systems of astrology (which inform such occult systems of alchemy, and so on), regard the earth as being at the spiritual centre of the cosmos: the earth is the crucible in which the spiritual beings work to perfect man. The melancholic is right, for the Earth element in all of us is the heavy cross of destiny which, whether we wish it or not, we must carry and eventually redeem. The old Christian tradition that the cross upon which Christ died was made from four different types of wood, reflects this idea that the spirit of man is charged with redeeming the fourfold weight of elements which are manifest in the materiality of his body.

This is one reason why astrology, in the face of the theories of Copernicus, adamantly remains GEOCENTRIC (earth-centred) in its outlook. Whatever the cosmoconception of science, occultism insists that the earth is the spiritual centre of the solar system. The seven planetary figures which stand upon the mountain of the Michelspacher plate are guardians of the earth.

As we have seen, the occult tradition teaches that there are five elements, yet at first glance the plate does not appear to have symbolized the all-important fifth element. In fact, the symbol is so large that we tend to overlook it. The entire halo-circle, at the periphery of which is the zodiac, represents the FIFTH ELEMENT, or QUINTESSENCE, which has many names in the occult tradition. It is the invisible force which holds in pact the four elements of Fire, Air, Water and Earth, which is why Michelspacher has placed it in the centre of the four smaller circles, binding them together, as it were, in a secret geometry.

The seven figures which guard the alchemical hill are representatives of the seven PLANETS. Starting at the bottom left, and moving clockwise, we see the following.

VENUS

The female holding the flaming heart is VENUS, the planetary expression of love. In a horoscope chart, she represents the spiritual impulse as it is manifested through the physical body. Venus represents the capability of a person to cooperate with others: Venus is a warm planet, and works well in the warmth engendered by consciously shared aims. When strong in a horoscope, Venus lends a strong love for beauty, an appreciation of the finer things in life, and an attraction to music. When weak, she restricts cooperation, and suggests a retiring or emotionally confused disposition; the person may be lacking in confidence, lazy or opportunistic.

In alchemical imagery, Venus is often the symbol of sexuality – of delight in the physical. However, in the occult and alchemical tradition, there are two Venuses (astrologically, the Venus of Libra and the Venus of Taurus), one of which is the beautiful virgin, the other the wanton. Often, the Venus of Libra holds the balance, a sign of her inner equilibrium, while the Venus of Taurus holds a mirror, an outer sign of her vanity and concern for self. The Venus of this alchemical plate holds a mask, symbolizing her wish to dissemble and appear what she is not: she feels herself a wanton yet wishes to appear a virgin. In this duality of symbolism lies much of the occult mystery of the planet.

MARS

The male figure with sword and shield is MARS, the physical planet. In a horoscope, Mars is an index of the energy of the native, of his or her ability to endure: the sword

THE SEVEN DEADLY SINS

Not surprisingly, demon images proliferated in the religious images of hell and in those pictorial cycles which warned against the seven DEADLY SINS, or unredeeming actions, of which this early sixteenth-century woodcut is a splendid example. Each of the sins is identified by its name on the banderole-like sword. Woodcut by Baldung Grien: loose print, probably from *Das Buch Granatapfel*, 1511.

symbolizes aggressive energy, the shield the protection which endurance offers. A strong Mars means that the person is constantly on the go, always anxious to be moving or doing. In a horoscope, Mars is an index of the excess to which the person is inclined. Mars is enterprising, courageous, confident and proud, yet easily given to quarrelling. This last tendency explains why (in alchemical images, at least) he is often portrayed as a soldier, or as a swaggering braggard. Mars is opposed by the soft Venus, for while she is concerned with love, Mars is concerned with the sex drives. The Rosicrucian Jakob Boehme called Mars the "turning wheel of desire". The wheel is an excellent image, for it moves inexorably and will crush all those who try to impede it. When badly placed in a birth chart, Mars may be explosive, tending therefore to recklessness and destructive violence. POSITIVE MARS, which is the Mars of Aries, is usually pioneering and outward-looking. NEGATIVE MARS, which is the Mars of Scorpio, is usually domineering and inward-looking.

In occult symbolism, Mars represents the urge to incarnation, the desire to descend into flesh. Once that incarnation is complete (which is to say, once the armour of the soldier has been buckled on) Mars begins to direct its energies towards a redemptive process. As the sixteenth-century occultist Paracelsus says, "It is difficult for a prince or a king to be produced out of an unfit and common man: yet Mars acquires this position with a strong and pugnacious hand." Without Mars, there would be no spiritual advancement, no redemption. Through Mars, mankind may take upon himself the halo which symbolizes the spiritual realm, or the spiritual vision. Through the grit and determination of Mars, the mirror of Venus is transformed into a speculum of the spiritual realm, its circumference an image of the zodiacal belt. If this marvellous work is not undertaken, the energies of Mars may turn to mere violence, and the energies which might have been used for redemption will lie unused, stored up in some karmic vault, themselves awaiting redemption. This 'karmic vault' is the hell of the demons (*left*).

The crowned male with a wand of office is King SOL, an image of the SUN. In occult lore, the Sun is the creative, self-expressive power in the world – it is the image of a benign king, working his rules by fiat (hence the wand of office). In astrology and alchemy, it is an index of the life-force, of the spirituality of the person or substance. The Sun, in the material realm, is symbolic of the life-force inherent within an object; for example, the solar element in minerals is the virtue distilled from light.

SUN

In a horoscope, the Sun has a dual identity, for it is both positive and negative in its working. A positive Sun gives dignity, self-reliance, generosity and an affectionate, commanding nature. A Sun under pressure tends towards excess and prodigality – the person may be showy, over-confident and egotistical. The Sun is a symbol of the INTERNAL FATHER, of the inner Male principle, or Animus, and is contrasted in its workings with the Moon, which explains why the female personification of this planet stands on the opposite side of Michelspacher's hill.

MERCURY

Standing in glory at the top of the hill, balancing on one foot as though to show that he is so refined as to scarcely belong to the earth, is MERCURY. This is the planet of volatility and communication, and he carries in one hand the CADUCEUS (a wand entwined by two snakes). This marks him out as the messenger of the gods, the go-between who carries the initiation wisdom. (Initiates were sometimes called SNAKES, for they could wriggle into the dark secrets preserved at the interior of the earth.) On his feet are wings, symbols of the rapidity with which he can transform from earth-creature to god.

A strong Mercury in a personal horoscope makes the native quick in mind, and highly expressive – fluent in talk, and quick to grasp the intentions or thoughts of others. Mercury is the one planet which will take rather than give, so the mercurial mind tends to live off the ideas of others. This tendency to take or borrow is an important aspect of the mercurial nature, for it works as a catalyst, absorbing into its nature the characteristics of other entities with which it is in contact. This perhaps explains why Mercury is regarded as being sexless, and why it is called the ANDROGYNE, for it will borrow femininity from a female contact, and masculinity from a masculine contact. Its androgyne nature is unique among the planets, which is one reason why it stands at the pinnacle of the mountain. A reminder of its dual nature is seen in the symbolism which has only one foot resting on the female (Mother) earth.

In alchemy, Mercury is one of the THREE PRINCIPLES, the communicating principle between the cold, cerebral activity of SALT, and the febrile will-forces of SULPHUR (*see page 34*). Since one of the searches in alchemy is for a union between these three principles, Mercury is sometimes said to be the name of the STONE. According to the Swiss occultist Paracelsus, Mercury is the alchemical AZOTH, the SECRET STONE OF THE WISE, the DEW OF HEAVEN (*see page 25*), the VIRGIN'S MILK, and so on. In alchemy, each of the planets has its own Mercury, or secret diluent – a spiritual energy stolen by the thief Mercury.

Descending clockwise from Mercury, we see the female figure which holds in one hand a lighted lamp, in the other a spear. On her head she is crowned with a crescent MOON, to leave us in no doubt that she is intended to represent this luminary. The Moon is the symbol of the imaginative, reflective, interiorizing power in our world. In astrology and alchemy, the Moon is an index of the withdrawal principle, and of the subconscious, or hidden side of life (sometimes called the DARK WORLD), in contrast to the light world of the Sun. The Moon governs the receptive, secluded and sensitive side of human nature. It represents the principle of growth, the proliferation of form, the fecundity of the womb of nature.

MOON

It is said in occultism that the Sun will inhabit the forms nurtured by the Moon; this is another way of expressing Blake's remarkable dictum, "Eternity is in love with the productions of time." The Moon rules the productions of time, that which unfolds from eternity into the dual world that dwells in time.

In a horoscope, the Moon has a dual identity, for it is both positive and negative in its working. A positive Moon gives sensitivity, impressionability, changeability, and (sometimes) a retentive shrewdness and practicality. A negative, or "baleful", Moon, which is under pressure, intensifies imagination to a point where it tends to lose contact with reality: the crescent becomes a heavy weight, which dulls the brain to feverish sleep. Under these circumstances, the subject becomes morbidly concerned with self, and strangely subject to the mutability of fortune. The Moon is a symbol of the INTERNAL MOTHER, or Anima, of the inner Female principle, and is contrasted in its workings with the Sun.

In occultism, the term SUBLUNAR, or "below-moon", has a particular meaning. It was believed in ancient times that the earth was encased not only in its own spiritual aura, but also in the spiritual aura of the moon. The earth was under the lunar influence, and was itself sublunar. In occult mythology, the earth is under the seductive and baleful influence of the Moon – a belief expressed in the mythological story which tells how the goddess SELENE (the Moon) falls in love with the sleeping shepherd, ENDYMION.

In the mystery wisdom, it was maintained that the cosmic rules on the sublunar plane were different from those on higher planes. For example, Aristotle taught that beyond the orb of the Moon everything conspired to move in spiritual circles, whereas on the sublunar plane, everything conspired to move in straight lines. This distinction, which is a spiritual view of the contrast between matter and spirit, became fundamental to occult thought. The sublunar world is mutable – its most fundamental phenomenon being change. In contrast, the spiritual extra-lunar world was long supposed immutable, unchangeable.

It is said that the NOVA, or new star, that appeared in the constellation Cassiopeia in November 1572 (which was observed telescopically by the astrologer Tycho Brahe) demonstrated for the first time that the heavens were subject to mutability and were not perfect. This perception had a baleful influence on human thinking, for it removed any last notion of there being an incorruptible sphere in the cosmos. After 1572, there was no longer the certainty that there was a spiritual place in which one might rest secure. A nova is a sudden increase in brightness of an existing star, but in the days before telescopes, a nova had all the appearance of being the creation of a new star *ex nihil*, from nothing.

At first glance, the next figure on the mountain might be taken for a female, wearing a dress. However, the wand of office and the bundle of thunderbolts grasped in the right hand reveal it to be JOVE, or JUPITER, the god of thunder and lightning. Jupiter is the planet of spiritual expansion and represents the speculative thought of the human being – that kind of thought which carries one beyond the confines of matter into the realm of the arcane, or spiritual. Jupiter governs the moral life (for better or worse) so that a well-developed Jupiter in a horoscope gives

JUPITER

a morally sound, generous, optimistic, loyal, popular and successful personality. A poor Jupiter brings almost the opposite characteristics, such as self-indulgence, prodigality and a recklessness in regard to the material well-being of self and others. This powerful duality is well-noted in alchemy, where the ancient texts emphasize that the planet has, hidden

SATURN

within its nature, a great deal of gold (Sun) and not a little silver (Moon) – a mixture of Fire and Water. No doubt, this feminine element is represented in the dress which the Michelspacher Jupiter wears.

The seventh figure, carrying the distinguishing scythe, and grasping in his right hand a baby, is SATURN. Both these symbols represent Time, reminding us that Saturn was once called Cronos. (The Greek word *kronos* means "time" and is the original of our own words chronology and chronometer.) The scythe is the great knife which cuts down all men and women when their time is up. The baby is not a symbol of the New Year (as our New Year greeting cards would have us believe), or even of the newly reincarnating soul, but a reminder of the myth which has Saturn devour his own children. This is yet another symbol of death to which all form is heir. In the myth, the children were saved when a stone was substituted in the place of one of them. The stone Saturn devoured was the secret stone of the alchemists – the stone of power which would preserve eternal youth.

Saturn, with his cruel knife, and his eyes fixed on the produce of his own loins, is the planet of restriction. When strong in a personal horoscope, Saturn represents the ability to concentrate, to persevere, and introduce structure and order into a situation. It is an index of reliability, reminding us that the planet rules over the skeletal frame, which keeps the human being erect, and prevents us from giving way to the earth's gravitational pull as useless amoebic jellies. When weak, Saturn becomes rigidified – conservative, emotionally cold, and despondent to the point of acute melancholia. The astrologer examines Saturn in a chart to determine the motivating fears of the person. The planet governs bureaucracy, which may organize society, and enhance creative life, or which may degenerate into legalized tyranny, and make creative life impossible through its own intolerable concern for minutiae.

In alchemy, Saturn is another name for lead, said by some to be the first matter of the philosophers (the alchemists) because its very inertness makes it a fine receptacle for the injection of life. It is no accident that the sixteenth-century alchemists who sought to manufacture androids, or ARTIFICIAL MEN (see page 118), used skeletons from charnel-houses, for bones are ruled by Saturn. The secret stone which the alchemists seek is said to be made of lead, and is hidden in the centre of the earth. This stone is made from the energies of Saturn, the time-spirit, who used to stand at the furthest limits of the planetary orbs, in the Ptolemaic planetary system, beyond which were the time-free entities that had rule over the stars, the zodiac and the great Prime Mover. This outer rim of time-bound Saturn marked the outermost limit of man's experience. The discovery of the more distant planets, Uranus, Neptune and Pluto, has put an end to this meaningful cosmic vision, yet Saturn still remains the time-barrier which only the secret lead of the alchemists may break.

LUMINARIES

On the rooftop of the magical house which is found in the interior of Michelspacher's alchemical mountain are symbols of the Sun and the Moon. Personifications of these already stand guard on the mountain, so we must assume that these are interior lights, which lighten the inner darkness of the mountain and the inner life of the weary alchemist. These are, indeed, the LUMINARIES. In medieval times, it was believed that some of the light from the Moon was autogenetic (though, of course, the principle of reflected solar light was understood); this is why our own satellite, which we now know to have no light of its own, was regarded as a source of light.

In alchemy, the two Luminaries are the solar ANIMUS, or spirit (which finds expression through the consciousness principle), and the lunar ANIMA, or soul (which finds expression through the unconscious). In Michelspacher's mountain (which also represents COSMIC MAN, or the archetypal man and woman), the spirit and soul are the living principles which make the earth, or sarcophagus of flesh, alive. The Sun and Moon are in the starry sky (one may see ten stars around the Moon), which is the astral sky, pointing us to an arcane term which needs some definition.

The word ASTRAL is derived from the Greek for star (*aster*), and used to denote the higher world, regarded as synonymous with the starry world. In the Michelspacher plate, the astral world is symbolized by the huge circle, fringed by the zodiacal band, which relates to the realm of stars. The astral is the spiritual realm which remains invisible to ordinary sight, but which is perceptible to clairvoyance. In the HIGHER ASTRAL dwell the angels, and higher spiritual beings. In the LOWER ASTRAL dwell the demons and the various SHADOW-BEINGS or ASTRAL SHELLS, which the cabbalists call KLIPPOTH. The higher astral is the proper home of the human higher principle, which is called the ego (*see page 55*). The ten stars around the Moon refer to the nine spiritual hierarchies, or angelic beings, and man, who is sometimes called the TENTH HIERARCHY.

The astral body is the spiritual seat of the emotional life, called by the ancient alchemists and Rosicrucians the SIDEREAL BODY. The astral body of man has the function of acting as a bridge between the ego (which cannot perceive the material world directly) and the physical body. Just as there is a higher and a lower astral in the cosmic realm, so there are a higher and a lower astral (stars and flames) in man (*illustration, page 56*).

Clairvoyants describe the astral body as being of a fine, highly luminous and vibrating nature, flooded with colours of indescribable beauty. When a seventeenth-century occultist was asked to draw the higher astral body, he could do no better than portray the physical frame studded with stars (*illustration, page 56*). The astral body may be seen by clairvoyant vision as all but detached from the physical body, when the latter is asleep, or in a swoon or trance.

It is the astral body which has the capability of ASTRAL TRAVEL, or travel in the starry spheres. Special discipline or occult training is usually required to undertake this astral travel consciously, and to remember afterwards the experiences such travel offers. Dreams are usually the shadowy memories of astral travel. Generally speaking, however, all people travel in the astral during sleep, although they will not remember their experiences or be able to undertake such travel consciously without special preparation.

It is essential when considering the astral forces to glance at another occult term – ETHERIC. The etheric forces are those invisible powers which work into the physical to make this a suitable recipient for life. When a body is in cellular activity it is bathed in an etheric force: when a body is in molecular activity (but not in cellular activity) it is not bathed in an etheric force. All living beings have etheric bodies; when the etheric forces are withdrawn, then the body, formerly alive, drops to the earth in death, and resolves itself back into its constituent elements. This is one reason why the etheric body is called the LIFE-BODY, or the BODY OF FORMATIVE FORCES. Curiously, the medieval occultists called it the ENS VENENI, or principle of poisons, probably because it could be used to heal the physical body by drawing away from it poisons and evils.

We cannot leave the remarkable Michelspacher plate without asking about the two figures in the foreground. Who are these men? One is blindfold and represents the ordinary man, the MUNDANE MAN, sometimes called the

THE FOOL

The Fool card of the Tarot pack. In terms of a non-esoteric interpretation, the Fool is an ordinary man, but this is a facade designed to hide the initiate who has exteriorized his inner anger. This exteriorization is the dog at his feet. He is a wanderer on the spiritual plane as much as on the material. Each of the Tarot images has been designed to contain both an exoteric and an esoteric interpretation.

FOOL, who is oblivious to the mysteries before him. In the arcane system of the Tarot deck, the unnumbered first card is just such an ordinary man (*above*); the world of mysteries is before him, symbolized by the remaining arcana of twenty-one mystery cards of the pack. The Fool is the one unprepared – the one who cannot read the signs of the time, and the meaning of the world. He is the one who neither seeks, nor will receive, initiation. The hare which runs away from him is symbolic of the opportunity for initiation that will soon be lost in the interior of the earth.

The other figure, at the bottom left, is using a ferret to dig his hare from the labyrinth beneath the magical mountain. This action symbolizes an arcane alchemical axiom, contained in a word from the Language of the Birds – VITRIOL. The word is made up from the first letters of an alchemical Latin adage, found in many occult texts:

Visita Interiora Terrae Rectificandoque Invenies Occultum Lapidem.

Some claim that all alchemical secrets are contained in this adage, which may be translated as:

Visit the interior of the earth, and by rectifying, you will discover the hidden stone.

The hidden STONE is the PHILOSOPHERS' STONE, the secret stone which will heal all sickness, preserve youth eternally, and transmute dross matter into gold. It is the secret of life, the stone which, in the myth, Saturn was made to eat in place of his own son.

The "house" in the cave of the mountain is in the form of a hive, reminding us that the alchemists often wrote of the heavenly dew, or stone, as a honey. In the beehive was found the sacred stone. The stone was called the DEW OF MAY, the HERB OF SATURN or the VEGETABLE STONE in the Language of the Birds, and whatever the secret meaning in these terms, it is evident that the stone is not an ordinary stone at all, just as Michael Scot's bee was no ordinary bee.

In fact, now that we have glanced at the meaning of a few arcane terms, we are in a better position to consider once again the Language of the Birds, the secret symbolism of the occultists. On page 8 we examined something of the meaning of the bee in this language, and saw that it was a reference to the human soul, dwelling in the hive of the physical body. Now, because we have learned a few occult terms, we may look at this bee from a different standpoint.

Let us consider again the bees and honey to which Michael Scot referred. The Latin for bee is APIS. This word also happens to be the Latin name for the sacred bull, which was worshipped at Memphis, in ancient Egypt. The fact that the bee and the bull were considered together in the Greek and Roman mystery religions is confirmed by the fact that images of these two creatures are found on the body of the multi-breasted goddess, DIANA

DIANA OF EPHESUS

The bees sculpted upon the body of the ancient statue of Diana of Ephesus, now at Selkuc, Turkey, are a reminder that the bee was one of the sacred images, widely used in the Mystery Schools. Diana of Ephesus was the most important female cult goddess of the ancient world, until her role was taken over by the Virgin Mary.

THE HERMES BIRD

The Hermes Bird stands amidst the seven feathers which pierce the waters from which it will be reborn. The solar water which falls in droplets around the bird is a symbol of rebirth, or reincarnation, which is the destiny of the phoenix-like bird. From a copy of George Ripley's alchemical scroll, circa 1470.

OF EPHESUS (*photograph, page 25*), a cult image directly from the ancient mysteries relating to the feminine spiritual principle. This Diana is a prototype of the pagan Egyptian goddess, Isis, and the Christian Virgin Mary.

In the Language of the Birds, the word Apis refers to a duality of nature – to the creature of flight, and to the heavy creature of earth, the sacrificial bull. This duality made the bee a useful symbol for the initiate, who, as we have seen, was the inhabitant of two worlds: the initiated human was free to wing through the astral realms, yet remained also a dweller on the lower physical plane, in the familiar human body.

The Rosicrucians who preserved the word Apis, and the image of the bee, were aware of these different levels of meaning, and could speak in their esoteric language on a level which was beyond the comprehension of the uninitiated. The bee symbol was more than merely an image of the soul – it was an image of the initiate soul, of the BULL-BEE, or WINGED BULL, which had the power granted the initiate to live in the two worlds. In the Rosicrucian print (*page 8*), it is not mere souls which are seeking the honey of the mystic rose, but the souls of initiates. The Latin *Dat Rosa Mel Apibus* translates as, "The Rose gives honey to the bees," which means that the mystic rose (which is Christ) gives spiritual sustenance to the initiates.

We note that this splendid rose, tended by the three bees, is supported on a cross, rather than a rose-branch, to indicate that the symbolism is Rosicrucian (Rose + Cross) in origin.

Since the bees are initiate souls, the hive becomes, by extension, not merely a symbol of the physical body of an ordinary man (nor even a community of ordinary men) – it is the place wherein dwells the initiate soul, or the place wherein the initiates work together. It is the temenos, or sacred site around the temple, or the Mystery School itself. Inside the cave of the philosopher's mountain (the MONS PHILOSOPHORUM, as the alchemical hill is often called) of the Michelspacher plate (*page 14*) is the sacred hive, or school, which dispenses wisdom and knowledge to the world outside.

Beyond the mountain, yet centred on this inner school, is the great circle of the spiritual realm. Earlier, we saw that this circle is the protective Quintessence. It is more, however, for it is a symbol of the SPIRITUAL WORLD, which bathes all created things in its glory. At the very centre of the circle is the PHOENIX, a symbol of the resurrection, rebirth and reincarnation. It is at the centre because in occult lore the centre is always striving to reach the periphery: God is defined as a circle, whose centre is everywhere. The phoenix seeks to fly to the fires of the stars, which will consume him, yet he will be born again. The centre will become the circumference, which will, in turn, enfold upon itself, and emerge at the centre.

At the periphery is the zodiac with its twelve images. These are the images of the zodiacal signs – yet they are more. The twelve signs of the zodiac have the same names and symbols as the twelve CONSTELLATIONS.

The constellations, or ASTERISMS, are star patterns in the skies, in which distinctive figures have been traced. Although many of these asterisms have great antiquity, some are fairly modern. The star groups for different civilizations are not always the same, for it is possible to trace fanciful figures in a variety of different star groupings.

The asterisms are made up from distinctive FIXED STARS. This term is something of a misnomer these days, since in terms of ordinary human time, all stars appear to be fixed. The term was used originally to distinguish those stars which appeared to remain embedded in the sky's diurnal motion from the moving planets. This last word is from the Greek which meant "wanderers". The unmoving stars, all embedded in the same orb looked down serenely from their outermost position, into the concentric circles, or orbs, in which ran the planets. This explains why the Sun, which is technically a star, is still called a planet in astrology, for it had all the appearance of being a wanderer. The Moon, the most volatile-seeming of the heavenly bodies, was also classified as a planet, for similar reasons. Originally the planetary orbs were the imaginary concentric pathways, or belts, in which the planets moved, as they careered around the earth. Eventually, the name was confused for the bodies of the planets themselves.

The great auric circle of the magic mountain symbolizes one further thing: it is the GREATER WORLD, or cosmos. It is the universal womb which is attending the birth of humanity, the LESSER WORLD, or microcosm. The occultists rightly symbolize this greater world as a circle because it is a spiritual realm which has neither beginning nor end. This is also true of the Lesser World, which is man, whom occultists regard as being a small image of the cosmos, a potentially creative power, or star in the making, a nova.

Occultists teach that the Lesser World has no beginning or end because the human spirit, which dwells in the physical frame and is the real man, has always lived and will live for ever. The spirit, like the phoenix at the centre of the circle, dips again and again into physical form, and consumes it, in cycle after cycle of rebirths. For this is an occult truth – while the mythologies insist that the flames burn the bird to death as it rides its sea-born nest, the occultists know that the opposite is true. They know that it is the phoenix, or human spirit, which consumes the body with its own ardent desire for life. The phoenix, which the ancient alchemists called the HERMES BIRD (*left*), is the secret bird of the hermetic lore. This is, of course, the lore of Hermes, the Greek Mercury, who was master of all initiation. This bird is extraordinary, for it lights its own fire, lifetime after lifetime, and sails our earthly seas on waters that have no power to quench the flames.

THE OCCULT WORLD

Beneath the broad tide of human history there flow the stealthy undercurrents of the secret societies, which frequently determine in the depths the changes that take place upon the surface. These societies have existed in all ages and among all nations ...

(ARTHUR EDWARD WAITE, *THE REAL HISTORY OF THE ROSICRUCIANS*, 1887)

 remarkable engraving, used by the psychologist J.C. Jung in his study of flying saucers, has had a profound importance in occultism. This picture (*page 30*) is cut into two divisions by the arc of a circle, which separates the spiritual world from the material world. In the material realm we see the familiar symbols of the four elements. Fire is represented by the sun, Earth by the tree (which is rooted into the soil), Water by the lake in the distance, and Air by the star-studded sky.

The other division of the picture, to the left, represents the higher spiritual world. In this, the symbols of the four elements are not materialistic at all: we see the flames of Fire, the clouds of Air, and the rainbow which represents Water. The Earth itself has no place in this higher world. Above the symbols of Fire, Air and Water are the circles which represent the perfect circular movements of the planets.

The curious wheel-like object in the top left has been taken by Jung to be a UFO, or unidentified flying object. However, Jung was mistaken. It is not unidentified, for it is a well-established iconographic reference to the vision of the biblical Ezekiel, who was enabled to see into the higher realms of spirit.

MACROCOSM AND MICROCOSM

(*Left*) The schema of the spiritual world revealed, with the correspondences between the ideal realm of the MACROCOSM, and the earthly realm of the MICROCOSM. Detail of folding plate from J.D. Mylius, *Opus Medico-chymicum*, 1618.

A similar arrangment of wheels is in the early sixteenth century illustration (*right*), from a religious text which makes no pretence to occult lore.

Centuries ago, the Greek philosopher Aristotle claimed that in the spiritual world all things moved in circles. In contrast, all things moved on earth in straight lines, under the influence of what we now call gravity. The grave, majestic movement of the planets was in rhythms which followed sacred circles. This is why it was a commonplace for images of the spiritual world to be conceived in terms of circles.

The seventeenth-century print (*below*) is unique because it shows a man breaking from the lower world into the higher. The man is struggling through the thin veil which separates the earth from the supernatural realm of spirit. This is the clearest image one can have of the experience of INITIATION. This man truly belongs to the TWO WORLDS. The man is kneeling, as though he has been petitioning the higher world to be granted this vision. He is carrying a walking stick, as symbol of the fact that, hitherto, he has been a wanderer on the earth, tapping like one blind against the mysteries of the world. One hand rests on the earth, while the other is held towards the heavens, as though to ward off the brilliant light which almost blinds him. The only reason he is not blinded in this intense light of the spirit is because he has been prepared by the sacred teachings, meditations and rituals to adjust to the new vision.

Although this is not the earliest picture of initiation, it is probably the first to reveal in such a simple way the nature of initiation, the act of breaking through from the ordinary realm of nature into a vision of the supernatural world. The kneeling man is allowed a vision of the higher realm, which until that moment was "occulted", or hidden from his earth-bound eyes.

Occultists have always believed that the hidden, or OCCULT, world is far more important than the visible material world. This is understandable, for OCCULTISM is the study of these secret realms, of the principles which lie behind the physical appearance of things. Although the seventeenth-century artist symbolized the spiritual world by means of circles and wheels, the truth is that the hidden realm is populated by spirits – in the higher realms by angels, and in the lower realms by demons.

Occultists also maintain that the earthly realm is populated by spirits. Between the angels and demons is the world of man, who is surrounded by

A DENIZEN OF TWO WORLDS

In this seventeenth-century engraving, the INITIATE is breaking through the invisible veil which separates the physical realm from the material. The spiritual realm is characterized by the symbolic devices of Fire, Air and Water (the rainbow); however, Earth itself is too solid to find a real existence on this plane. The material realm contains these three elements in material form – Fire and Air in the star-studded skies and Water in the lake – and also Earth in abundance.

A HIGHER COSMIC VISION

Detail from early sixteenth-century breviary, showing the vision of Ezekiel, with two versions of the Four Creatures. Some ufologists (those who study UFOs) have attempted to claim this vision as being of an extraterrestrial entity, but it is a record of higher cosmic vision of the Seraphim and Cherubim. Note the similarity to the wheel-like object in the seventeenth-century engraving (*left*).

the secrets of nature, itself inhabited by fairies, gnomes and other creatures invisible to ordinary sight. The tree of the seventeenth-century print (*left*) would be the habitation of the GNOMES, the lake would be the dwelling of the UNDINES, the air would be filled with SYLPHS, and the warmth of the stars and fires would be the dwelling of the SALAMANDERS. This teaching means that those men and women who dwell on the earth plane, and who have not broken through the veil of illusion which separates it from the spiritual realm, do not see the earth aright. Such people have not refined their vision to a point where they can see the living forces behind the appearances of things. For such men and women, the earth is still a MAYA, or illusion.

In the course of history, occultists have studied these invisible worlds from a number of different standpoints, among which the more important are alchemy, Rosicrucianism, cabbalism and astrology. To understand the nature of occultism more fully, we must glance at each of these studies in more detail, before turning to several modern outgrowths, wherein these traditional studies have been continued.

ALCHEMY

LCHEMY is the art of transformation, and may be described as a method of investigating nature in a spiritually creative way. Just as an artist takes colour pigments and oil from the earth and combines these so as to incorporate on canvas his own inner vision (thus transforming nature into mental images), so the alchemist seeks to work with the material of nature, and impress upon it something of the power of the invisible spirit.

Since, in ancient times, the Sun was seen as the physical embodiment of spirit, and since the metal of the Sun was gold, the quest of the alchemist was succinctly said to be the search for the art of GOLD-MAKING.

Ancient Egyptian alchemical documents, and some later Greek texts indicate that the early metalworkers had learned various "secrets" for making gold, in a very materialistic sense. Among these was the method of doubling gold (DIPLOSIS, to the Greeks) which depends on the addition of silver and copper to gold, to increase the weight without significantly changing its colour. Medieval European alchemists were frequently reputed to have a secret powder, which some called AZOTH, or PROJECTION POWDER, which had the power to transmute base metal into gold, and many alchemists worked for royal families as official gold-makers.

The alchemist Kaspar Harbach worked for Christian IV of Denmark in the early seventeenth century in this capacity, and, in 1644 and 1646, several ducats were struck from the gold made through such alchemy. At about the same time, an alchemist named Hofmann worked for Ferdinand III in Nuremberg. From the gold manufactured by this adept, the Emperor had a beautiful medal struck, its obverse and reverse set with enigmatic designs, bearing an inscription to the effect that the gold was made from five

THE SECRET OF ALCHEMY

This portrait of the great Swiss occultist and alchemist Paracelsus shows him carrying a sword, on the hilt of which is written the word ZOTH, a form of the mystical word AZOTH, the secret of alchemy. Symbolically this reveals that he was an initiated alchemist who had the ability to take in his grasp the power of Azoth whensoever he chose. The woodcut has led to the erroneous belief that Paracelsus kept this magical powder in a secret container in the hilt of his sword! The Latin motto at the top of the woodcut reads: "Let no man who may belong to himself belong to another." This was the principle of the New Age which the occultists of Paracelsus's time saw dawning in Europe. From Paracelsus, *Opuscula Astronomica et Astrologica*, circa 1570.

drops of a secret ELIXIR. "For truly," wrote the seventeenth-century alchemist Jean Baptist van Helmont in his *Life Eternal*, "I have divers times seen [the philosopher's stone] and handled it with my hands." He recorded that that one grain of the stone was so powerful that it "transchanged 19186 Parts of Quick-silver ... into the best Gold."

Whereas the search for the secret of making gold from base matter has always remained the EXOTERIC, or non-secret, art of the alchemist, the search for inner transformation, for the secrets of creativity, have always been the ESOTERIC, or secret, work of the alchemist.

The search for a way of injecting spirit into matter has a parallel in the FRANKENSTEIN story, in which Dr. Frankenstein sought a way of injecting spirit into bones and dead flesh (*right*). Although this was a "transformation" story, undoubtedly linked with the notion of initiation, and the shadow-realm to which initiation gives rise, it is also rooted in historical fact. Mary Shelley undoubtedly knew that at Castle Frankenstein, in Germany, a real alchemist, Konrad Dippel, had worked at precisely the same quest. The moral of the Frankenstein story, as it has come down

THE FRANKENSTEIN STORY

The monster of Dr. Frankenstein, born of the imagination of a Victorian woman, Mary Shelley, had its origins in the life and work of Konrad Dippel, an alchemist who was born in Castle Frankenstein, near Darmstadt. One important difference between the historical Dippel and Mary Shelley's doctor was that Dippel believed that life could be injected into dead bodies by magical means. He therefore belonged to the ancient tradition of black magic, while the doctor of the story was an unconventional scientist, seeking for life secrets in the world of chemistry and physics.

to us in its various amended forms, is that this monstrous creation destroys its own creator – and there is, indeed, an element of spiritual truth in the notion that the creative artist is consumed by his quest to inject spirit into matter.

A detail (*page 34*) from one of the most famous of all alchemical documents, a fifteenth-century manuscript over five metres (eighteen feet) long, called the RIPLEY SCROLL (sometimes the Ripley Scrowle), after its author, Sir George Ripley of Bridlington, shows the alchemist driven to distraction by his inability to find the SECRET STONE of the alchemists, and by the poverty to which this has reduced him. The moral here is that the alchemical search is a difficult one, and that only a very few attain to the initiation which is the true esoteric aim of the alchemist.

We have already glanced at another detail from the same scroll showing the redemptive element in man, the so-called HERMES BIRD (*pages 26-27*) which is reborn every 500 years, in a series of reincarnations. This is a symbol of the almost-perfected alchemical Work, for the Bird is the soul, and HERMES is a name for Mercury, who is reputed to have brought to earth the secrets of gold-making, from the gods. The irony behind the image is that even this creative bird, which is aware of the cosmic rhythms, and of the essential spirituality of the cosmos, is biting into its own flesh. This, as with so many alchemical pictures, is partly an intimation of Christian imagery, for it calls to mind the MYSTIC PELICAN (the Christ) who puts its beak into its own breast (causing itself great pain) that it might feed its young. This is the type of suffering experienced by the initiate, who must remain on the earth plane, alienated from his beloved spiritual world, to help the less developed, who are still bound to the earth plane.

It is commonplace for modern historians to trace the development of modern chemistry to alchemy. However, the truth is that modern chemistry began as a materialized and exoteric form of alchemy. In a sense, chemistry began when the later alchemists began to classify nature in a new way – when, for example, they set aside the old view of nature as being a union of the FOUR ELEMENTS of Fire, Earth, Air and Water, and replaced these with a multiplicity of elements. As with all new developments, much of the inner quality of the old alchemy was lost when this "modern vision" of nature was developed.

Among the traditions which were lost – or which were soon regarded as being unscientific – was the idea of the THREEFOLD NATURE, which the alchemists had termed the TRIAD, the SACRED THREE, the TRIPLE SECRET, and so on.

The literature of the alchemists insists that every living organism (which is, in effect, every entity in creation) is a result of the working of the sacred three. In many texts this triad is called Sulphur, Mercury and Salt.

MEDIEVAL ALCHEMIST

This detail from George Ripley's alchemical scroll, circa 1470, shows the distracted alchemist, apparently reduced to penury through his search for the philosophers' stone. As with all Ripley's arcane symbolism, the meaning of this image is very different from what we first imagine. The point is that the soul must sense its own lack of intrinsic worth before initiation into the higher mysteries may proceed. This is the state of the true alchemist at the beginning of the Great Work – which is why Ripley has placed it at the bottom of his famous scroll, rather than at the top, where completion is symbolized.

In alchemy, these are not the inert chemicals of the modern scientist, but "living principles", or the THREE ESSENCES, "the triple secret of the Art".

It will be instructive to examine this triad as it manifests in the human being, the most complex of created entities. SULPHUR represents the (presently) inchoate forces within the human subconscious realm of Will. SALT represents the death-process in human thinking. MERCURY represents the breathing-controlled emotional centre in man, which regulates the polarities of will (that is, Sulphur) and intellect (that is, the death element represented by Salt).

Man, like the cosmos, is seen as a merging of three principles – the life-force of Sulphur at one extreme fighting against the death-force of Salt at the other extreme, both yoked together by Mercury. The life-power of Sulphur is located in the stomach, or in the sexual region, while the death-power of Salt is located in the head, in the thinking centre.

Mercury is the reconciler of these two principles, and is sometimes called the HARMONIZER. This is one reason why Mercury is called the HERMAPHRODITE (for it has neither the female salt tears, nor the demonic sulphuric laughter of the male), and why the CADUCEUS (the ancient symbol, or wand of office carried by Mercury) shows two polarity snakes entwined around the central stick in a semblance of harmony. In this sense, Mercury may be said to have an identity only in so far as this is received from either Sulphur or Salt. Its cosmic aim is to balance these two opposing principles of life and death, of light and darkness, and all such cosmic dualities. Mercury is the healing force, and it is no accident that the caduceus has been adopted as a symbol of the healing fraternity, and of pharmacies.

ALCHEMICAL SULPHUR

In the final plate from Michael Maier's masterpiece of 1618, *Atalanta Fugiens* ("The Fleeing Atalanta"), the winged serpent, or FIERY DRAGON, represents Sulphur, which (uncontrolled in this instance) is destroying the woman, who lies in the grave of earth. Without the other polarity of Salt, and without the reconciling power of Mercury, the will forces and sexual energies prove too powerful for the body. The irony is that the serpent which squeezes this woman to death will die itself, because it is killing its host. (For all that Maier identifies the woman in the grave with Mercury, she is in fact Venus, in her role as ruler of the physical body.)

The main centre of the Sulphur realm – that is, of the unconscious – is located in the stomach and sexual regions, and is associated with the excretory system. Now, the Greek word for VENUS (KUPROS) gave us the name for the island Cyprus where the goddess was supposed to have emerged from the eternal realm, onto the material plane, on a rocky beach near Paphos. Besides being the "Island from whence copper came", it was also the "Island of Venus".

In the esoteric tradition of the Green Language, the Greek word for Venus (*Kupros*) is said to be the same as Sulphur (SOUPHROS) because of the similarity in sounds in the Greek words. The enigmatic occultist and alchemist Fulcanelli tells us that Souphros has the meaning of "manure and ordure", which is why the alchemical texts insist that the stone of wisdom, the pearl of great price, the alchemists' secret and magical stone, will be found in the dung heap. This association throws some light on why the realm of Sulphur in man should be linked with the stomach and excreta. Venus hurts her feet when, newly arrived

ALCHEMICAL LABORATORY

The alchemist at prayer in his laboratory, kneeling before the tent-like oratory. The forceful perspective of this image creates the impression of gazing into the interior of a cone. The eye is drawn inexorably towards the open door at the distant centre – this is the still-point, the light, to which the growing soul aspires. Engraving from Heinrich Khunrath's cabbalistic–alchemical work, *The Amphitheatre of Eternal Wisdom* (usually referred to as the AMPHITHEATRE), which he completed towards the end of his life, in 1602. The drawing for this remarkable plate was made by Hans de Vries, a member of a family of esotericists.

from the light-filled spiritual realm, she has to stand upon the hard, pebbled beach of Cyprus. She is no longer spume-made, but earthly, and must learn to live in the dung-heap which, symbolically speaking, is the earth.

There is no hint of the dung heap in the beautiful circular portrayal of an alchemist's LABORATORY in Khunrath's engraving *(left)*. This roundel portrays the higher aspirations of the art, and the alchemist is seen at prayer in front of a curious tent-like tabernacle, or ORATORY, which contains admonishments in Latin and cabbalistic Hebrew. From the censer (incense-burner) to his left rises a pall of smoke in which is written, in Latin, "Prayer ascends like smoke, a sacrifice acceptable to God." On the further side of the room (symbolically balanced by the table bearing instruments of creativity) is the fireplace where the practical alchemy, the experimental art, the Fire-art, may be pursued. The division between the place of prayer and the place of work (both legitimate areas of alchemy) is emphasized by the play on the words "laboratory" and "oratory", for the latter is contained in the former.

Once again, mottos set the theme. On the moulding above the fire are the Latin words, "That which is wisely attempted again will sometimes succeed." On the ceiling above the table, is the most important of all occult maxims: "Without Divine Inspiration, no man is great."

Some scholars claim that the first three letters of the word Rosicrucian are not from the Latin for "rose", but are from the Latin for "DEW" (also *Ros*, in Latin), symbolically the sacred liquor which descends from heaven. Certainly, some of the early alchemists (who were also Rosicrucians) seem to have believed this. Among them was the seventeenth-century Dutch alchemist Dr. Tolle (writing under the pseudonym Altus), whose strange "Wordless Book" (MUTUS LIBER) contains many allusions to the dew.

In one of the plates *(right)* he shows the alchemists gathering early morning dew in sheets, and squeezing the precious liquid for use in their experiments. Many of the elements in this picture appear strange to the uninitiated. However, they become clear when the true nature of the alchemical operation is understood. The alchemists (who are also Rosicrucians, as is indicated in the symbolism of this strange book) have gathered the ALCHEMICAL DEW (*Ros*) in a secret country

THE ALCHEMICAL DEW

Rosicrucian alchemists gathering early morning dew in sheets and squeezing it for use in their experiments. The dew was gathered at an appropriate time in the year, when the Sun left Aries and entered Taurus, as indicated by the Ram and the Bull. The square-shaped waterfall of dew passing into the circular dish symbolizes matter being transformed into spirit. Plate 4 from the *Mutus Liber* ("Wordless Book"), 1677.

place at a cosmically appropriate moment. This special time is indicated by the Ram and the Bull, which stand to either side of the line of two spread sheets – a reference to the time when the Sun leaves Aries the Ram, and enters Taurus the Bull (in terms of a modern calendar, about the 21st April).

The arrangement of the sheets is significant. If the one being squeezed by the couple in the foreground were placed in its original position, at the far side of the others, the six sheets would make the figure shown on the next page.

This MAGIC TRIANGLE, or numerological progression, is intended to echo on the earth plane the huge triangle behind the city, which represents the spiritual influx from heaven – the secret and sacred dew. The triangle in this form is one of the most deeply significant of all occult symbols, and is worth close examination, for its magical nature will explain much which is hidden in the *Mutus Liber* plate (*page 37*).

The triangular form itself symbolizes pure spirit, the celestial fire (the old alchemical symbol for Fire was a simple triangle). The great celestial triangle which dominates (*right*) is the GREAT FIRE which the furnace fires of the alchemists seek to imitate. This is why alchemy is frequently called the FIRE-ART, or the ART OF FIRE, with the great mythological smith HEPHAESTUS, the Greek god of fire, as its patron. The symbolism explains why alchemists were often referred to in a derogatory way (by those who did not understand their secret search) as PUFFERS, for they used bellows to puff away at their flames – a symbol of their persistence in the laborious process of the Fire-art. The three-lined structure of the triangle (symbolized in the arrangement of the sheets) is capable of infinite extension from a single point (the Godhead) into space and time:

In this form, it is called the TETRACTYS, and linked with the name of god IHVH. The great seventeenth-century occultist Kircher showed that the four levels of the tetractys have numerological equivalents which add up to the mystic number 72:

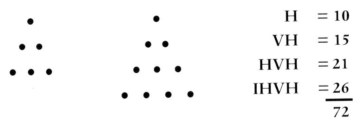

H	= 10
VH	= 15
HVH	= 21
IHVH	= 26
	72

Viewed from the point of view of the tetractys, we see a meaningful progression in the activity of the man and woman in the foreground. The dew being squeezed from the foreground sheet pours out in a distinctive waterfall in the shape of a rectangle or square. Because a square has four sides, it is usually taken as a symbol of the realm of matter, which is fourfold, being composed of the four elements of Earth, Air, Water and Fire. Thus, we see what was originally in a spiritual triangle being transformed into an earthly square.

This dew is falling into a circular dish. The MAGIC CIRCLE is the standard alchemical symbol for the realm of spiritual life – among other things, it symbolizes the great circling wheel of the planets and zodiac circling the geocentric earth. When in alchemical diagrams a rectangle stands upon, or within, a circle (*below*), it is a symbol of the "Squaring of the circle", an alchemical process of transformation. The passing of the earthly square (dewfall) into this spiritual circle (dish) is symbolic of the difficult and delicate art (which some see as a symbol of the alchemical process of TRANSMUTATION itself) by which matter is transformed into spirit.

The three stages – from triangle, through rectangle to circle – represent the alchemical stages by which a heavenly power (dew) is brought down to earth (square sheet), and magically treated (square dewfall) so as to lift it to a higher spiritual level (circular plate), where it may be of service to man. Such a delicate art requires the cooperation of the cosmos, and certain correspondences on the earth plane. This is why the male alchemist stands beneath the Sun (symbol of the ANIMUS, and spirit-life of consciousness) and the female alchemist stands beneath the Moon (symbol of the ANIMA, the soul-life of our imaginative realm).

It is evident that, since the alchemists were dealing with inner things, with secret principles, the pictures they used to illustrate their texts often appear to be enigmatic to the point of obscurity. However, if these images are related to their beliefs, much of this obscurity falls away. The engraving on page 41 is from Michael Maier's ATALANTA FUGIENS, one of the most remarkable of the seventeenth-century alchemical books published by Theodor de Bry. This book contains no fewer than forty-nine plates of a similar quality to the one reproduced here, along with, as the Latin title puts it, "some fifty musical fugues in three parts", and a number of epigrams, the "whole to be seen, read, meditated, understood, judged, sung and heard".

Michael Maier was born at Rendsberg (Holstein) in 1566, and after a career as a physician, was enobled by Rudolf II, a king deeply interested in occultism. It is clear that Maier was himself involved in the Bohemian Rosicrucian movement at Heidelberg, where the original alchemical laboratory is still preserved. His influence

SQUARING THE CIRCLE

A rectangle standing upon or within a circle represents the "Squaring of the Circle" as illustrated in Michael Maier's *Atalanta Fugiens*, 1618. The Latin text insists that this mystic circle must be made "from a male and female", and that its construction marks the beginning of the alchemical manufacture of the secret stone of the philosophers.

on alchemical thought was profound, and it is worth observing that Sir Isaac Newton, who contributed so much to the development of modern science, was deeply impressed by his writings, to the extent of copying out long extracts from his alchemical works. From the point of view of the plate studied here (*right*) Maier's main original contribution to alchemy was his interpreting of ancient mythology in terms of spiritual processes and alchemical lore.

The plate depicts, as the translation of the Latin puts it, "The Rebis, like the Hermaphrodite, born from the twin mountains of Mercury and Venus". The image is of the planetary gods Mercury and Venus in the act of love-making. What is this curious Rebis, to which the Latin refers? The REBIS is one of the most mysterious terms in alchemy. It is a word from the Green Language, which refers, in part, to the prime matter which is being transformed in the alchemical operation. The Green Language meaning behind the word is as follows. *Re* is the ablative form of the Latin *Res* (which means "thing"). *Bis* means "twice". Therefore, the Re-bis is "concerning the thing twice", or a "double matter". It is a double matter because, besides consisting of the dung of the elements, it also contains the spark of light (the gold) which the alchemical operation seeks to liberate. This is why the Rebis is sometimes said to be the "ordure", which, as we have seen, is linked with the beautiful body of the goddess Venus (*see page 17*). It also explains why the Rebis is sometimes said to come in an egg, for the egg is the beautiful yet fragile body, which cannot take the shocks and vibrations of the material world, yet protects new life within. Finally, in the Green Language, Rebis is also an epenthesis for Rebus, a riddle, suggesting that this mysterious double matter is in itself a great secret.

The image of the planetary gods Mercury and Venus making love is an excellent way of showing how the light element (love, or even a child) may be made from mingling in the body of earth. The androgyne figure above their heads is the Rebis which emerges, dual in nature, from this love-making.

In terms of alchemical symbolism, and the sequence of plates in Maier's *Atalanta Fugiens* of which this is part, the alchemical process pictured in this remarkable image is the emergence of the "Androgyne of the Wise" from the impacting into union of Sulphur and Mercury. The externally beautiful Venus of this plate rules over the internally "ugly" realm of inchoate will. Only in the initiate is the realm of will under control, and of the kind which can (literally) move mountains.

When not under control, this same realm of WILL is a liability for man. As an example of this, we might consider only one aspect of will, that SULPHUROUS FIRE within, which is the sexual drive – in alchemical psychologies, called MARS. When the sexual drive is not under control (as, indeed, is the case in the normal "earthly man", caught in an aspect of time, rather than in the aspect of eternity), then it is the equivalent of a raging fire, as is intimated in a previous plate from the same alchemical text. When the mediator, Mercury, is called to control this fire (in his role as mediator of the two poles in man), then he is

THE MYSTIC TRINITY

The Hermaphrodite, born from Mercury and Venus, is another play on the alchemical triplicity (Sulphur, Mercury and Salt) in the human being. In this case, the Rebis is Salt, or the spiritual activity of pure thought. Plate 38 of Michael Maier's *Atalanta Fugiens*, 1618.

blasted by its power. Eternally seeking an identity, he willingly takes on the warmth, ardour and inner chaos, and turns into Mars himself. Thus, we see in this Maier plate that Mercury, always associated with the caduceus, has actually thrown his wand of office on the floor, and has taken on the role of Mars, reaching out for Venus.

Mercury has relegated his role, and has become inflamed by the lower urges of the will, presumably because Venus has revealed the tantalizing beauty of her form – she has bared her breasts. Venus is the hunted huntress, and her quiver of arrows is symbolically represented in phallic form, raised up by the cupid to her left. Mercury is debased from his ambivalent role as mediator, for he has been seduced, and lost his true nature. Venus also is debased, for she is pulled down from her role as spiritual "eternal feminine" (Goethe's phrase). This is why they sit on the earth – two gods of the spiritual realm, fixed to the material plane, their symbols of office also thrown to earth.

Born from this union, emerging from their heads, from which all imagination (image-making) proceeds, is the monstrous image of the Androgyne, "born from the twin mountains", as the Latin text below the illustration puts it.

Alchemically speaking, the situation arises because Mercury is no longer acting as a harmonizer, a giver of union, but has become actively involved in a single polarity himself. There is no trace of Salt, the third of the triplicity, in this image, and it is upon this absence that one is invited to meditate.

The mystic PHILOSOPHERS' STONE, which would grant its possessor eternal youth, freedom from death and sickness, and all inner knowledge, was sometimes called the QUINTESSENCE, or FIFTH ELEMENT. The ancients believed that all natural forms were a result of the workings of the four elements of Earth, Air, Fire and Water. These FOUR PRINCIPLES were of antagonistic natures – for example, Water would extinguish Fire, and Fire would parch Earth. They were united – "yoked together", as the alchemists claimed – by the fifth element, which remained invisible to ordinary sight. This was the secret essence, the unifier, the SECRET OF SECRETS, which the alchemist sought. Anyone who had the secret of secrets in his grasp could control nature. We see, therefore, in this notion of the power which the acquisition of the philosophers' stone would give its possessor, the roots of the Frankenstein-like nature of the modern scientific search to dominate nature. The alchemists of old maintained that if nature was not approached in awe and love, then it would destroy the one who came too close.

THE MERCURIAL DRAGON

This strange being, from the 1612 edition of Martin Rutland's *Lexicon Alchemiae*, may appear to be merely a monster, until one considers that the three heads are symbolic forms of the Sun, Moon and Mercury – equivalents for Sulphur, Salt and Mercury, respectively. In this picture, the three principles emerge from a monstrous body, with wings and a pair of taloned feet. This is the image of the human being, presented as a biped whose lower parts are monstrous, but whose upper parts offer the opportunity of redemption from this state. The woodcut is a vision of undeveloped human form, which houses the subconscious, inchoate and unrefined natures. The purpose of alchemy is to use the upper three principles in such a way as to transform this monster into a human being – making of it a godlike or angelic creature, the BIRD OF HERMES, or HERMES BIRD.

ROSICRUCIANISM

The term ROSICRUCIAN was first used in the fifteenth century, and applied to the disciples of an enigmatic German initiate called Christian Rosenkreuz, who established a number of esoteric schools in Europe, to prepare for the religious and spiritual reforms of the coming centuries. In the seventeenth century these reforms were desperately needed to counter the growing materialism which eventually found its outer expression in the Industrial Revolution.

Rosicrucianism, with its profound interest in the cosmic significance of man and the earth, was ideally placed to offer this reform. The esotericist Rudolf Steiner wrote that Rosenkreuz "felt it to be his mission to make it possible for every human being, no matter where he stands in modern life, to rise to spiritual heights". This was a return to the old Christian values of the Gospels, infused with a feeling for democracy which was beginning to stir in Europe.

The Rosicrucian movement, which was one of the first non- heretical groups openly to propose occult tenets, came to public notice in the seventeenth century. The existence of a European group of occult initiates, loosely tied together as a fraternity, was first announced in a publication known as the FAMA, in 1614. The first important text which may definitely be linked with this movement is *The Chymical Wedding of Christian Rosenkreutz*, which was probably written by Valentin Andreae, and which appeared in print in 1616. The roots of Rosicrucianism are much older, however, and are probably to be found in the Bohemian castle at Karlstejn, near Prague, which was built by the Emperor Charles IV. This highly cultured Bohemian king has been described as the last initiate ruler to sit on a European throne.

The image of the rosy-cross was developed into a highly complex symbolism by the Order of the Golden Dawn, which was derived from Rosicrucian sources. Detailed instructions relating to the arcane meaning of the symbol were drawn up, and each of its members of a certain grade of initiation was required to make his or her own "cross" to wear during rituals. The four terminations of the cross were linked with the four elements, the central part with the fifth element or Quintessence, wherein dwelled the Christ. The twenty-two petals of the rose symbolize the twenty-two secret paths of the cabbalistic system, of the Tarot cards (the picture deck of which consists of twenty-two cards) and the Hebrew alphabet. The inner trefoil arcs, on the short arms of the cross, are marked with the sigils (secret signs) for Salt (left), Mercury (top), and Sulphur (right).

The purpose of Rosicrucianism was to study and promulgate esoteric Christianity within a framework of meditative disciplines. This it did by means of arcane astrological, alchemical and occult imagery, designed to hide the Rosicrucian teachings from the uninitiated, and from the Church, which might prosecute the movement for heresy. In

Heidelberg, which was the main centre of Rosicrucianism in the seventeenth century, is the castle used by the alchemist ROSICRUCIAN KING, Frederick V of Bohemia, which once had gardens designed on Rosicrucian principles, and in which is now a bust of the greatest Rosicrucian of them all, the German writer and philosopher Goethe. On the facade are arcane statues of planetary beings and mythological figures linked with Rosicrucian lore.

One of the most important of the early English Rosicrucians was Dr. John Dee (who had spent some time in Bohemia). A mathematician, alchemist and astrologer, he wrote widely on occult and cabbalistic subjects, and designed an occult figure, which he called the MONAS HIEROGLYPHICA (*below*). This combined in one figure, or sigil, the three symbols for the zodiacal sign Aries, the Sun and Mercury: ☿

Its fame among modern occultists stems from the fact that it was adopted as one of the distinguishing emblems of the Rosicrucian movement. The Monas was often used as a sign – sometimes as a colophon (a printer's device) – to show that the contents of a book in which it appeared were intended especially for the eyes of the Rosicrucian fraternity. Dee regarded the sigil as expressing the deeper secrets of the cosmos, and he wrote an entire book on the secrets of its form, to describe the different levels of symbolism within its simple-seeming, yet enigmatic structure. So widespread was Rosicrucianism in the seventeenth century that it has been claimed that its members included such figures as Shakespeare and Francis Bacon. Historical documents show that Henry More, Ralph Cudworth, Robert Fludd, Christopher Wren and Thomas Vaughan were members, and it was a translation of a work of Vaughan, *Anthroposophia Theomagica*, which seems to have introduced Goethe to the fraternity, around about 1784. It is this last name which, by direct ancestry, brings us to MODERN ROSICRUCIANISM (*see page 74*), for the Goethe-scholar Rudolf Steiner was the one who revitalized the Rosicrucian impulse in the twentieth century.

THE ROSY-CROSS

The ROSY-CROSS emblem which was constructed personally by each member of the ORDER OF THE GOLDEN DAWN, according to a closely prescribed system of symbolism. The Latin *ros* means "dew", as well as "rose". The Latin *crux*, which gives us "crucian", means "cross". This means that the rose of this rosy cross is the heavenly flower (Christ) which is renewed each day, yet which hangs on the "cross".

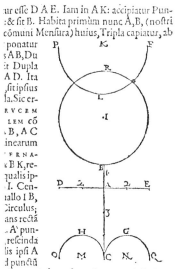

THE MONAS OF JOHN DEE

The secret sigil of the Monas of John Dee, represented here as though in a geometric proposition, within the main body of his text, *Monas Hieroglyphica*, 1564. The Monas is one of the most profound works in Dee's occult canon.

THE CABBALA

The CABBALA, sometimes transliterated as QABBALAH, is the esoteric lore of the Hebrews. It appears to have developed as an arcane philosophy following the dispersal of the sacred lore which took place after the plundering of the temple in Jerusalem, in 54BC. Probably, before that time, such esoteric secrets as are found in the cabbala were studied only within the confines of the priestcraft.

A great deal of the cabbala is highly complex, and much of it consists of interpretations of the sacred books and scriptures of the Jews, such as the Zohar and the Sephirah Yetzirah. After the thirteenth century, many Christian writers interested themselves in this secret tradition, as a result of which a specialist form, later called CHRISTIAN CABBALISM, developed. A great deal of the cabbalistic writings of such occultists as Cornelius Agrippa, Dr. John Dee and Robert Fludd really belong to this latter stream of thought. In both these forms, the cabbala has had a most profound influence on the development of European occultism, especially in the realm of OCCULT ALPHABETS, such as gematria, notaricon and temurah. Each is a form of word- and number-play which lends itself easily to Hebrew, and which has been adopted (not always with the most grace or utility) for the European alphabetical system.

SECRET ALPHABETS

Several occult alphabets, preserved in the late fifteenth century by Cornelius Agrippa, are still used in modern times and are frequently found on magical objects designed for the purpose of angel magic and similar rituals. (*Top*) The secret alphabet which is attributed to Honorius Theban, with its corresponding Roman letters. It is now called the Alphabet of the Thebans. From Cornelius Agrippa's *De Occulta Philosophia*, 1534. (*Above*) The Theban script, or secret alphabet, can be seen here engraved on the bone handle of an athame, or dagger, used in wicca rituals. Private collection, Toronto.

A large number of the occult alphabets that are still used in occult circles (*above*) are derived from various forms of the Hebraic and related alphabets, which have been given deep levels of significance by a succession of occultists.

GEMATRIA is a system of numerical writing based on the fact that the twenty-two letters of the Hebrew alphabet have been accorded numerical equivalents. Because of this, every word has a number-value, which is the sum of its letters' numerical equivalents. For example, the word SORATH has the numerical equivalent of 666, and this has been used by some occultists to explain this number, reported in the Apocalyptic literature as the number of the GREAT BEAST of Revelations.

In the cabbalistic system of interpretation, words of a similar numerical value are perceived as having analogy, or some meaningful correspondence. The system is designed to abstract hidden meanings (or supposed hidden meanings) from words and sentences in holy writ and in occult texts. A classic example of a gematric relationship is found in the Hebraic words Nachash (Serpent) and Messiah (the Coming Lord), both of which have the numerical value of 358.

NACHASH in Hebrew: נחש   MESSIAH in Hebrew: משיח

נ ח ש
300 + 8 + 50 = 358

מ ש י ח
8 + 10 + 300 + 40 = 358

This correspondence permitted cabbalists to claim that the image of the brazen serpent of Moses (mentioned in Numbers XXI: 9) was a prefiguring of the Messiah, or Christ on the Cross. The cabbalistic image of a serpent twisting around a cross is usually intended as a reference to this gematria, and to the Messianic number 358. In Numbers XXI: 9 we learn that a man poisoned by a serpent could be kept alive by gazing at the brazen serpent – a reference to the redemptive power of the Messiah in the face of the poison of the OLD SERPENT, who was the Tempter.

NOTARICON is a form of cryptography in which each letter of a word is conceived as being an abbreviation of another word. For example, the word AGLA, which appears in so many magical texts and formulae, is notaricon for the Hebraic phrase, "Atha gibor, leolam Adonai" (Thou art mighty for ever, O Lord). The word VITRIOL, which was discussed on page 25, is another example of notaricon.

Another good example is found in the word CROMAAT, used in certain Modern Rosicrucian rituals. MAAT is an Egyptian god-word meaning "truth". Prefaced by "Cro" it means (among other things) "in truth". The reversal of the conjoined words gives TAAMORC, an acrostic for "The Ancient and Mystical Order Rosae Crucis", the full title of the American Rosicrucian Society, AMORC (see page 74).

TEMURAH is the name given to a method of interpreting texts by means of verbal analogies. Words and letters of an occult or sacred text are altered by the simple expediency of substituting one letter for another, or by changing the orders of letters in words, according to definite principles. For example, the

THE GREAT BEAST

Portrait of the occultist Aleister Crowley (1875–1947), who was learned in the laws of gematria. The number 666 at the sacred point in the space of the Third Eye is linked with his own numerological interests: Crowley saw himself as an incarnation of the Great Beast of Revelations, whose number is 666. According to the occult tradition, however, this number pertains to the sun-being, Sorath. Portrait by Gordon Wain, commissioned by Charles Walker.

alphabetic order ABCD … etc., may be substituted by the reverse order, ZYXW … etc. Thus, in this temuric change, the original word BAD would read YZW. This form of permutation creates new words which may be interpreted by means of analogical inferences.

A unique tenet of Jewish occult lore is the notion of the SEPHIROTHIC TREE, or TREE OF LIFE, which has had a deep influence on Western esotericism. This is a graphic representation of what is, fundamentally, a three-dimensional visualization of the structure of the spiritual world. Many interesting images have been produced through the ages to represent this Tree of Life.

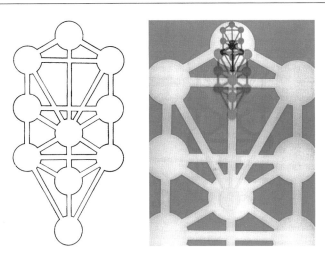

SEPHIROTHIC TREE

The Tree of Life, or Sephirothic Tree, is sometimes represented in a strictly diagrammatic form, almost as a geometric proposition, pointing to the harmonics which underlie the cosmos. This simple diagram (*above left*) of the tree shows the twenty-two paths between the sephiroth. It is one of several related patterns, used in cabbalistic meditation.

In this picture (*above right*) combining photography and computer editing, by James Thorn, the Sephirothic Tree is seen in three dimensions, growing from within a sephirah (Kether) and emanating by proliferation into another sephirah (Tiphereth). For the interactions between the sephiroth to be significant, it is necessary to take into account the legitimate pathways between them, with each of the sephira interacting with the others in two, three, and perhaps even four, dimensions, as here. Such a schema indicates the profound significance of the fact that one may proceed from Tiphereth to Kether by a pathway which "tests" the ascending initiate at Daath, yet one may ascend by way of Chockmah or Binah from that same Tiphereth without having to pass the testing ground of the Abyss. The questions raised by such a survey of the schema are the very substance of true meditation.

Most usually, however, the tree is visualized literally in arboreal form, growing downwards (being rooted, like all created things in the heavens) through the spaces of what the cabbalists call the FOUR WORLDS. These four descend, step by step, from refined spirituality into dense matter.

The first, ATZILUTH, is the World of Origins, where God-aspects begin to take on the shadow of spiritual form. The second is BRIAH, the World of Creation, wherein the ethical and moral realities have their source, and where the archangels rule. The third, YETZIRAH, is the World of Formations, where forms (or archetypes) that will eventually materialize begin to manifest. The fourth is ASSIAH, the World of Expression, which is the familiar material world; the lowest of the four, it is a projection of the picture-making faculty of our own senses.

The tree penetrates the four worlds, finding expression and fulfilment on each of the four levels, and each in turn reflecting the other. To grasp the philosophical grandeur of this conception, one must trace the growth of the tree downwards, from sublime spiritual levels into dense matter.

At the highest level of the tree is AIN SOPH, Nothingness, out of which everything comes. This region, which includes the AIN SOPH AUR, has been described by one modern cabbalist, William Gray, in his excellent work *The Ladder of Lights*, as the "Three Negative Veils".

The topmost sephiroth is called KETHER, the Crown, which corresponds to the ancient Primum Mobile, or source of the First Motion of the created cosmos. The mighty being who rules over Kether is called METATRON.

CHOKMAH, Wisdom, is the second level, corresponding to the zodiac, and guided by the spiritual being RATZIEL.

The third level is BINAH, Understanding, corresponding to the orb of Saturn, and governed by the ARALIM.

Between Binah and the next level of the tree (Chesed) is the ABYSS, called by cabbalists DAATH (Knowledge). Daath is a bridge of knowing by which human beings may cross the "Abyss of Masak Mavdil".

The fourth level of the tree is CHESED (Mercy), the equivalent of the orb of Jupiter, ruled by the CHESMALIM.

The fifth level is GEBURAH (Severity), the equivalent of Mars, ruled by the SERAPHIM.

The sixth level is TIPHERETH (Beauty), the equivalent of the Sun, ruled by the mighty MICHAEL.

The seventh level is NETZACH (Victory) the equivalent of Venus, ruled by the ELOHIM and the archangel HAMIEL (sometimes called Phanael or Auriel).

The eighth level is HOD (Splendour), the equivalent of Mercury, ruled by the BENI-ELOHIM.

The ninth level in the tree is YESOD (Foundation) the equivalent of the Moon, and ruled by the AISHIM.

The lowest level is MALKUTH (the Kingdom), the equivalent of the earth, ruled by the CHERUBIM.

The description of the sephiroth in this form tends to obscure the fact that the tree penetrates the four worlds at every stage. At the earth plane (Malkuth), the angelic ruler of Atziluth is the ADONAI MALAKH, "the Lord King", who rested his feet on the "footstool

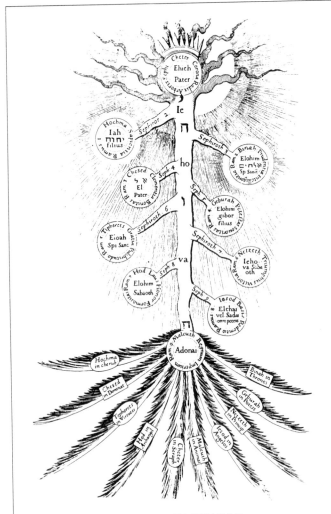

ROOTED IN HEAVEN

The variety of sephirothic schema may sometimes be misleading. The simple tree used by the English esotericist Robert Fludd in 1617, in *Utriusque Cosmi Maioris*, sets out the structure very graphically, but is not suitable for meditative purposes. Since the tree is rooted in heaven, it is represented, in this Fludd picture, as being upside-down, with the earth and its emanations the "flower" of the tree.

of God", which was the earth. The ruler of Briah is the being SANDALPHON, a name for the Archangel of the Presence, who stood behind the divine chariot. The Cherubim, who have a special connection with the four elements (symbolized in their forms as composites of Bull, Lion, Eagle and Man, the four fixed signs of the zodiac – respectively Taurus, Leo, Scorpio and Aquarius), have dominion over the World of Yetzirah. In the realm of Assiah, the ruling spiritual being is man.

Complex as the Tree of Life is, when perceived as a three-dimensional extension in space and time – and even as four-dimensional, which is to say, "out of the limitations of time" – its detailed structure serves the cabbalist and Western occultist as a powerful tool for meditation. Indeed, the Tree of Life may be regarded as the most useful of all meditative devices in Western occultism. It is of little wonder that the sixteenth-century cabbalist Reuchlin should describe the tree as setting out the "ten steps by which we ascend to the knowledge of things". The "FIFTY GATES of intelligence", to which Reuchlin also refers in his commentary on the tree, is a reference to the fourth-dimensionality of the tree, with its four worlds, each penetrated by the ten sephiroth, and the Ain Soph.

One of the riches of the tree lies precisely in the fact that it is a tree – a growing organism – which (all being well) will fructify with the passing of time. Man is visualized as involved in this growth: he is no "finished work", lost in the remoteness of spiritual space, but a being in creation, a potential flowering for the tree – perhaps even its most extraordinary fruit. Whether the tree will yield a rich fruit, or will wither, and have to put out new tendrils at a later point, depends very much upon mankind itself.

THE THREE WORLDS

Because occultism deals with the hidden realms, the models of the universe proposed by occultists are very different from the more familiar models of worldly knowledge. Ordinary knowledge tends to concern itself with the one visible realm, of which man's physical body is an important part. Occultists, however, claim that there are THREE WORLDS – the worlds of angels, man, and demons.

Just as the angels and demons are normally invisible, and reveal themselves to human eyes only under exceptional circumstances, it is also true that the human being is invisible. It is an important occult teaching that we are all invisible: what is visible about us – our physical body – is really the least important aspect of our self. According to the occultists, what is of paramount importance about mankind is the invisible spiritual bodies.

Man stands between the angelic and demonic realms, and belongs partly to each. According to the arcane tradition, man may contact the angels by means of PRAYER; he may also contact the demons by means of INVOCATIONS – though all occult systems maintain that it is extremely dangerous to attempt to raise demons without adequate preparation. In ancient times, a priestcraft existed charged with the duty of prayer and invocation. Prayer was usually offered in TEMPLES, which were designed to enable gods and angel-beings to descend to the earth plane from the heavens. Invocations for demons were made in a specially constructed underground cave or chamber, called a NECROMANTEION.

Occultists visualize the angels hovering around the heads of men and women. The circular HALO which appears in paintings and drawings in medieval Christian art, as in Buddhist art, is a reminder that the spiritual realm touches man at his head.

In contrast, the demons work most effectively through the lower parts, centred on the sexual organs. The sexual organs are visualized as being at the centre of a circle which describes the outer limits of the spiritual bodies of man. When a magician, anxious to raise demons, stands at the centre of a protective circle, in which he has inscribed a number of secret symbols, he is externalizing his spiritual power. The circle announces to the demonic hordes that he is available (naked, so to speak) for communication with their realm. The outer circle both protects him and makes a sign to the lower spiritual world that he is wishing to make contact with it.

In occult terms, the two extremes of man's physical body are the sexual centre, wherein mankind may be sucked into a too intense relationship with the demonic world, and the head, wherein mankind may be sucked into deep relationship with the angelic realm. Both polarities represent threats to man's development. Too deep a contact with the demonic tends to debase mankind, and leads eventually to the subconscious overwhelming the individuality, leaving the mind demented. Too deep a contact with the angelic tends to make mankind etherealized, too remote from the physical realm.

The medieval occultists insisted that the SPIRITUAL WORLD above the earth was filled with angelic beings – there were, it was claimed, more angels than the milliards of stars. This spiritual, or ETHEREAL, space was also resounding to the sound of a wondrous celestial music, and filled with colours of superior unearthly beauty. Of course, the occultists recognized that the angels and colours were invisible to all except the initiates, just as the MUSIC OF THE SPHERES was inaudible to all but the highest adepts. This did not stop artists portraying the secret geometry of this spiritual music in earthly colours, nor did it dissuade philosophers from constructing detailed lists of the names of the angels, or CELESTIAL HIERARCHIES.

A striking image of what was often called the CHAIN OF BEING, which stretched from the highest spheres where God dwelled, down to the earth itself, is from a book on occult and cabbalistic lore by Robert Fludd (*left*). The human figure in this engraving is the ANIMA MUNDI, or SOUL OF THE WORLD, a personification of the divine essence which unites all created things. This naked female represents both the soul of the world and the archetypal man. She stands literally poised between the higher realm and the lower realm, for she is chained by her right hand to God (the cloud contains the name of God in Hebraic letters) while her left hand holds a chain fastened to a monkey, which represents the lower part of her being, the chattering simian which dwells in all humans.

Around Anima Mundi are the ranks of the celestial hierarchies, or the NINE ORDERS of the angels. In the occult tradition these are linked with the planetary spheres which, it was believed, swung around the earth in gigantic circles. Each sphere had a group of angelic beings, or celestial hierarchies, who were in charge of the activities of the particular sphere. Usually the names were listed in Latin or Hebrew, but sometimes they were given in Greek. Each activity was linked with one of the planets or zodiacal powers.

The first sphere was that of the CHERUBIM, who ruled the sphere of the zodiac. The second sphere was that of the SERAPHIM, who ruled the sphere of the fixed stars. The third sphere was that of the

THE SOUL OF THE WORLD

Anima Mundi, the Soul of the World, her head sheathed in a halo of stars, and with sun and moon on her breasts. She is chained by her right hand to the Godhead, and holds in her left hand a chain binding the lower monkey, which measures the Earth. Anima stands with one foot on the Earth, the other on Water; her body is surrounded by Air, and she has the warmth of spiritual Fire inside her physical frame. Behind her is the sequence of planetary spheres, culminating in the spheres of the Cherubim and Seraphim. From Robert Fludd's *Utriusque Cosmi Maioris*, 1617.

TRONES (or THRONES), who ruled the sphere of Saturn. The fourth sphere was that of KYRIOTETES, or DOMINIONS, who ruled the sphere of Jupiter. The fifth sphere was that of the DYNAMIS, or VIRTUTES, who ruled the sphere of Mars. The sixth sphere was that of the EXSUSIAI, or POTESTATES (Powers), who ruled the sphere of the Sun. The seventh sphere was that of the ARCHAI, or PRINCIPALITIES, who ruled the sphere of Venus. The eighth sphere was that of the ARCHANGELS, who ruled the

THE SALAMANDER

A rare two-legged salamander, which winds around the twelfth-century font in the parish church of All Saints, Youlgreave, Derbyshire. Its placing on a font indicates that it was formerly perceived as a highly spiritual creature.

sphere of Mercury, while the ninth sphere was that of the angels themselves, who ruled the sphere of the Moon. Man, who rules the earth, is sometimes called the TENTH HIERARCHY. While mankind remains at the very bottom of the orders, the interesting thing is that the activities of this vast ladder of being are directed towards ensuring that the world of humans finds its evolutionary fulfilment.

Although the entire realm of celestial beings is guardian to the earth, there are four angels – more properly speaking, four archangels – who are directly concerned with earthly matters. These are the archangels of the four elements. MICHAEL is the archangel of Fire (associated with the Sun); RAPHAEL of Air; GABRIEL of Water (associated with the Moon); and URIEL of Earth. Three other angels unite with these four to make up the seven SECUNDADEIANS, each of whom, in the occult tradition, rules definite periods of human history, lasting 354 years. Since approximately 1881, world history has been under the charge of the archangel Michael, which is why the present epoch is sometimes called the MICHAELIC AGE.

The four archangels call to mind another fourfold classification of invisible beings. Some modern occultists call these beings DEVA (a word from the Sanskrit meaning "beings of light", and really the Oriental equivalent of angels), but the more traditional name is ELEMENTALS. There are four types of elementals, each one linked with one of the four elements of the alchemists.

The elemental of Fire is the SALAMANDER, a creature which delights in living in the flames of fire. Although invisible to ordinary sight, clairvoyants say that the salamander is a red-hued, lizardlike creature. In medieval times, however, the salamander was sometimes portrayed with six legs (though the sample drawn in the drawing above, which is from a medieval font, has two legs). The elemental of Air is the SYLPH, which corresponds to the air-fairies, winged gossamer-like creatures, with the colours of

WITCH FAMILIARS

A witch feeding demonic imps, or familiars, two of which are toads or frogs. The four elementals of the fairy tradition are demoted in witchcraft to base demonic form. The frogs, here being spooned with the witch's own blood, are the dark equivalent of the undines, or water-elementals. Woodcut from a witchcraft pamphlet, *A Rehearsall both straung and true …*, 1579.

rainbows. The elemental of Water is the UNDINE, a translucent water-creature, who lives in the waves and ripples of water (particularly waterfalls), and has a protean, rapidly changing body. The elemental of the earth is the GNOME, which lives within the earth and amidst the roots of trees, rarely choosing to venture into the light.

The functions of these four creatures are to regulate the elements and to see to the proper growth of plants. They work most effectively on the etheric plane of being. While they are definitely not angels themselves, they work closely with the angels in attempting to maintain and regulate the well-being of the earth.

In the witchcraft tradition, this notion of the invisible elementals is inverted (*see page 97*), and some writers maintain that the witch will have at her beck and call four visible workers (the so-called FAMILIARS), each linked with one of the elements. The frog is the water-creature, a bird (such as a black crow) the air-creature, the toad an earth-creature, and the demonic imp a fire-creature (the fire, in this case being the infernal flames).

The different occult systems have various ways of describing and naming the invisible bodies of man. However, in the West, the general arcane tradition insists that men and women possess several invisible bodies, the most important of which are the astral, the etheric and the ego.

ETHERIC is a word derived from ether, which means "airy". The etheric body of man is that spiritual body which maintains the physical body in a state of life. A physical body which has no etheric around and within it is "dead". A stone, for example, has no etheric body; on the other hand, a healthy plant does. A stone is matter in a state of molecular activity. A plant has a body in a state of molecular activity too, but it also has a cell-life, and thus may grow and die. The etheric body is linked with cellular life, and permits the forms of matter to increase or diminish. Every living thing has an etheric body which remains invisible save to clairvoyant vision. It is called by some the SUBTLE BODY, and, for obvious reasons, the LIFE BODY.

The word ASTRAL is derived from the Latin word *aster*, which means "star" (*see page 23*). The astral is the STARRY BODY, sometimes called the SIDEREAL BODY, or HEAVENLY BODY. The astral body is that which links living creatures to the starry world and gives them the potential for experiencing emotions. A plant (which has an etheric body) does not have an astral body; it therefore feels no emotion. On the other hand, all animals have both etheric and astral bodies, which is why all animals have emotions, such as joy and fear, love and anger. The astral body is the instrument by which creatures experience the world as "something outside", as an entity separate from self. All creatures with astral bodies have an emotional life which constantly drives them into motion (motion and emotion are words deriving from the same root). Sometimes, the astral body is called the DESIRE BODY. Desire springs from love of the world.

In the human being there is a fourth "body", usually called the EGO. This is the incarnating principle, the permanent entity which lives in the physical body, when such a body is available, and in the spiritual world when a body is not available. The word is from the Latin meaning "I". It is the one body which may be so named only by its possessor: no one may truthfully call another ego "I". In the occult model of man, the ego is eternal, the reincarnating vehicle, ever-hungry for experience on the material plane. The ordinary self, with all its myriad of desires, hopes and fears, is merely a faint shadow of the eternal and wise ego. Each time an ego chooses to dip into the physical plane, and incarnate in a physical body, it will forget its true origin (which is the spiritual realm) and remain immersed in a sort of shadow-dream forgetful of the true majesty of its own ego. Only by doing this – by uniting with the earth – may the ego gather experience, and grow. Some occultists call the ego the INDIVIDUALITY, and others call it the INCARNATING PRINCIPLE.

This model of man indicates that the invisible bodies act as a chain by which the ego may grasp the physical body. The body is granted life by the etheric, and emotional life by the astral. The latter is sufficiently refined for the ego to dwell in it. When the ego separates from the body, the body falls asleep. When the etheric separates from the body, that body dies. DEATH is merely the separating of the physical elements back to the earth: at this time, the etheric and astral elements dissolve back into spiritual spaces of the etheric and astral realms.

COSMIC MAN AND WOMAN

An eighteenth-century diagram which was constructed to illustrate a book by the Rosicrucian Jakob Behmen, depicts the astral or starry body of man quite literally, as a circle studded with stars. The circle is in the higher part of the human frame. A series of fold-out windows reveal "hidden" spiritual states of being. The flap at the feet of the man has been pulled back to reveal the demonic hordes, with flames issuing from the interior of the earth. This arcane picture is intended to indicate that man stands poised between the realm of stars, wherein the angels have their true existence, and the realm of the lower regions, or hell, wherein the demons dwell. From William Law's edition of Jakob Behmen, *The Teutonic Philosopher*, 1772.

Almost all occult systems insist that beyond the ego are even more refined spiritual bodies. These presently lie dormant, awaiting growth and unfoldment in distant incarnations. In modern times, they are formed, or partly formed, only in geniuses or initiates, men and women of very high spiritual develop-ment. The terms for the three higher bodies, introduced to the West by way of theosophy, are Atma, Buddhi and Manas.

ATMA is the highest human principle, and grows through conscious work on the physical body. Few humans are presently capable of such work, or of such development.

BUDDHI is sometimes called the LIFE-SPIRIT and grows through conscious work on the etheric body.

MANAS is connected with high-level mental energies, and grows through conscious work on the astral body.

The DEMONS are as numerous as the angels. The Jewish TALMUD says that if the eyes of man could perceive the demons, humans would be completely overwhelmed by the vision, for the demons are more numerous than we are. Although most occultists say that the gradation of spiritual order, which may be seen in the heavenly Chain of Being, is entirely lacking in the cacophanous CHAOS and disorder which is HELL, others have insisted that hell and PURGATORY are organized according to definite principles. The gradation of power in hell does not move from higher refinement in progressive stages towards the earth, however: it sinks in darkness, from the horror of a dark fire to the incredibly remote depths of an ice-cold lake.

This demonic order of being is an inversion of the Celestial Order, a dark mirror-image of the light. While God presides at the very top of the spiritual hierarchies, the Devil lurks at the very bottom of the INFERNAL HIERARCHIES. In the mid-point, between the angels and the demons, is man.

In the Rosicrucian image (*left*), the lower parts of the man are licked by flames. These suggest the flames of hell, in which the fallen angels are condemned to pass their time. The image is intended to remind us that mankind is as actively involved with the lower demonic

LUCIFER'S LAKE OF ICE

A sixteenth-century illustration of Dante's vision of purgatory and hell. Dante has the great monstrous Lucifer at the centre of the earth, encased in a lake of ice up to his private parts – a sign that Dante was familiar with the occult tradition relating to the connection between this part of man and the demons. Dante and his guide, Virgil, are watching Lucifer chewing on the soul of Judas Iscariot, the supreme type of spiritual denial. The message is that all who deny the reality of the higher spiritual world will become food for the demons. From Bernard Stagnino, *Opere del Divino Poeta Danthe*, 1512.

energies as with the higher angelic energies. It may be, indeed, that the demons of the occult literature are figments designed to personify aspects of man's lower nature – those base instincts which people have been unable to integrate in the personality. On the other hand, it could be that the occultists are right, and the demonic world is a realm of its own: a world of ferocious passions, enmity and darkness, in which hatred is the predominant emotion. This demonic world is sometimes called the LOWER ASTRAL.

Although the traditions of DEMONOLOGY insist that the trillions of demons which exist on the lower astral are monstrously ugly, with bestial faces, hirsute bodies, fanged tails and sharp horns, some demons have been singled out for more precise descriptions.

A statuette of the Babylonian demon, PAZUZU, has survived almost four thousand years, and reveals a creature with a dog-head and clawed feet. This was the demon of the East Wind. An inscription informs us that, when placed on a window ledge, the image of Pazuzu would protect the house – presumably from his brother demons.

Egyptian mythology abounds in demons, mainly because the afterlife played such an important part in Egyptian culture. It was believed then (and is still believed in many

WEIGHING OF THE HEART

The Egyptian gods Anubis and Amemit at the psychostasis, or weighing of the heart to determine the worth of the deceased soul. Jackal-headed anubis does the weighing, while Amemit, the Devourer, waits in anticipation of a meal. The heart of the deceased is being weighed against the feather of Maat. From the Budge edition of the Papyrus of Hunefer in the *Egyptian Book of the Dead*.

CROCODILE GOD

In this ancient Egyptian calcite statue, now in Luxor Museum of Antiquities, the crocodile-headed SOBEK, who stands as a sort of guardian to the youthful Pharaoh, Amenhotep III, has an inner nature corresponding to the crocodiles that infested the Nile in ancient times – a cold cruelty, which evinced no interest in human pain. Sobek was eventually demoted to the role of a demon in reptile-headed form.

cultures) that hordes of demons swirl towards a dying person, anxious to gain his or her soul. To prevent this, and to drive the demons back, the dying person has to have the help of priests, AMULETS and secret passwords. A liberal supply of CHARMS, TALISMANS and papyrus "Instructions to the Dead" were provided by the Egyptian priestcraft to see the deceased safely through AMENTI, the Egyptian equivalent of the post-mortem spiritual realm. Among the most interesting survivals of this cult is the so-called BOOK OF THE DEAD, in which demon-forms are pictured jostling with god-forms, or NETERS (*above left*). It is significant that these demon-forms, or god-forms, are represented with animal-like heads. This is one way occultists express the idea that these creatures exist on the astral plane, for all animal life is immersed in the astral (*see page 55*).

The neters and demons from this ancient papyrus illustrate another important aspect of Egyptian mythology which has survived into modern demonology. The Egyptian priests would use a head as a symbol of an inner nature, or propensity – for example, the jackal-head of ANUBIS (*above left*) reflected something in his nature which was found in the scavenger "desert dog".

It was precisely this interest in head-forms which survived into later demonologies. As we shall see, it is possible to trace the distinctive appearances of certain medieval demons back to their Egyptian or Babylonian prototypes by way of their facial appearance.

The dark books which preserved the demonic lore of the ancient world were called GRIMOIRES. Few of these books had any pretensions to literary quality, and few provided pictures of demons. When images of demons did appear in the grimoires, they were not descriptive portraits so much as crude conventions – ugly-looking creatures with horns, and sometimes with bat-like wings. The demonic pictorial tradition is surprisingly conservative.

Most of the medieval grimoires restrict themselves to providing descriptions of the demons, alongside their secret DEMONIC SEALS, or graphic signatures. One typical grimoire, a "Treatise on Angel Magic", incorporates the ANGEL LORE of Dr. John Dee. In this work are notes on the sexual demons, the INCUBUS and SUCCUBUS, on the Wicked Demons and on the power of necromancers, as well as a list of the seventy-two demons of the Solomonic and Enochian tradition. The treatise does not give one picture of a demon.

The English demonologist Reginald Scot followed this tradition in his seminal study of witchcraft, published in 1584. In this vast work, Scot includes descriptions of the seventy-two demons of Solomon, yet does not represent a single one in pictorial form. The few woodcuts which were used to illustrate this book were restricted mainly to drawings of demonic seals, conjuration circles and ritual objects. The only demon he portrayed was quite unimaginative – little more than a medieval stereotype, with horns and tail. This was a demon with the power to reveal hidden treasures.

Dr. John Dee and Reginald Scot had both learned their demonology from such ancient

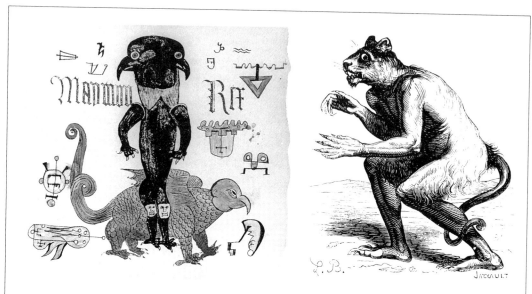

ANIMAL-HEADED DEMONS

Occasionally in a grimoire, a named demon surfaces as a direct reminder of the forgotten neters of the past, as in this sixteenth-century grimoire (*above left*). This bird-headed monster, MAYMON Rex (King Mammon), presumably is a relic of the Egyptian bird-headed HORUS. It reminds us that most demons were once gods, demoted by a new priestcraft anxious to stamp out the earlier cults. Another example is the cat-headed demon FLAUROS (*above right*) which is the later demonic descendant of the ancient Egyptian goddess SEKHMET, who was also feline-headed; wood engraving from Collin de Plancy, *Dictionnaire Infernal*, 1863.

Arielis erste Erscheinung.

DOG-DEMON, ARIELIS

A knowledge of a demon's seal, or magical signature, bestowed power over the demon. Thus, these three seals for the dog-demon Arielis, from a drawing for a mid nineteenth-century grimoire known as the *Faustbuch*, were of greater importance to the demonologist than the picture of this "first manifestation" to the magician of this canine beast. The importance of the seals and sigils explains why they were listed in all the best grimoires, even when the actual appearance of the demon was ignored. From Schiebel's *Faustbuch*, c.1860.

grimoires as the LEMEGETON, or "The GREATER KEY of Solomon the King". These grimoires provided descriptions and secret seals of the seventy-two demons known to the wise KING SOLOMON. The SEAL – a magical signature – was more important than the appearance of the demon, for it contained the magical power of the demon. The seal (sometimes called the demonic sigil) was as personal and powerful as the name of the demon, for anyone who knew how to draw this secret image could CALL (that is, evoke, and command) that demon in a magical CONJURATION CIRCLE. Such a conjuration circle was intended to protect the magician, by sealing him off in space and time. The demon was prevented from crossing the outer circumference of the circle, yet was held by the power of the call, ready to receive the instructions of the magician.

Alongside the grimoire tradition ran the rich pictorial art of the Christian fresco-painters and illuminators, for whom hell, purgatory and its weird denizens were ever-popular subjects. The images of demons, which were such an important part of Christian art, survived mainly in pictorial cycles linked with biblical illustrations, and medieval frescos or mosaic cycles.

The demon-imagery of the great artists – such as the painter of the Pisan Campo Santo fresco; or the mosaic workers who depicted LUCIFER in the Florentine Baptistry; or Signorelli, who painted the marvellous scenes of purgatory in the frescoes in the San Brizio chapel of Orvieto Cathedral (*page 62*) – is derived from the Christian tradition, rather than from the grimoire lore.

The realm of the demons offered a wonderful opportunity for artists to exercise their imaginations, yet it was generally necessary for the artists to please their patrons, and to work within established conventions. The most individualistic artist of the late eighteenth century, William Blake, delighted in a highly personalized portrayal of demons (*right*). However, Blake was rich in imagination and poor in patrons, and, on the whole, he worked in an hermetic–Christian, Rosicrucian artistic tradition, which makes his pictures and poems strange to those unfamiliar with these teachings. In some respects, his genius was far too advanced for him to found a competent school of followers who could explore his artistic discoveries, and his demonology remains unique, even today. It was Blake's fellow-Rosicrucian, Goethe, with his profound knowledge of the esoteric and occult lore, who first gave artists an opportunity to break free from both the grimoire and Christian iconographic traditions, by way of his play-poem, FAUST. This remarkable esoteric drama deals (among many themes) with the nature of demonic pact and modern consciousness. Undoubtedly, it was the literary excellence of this play which attracted so many talented artists to illustrate it with such inventive imagination.

Goethe was the Dante of his time. Just as the Italian's great *Divine Comedy* had attracted the most brilliant artists of his own period, and provided a channel for their creative genius, so Goethe enthused the artists of his own time. Dante encapsulated a cosmic vision, and presented man's predicament in terms of medieval theology; Goethe offered a vision of the modern spiritual predicament, in which he is guided, not by a dead poet, but by a sophisticated and urbane devil through an insecure world. It is highly significant that Goethe felt it necessary to deal mainly with the demonic side of man's nature.

The nineteenth-century French journalist Collin de Plancy (1794–1881) put an end to the grimoire tradition of visual silence, and created

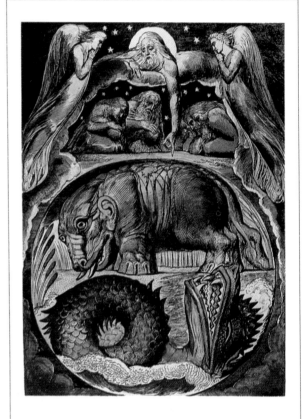

BIBLICAL DEMONS

Behemoth and Leviathan in demon-forms, as visualized by William Blake in his *Illustrations to the Book of Job*, 1825, are among his most impressive products. The hippo-like creature is Behemoth; the sea-monster, Leviathan. Hand-coloured print.

a popular demonology which reached almost absurd levels of personal inventiveness. De Plancy was among the first of a whole band of journalists who, in modern times, write with panache and conviction about the occult world, regardless of the fact that they know little or nothing about it.

Collin de Plancy had a feeling for what people wanted, and he went out of his way to provide this. His major work, DICTIONNAIRE INFERNAL, dealt with demons, witchcraft, and related subjects in a popular, badly organized and inaccurate manner. It was first published in 1818, while he was still a young man, and its many reprintings gradually made him both rich and famous. In this book, he introduced his readers to demons which, until that time, had no real existence. More important, he provided pictures, not only as an aide memoire, but also to titillate his readers and attract a wider readership.

After de Plancy, the illustrated "coffee-table book" of demons was to become an established element in popular occultism. The French journalist spawned a series of portraits of demons which were, in essence, little more than the dream-children of his own febrile mind. In spite of this, the de Plancy demons have become a standard repertoire of contemporary demonological lore.

Perhaps it is not important that these quaint demonic images are semi-modern inventions. What is of greater importance is the ancient occult tradition which influenced de Plancy in his choice of representative images. Where did the French journalist find the sources for these demonic images?

When Shakespeare, Marlow, Milton or Blake wrote about demons, they would – wittingly or otherwise – be using material garnered from the grimoire tradition. Collin de Plancy, while scarcely a Shakespeare, was no exception, and he dug freely into the grimoire tradition in order to prime his imagination, before giving instructions to

CHRISTIAN IMAGERY

The demons torturing the souls of the damned in hell, in this detail of a fresco by Luca Signorelli, circa 1502, in the Chapel of San Brizio in Orvieto Cathedral, Italy, are derived not from grimoire lore but from the Christian tradition.

his artists. Perhaps without knowing it, de Plancy was to be the first to give an illustrated version of the grimoire tradition – sanitized, of course, to meet the popular readership of his day.

The image of the elephant–demon, BEHEMOTH, which de Plancy invented (*page 64, left*), is almost as famous as his "Lord of the Flies" (*right*). The original Behemoth is mentioned in the Bible (Job 40:15), yet, while the Bible tells us that it "eateth grass as an ox" and its "strength is in its loins", there is no mention of its resembling an elephant. In fact, some specialists believe that the name for the demon is derived from the same root as the Arabic word "Bahamut", which is a huge fish in Islamic lore; this would suggest an origin in the Arabian Sea, rather than in the veldt of Africa or the forests of India.

The biblical description – "his bones are as strong as plates of brass ... his nose pierceth through snares" – led early interpreters to assume that the huge creature was something like a hippopotamus. Later, the English poet James Thomson, in "The Seasons", pictured it as a rhinoceros. William Blake followed this latter tradition, depicting his demonic Behemoth as a sort of plated hippo with tusks (*page 61*). Undoubtedly, what de Plancy had in mind when he produced his imaginative image of Behemoth is that found in the medieval tradition. Behemoth was a demon of gluttony. This tradition alone will explain the huge

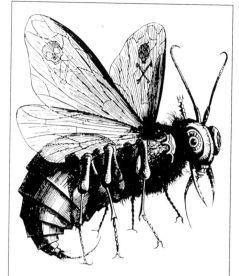

LORD OF THE FLIES

The classic demonic portrait by Collin de Plancy is the frightening image of the demon BEELZEBUB, whose name (according to some) means "Lord of the Flies". Note the nice touch of the skull-and-crossbones wings. Nowadays, this is such an enduring occult image that few stop to question its origin. The truth is that it is really no older than the early nineteenth century, when it was invented by the fertile, and historically unreliable, brain of de Plancy. From de Plancy's *Dictionnaire Infernal*, 1863.

belly upon which the de Plancy demon rests his hands. The elephantine trunk may be some attempt to explain why the Bible claims that the nose of the creature could "pierce through snares", while the tusks may reflect the idea that "his bones are like bars of iron".

In some respects, it is far easier to explain away the curious imagery attendant on de Plancy's picture of the demon ANDRAS (*page 64, right*). This creature is straight from the grimoire tradition, for he is one of the seventy-two named spirits who, according to the grimoire entitled "LEMEGETON", were bound to the service of KING SOLOMON. The legend tells how the king used his magical powers to gather together seventy-two of the most rebellious demons, and shut them up in a brass bottle, which he then threw into a deep lake. The Babylonians, hoping to find hidden treasure, drew up the bottle, broke it open, and thus allowed the demons to escape, to plague the world of man.

The rules of the "Lemegeton" were drawn up in such a way as to enable the magician to conduct the correct rituals and thus ensure his own safety. In this respect, the text was little different from hundreds of other demonologies. Almost all forms of magical CONJURATION were known to be dangerous, and had to be conducted inside a protective circle of signs and sigils which ensured the safety of the magician. The tribe of demons which he sought to bind to his service were unable to cross the consecrated circle, and the many magical figures and sigils kept them from leaping over the invisible bounds of the circle.

Andras is portrayed with wings, a sword and an owl-like face, and rides a wolf. All these attributes are explained by the grimoire entry for Andras, which reads:

> *Andras is a great marquisse, and is seene in an angels shape with a head like a blacke night raven, riding upon and blacke and a verie strong woolfe, flourishing a sharpe sword in his hand, he can kill the maister, the servant, and all assistants, he is author of discords, and ruleth thirtie legions of spirites.*

De Plancy has given Andras the face of an owl, in place of the more proper raven, and appears to have given claws to the angelic feet, but there is no great deviation from literary tradition here.

A more striking example of just how far de Plancy may go in personalizing his

BEHEMOTH AND ANDRAS

Behemoth, the demon of gluttony, was portrayed by the journalistic occultist Collin de Plancy in his *Dictionnaire Infernal*, 1863, as an elephant–demon (*above left*). This Behemoth makes an interesting comparison with Blake's vision of the same demon, on page 61. In the same grimoire de Plancy has the owl-headed, winged demon Andras riding a somewhat tame-looking infernal wolf (*above right*).

inventions is the image for the demon ABRAXAS (*near right*). In fact, Abraxas was not originally a demon at all, but a magical word, used in Gnostic texts. The modern stage magician's ABRACADABRA is probably linked with this Gnostic magical term. In Gnostic circles, another creature (which may not have been demonic) was called Abraxas; this was depicted as a cock-headed half-serpent, carrying a whip and a shield. The magical gems and amulets carved with this creature were called ABRAXAS STONES.

From these historical facts, we may see that the image of the demon provided by de Plancy is almost entirely fanciful. The all-important cock's head has disappeared – though perhaps it is de Plancy's sense of humour which has turned the cockscomb into a crown. The distinctive serpent-legs of the original creature have been demoted to serpentine feet. The only real survivor from the ancient tradition is the whip.

AZAZEL is one of the more important of the literary demons, but Collin de Plancy did

ABRAXAS AND AZAZEL

De Plancy's demon Abraxas has a knotted tail and bifurcating snakes for legs, which reveal his Gnostic origins. The original demonic Abraxas was cock-headed. Azazel, as depicted by de Plancy, also departs from demonic traditions. The original Azazel was a daemon, not a demon, and was associated with air, not water as the trident suggests. In popular lore, it is claimed that the scapegoat itself is Azazel, but the fact is that the goat is merely dedicated to Azazel, who was one of the ISCHIN (a group of exalted angels mentioned in the Jewish "Zohar", who mixed with the sons of men at the beginning of earthly incarnation). The flag is emblazoned with the image of a toad or frog. Wood engraving from Collin de Plancy's *Dictionnaire Infernal*, 1863.

not quite know what to do with him (*far right*). Almost in desperation, the Frenchman combined into one image a number of traditions, each of which was derived from sources as diverse as the Hebraic, the English poetic, and the medieval. The de Plancy version of Azazel reveals the French writer for what he is – an eclectic journalist, who steals like a magpie from different traditions, without really understanding the nature of the things that he steals.

Azazel's name is Hebraic, but by the time the famous magician Cornelius Agrippa included him in his occult book, *De Occulta Philosophia*, in 1532, he was a DAEMON of Western literature, linked with the element of Air. For all the similarity of sound, the daemon is not really a demon, but a creature who (under normal circumstances) bears the well-being of man in mind. Presumably, Collin de Plancy was ignorant of this tradition which links Azazel with the element of Air, for he gives his demon a trident, which is the standard symbol of the sea-gods. However, the English poet John Milton called Azazel the standard-bearer of the rebellious angels, which explains why de Plancy's version carries a flag on the same trident.

In Mohammedan demonology, Azazel is a DJIN – a general name for a spirit, from which we derived our word GENIE. When he is commanded to worship the newly created Adam, Azazel refuses, claiming that he, as "one of the sons of smokeless fire" (that is, as an angel), should not bend to a son of dust. Some say that it was this refusal which led to Azazel being demoted to demonic rank, and thrust from heaven.

The popular grimoires tell us that Azazel is the guardian of the goat (which, once again, explains the de Plancy imagery) because his name is connected with the Hebraic scapegoat ritual.

Blavatsky, a great exposer of esoteric traditions (*see page 67*), informs us that Azazel was one of the chiefs of the transgressing angels. When they descended to earth, Azazel occupied himself in teaching mankind how to make swords, shields, knives, and other cutting tools, as well as how to make mirrors, including MAGIC MIRRORS, in which man might learn to see the future and the past. Perhaps the trident carried

TRUMPETS AND HORNS

Also by de Plancy is this wood engraving of the unicorn–demon, Amduscias, a grand-duke of the infernal legions, who is conjured mainly for his power to command sweet music (hence, the trumpets). This demon has a special connection with musicians, for he is conjured to provide imps, or demonic familiars, for those musicians who feel the need of such companions. Wood engraving from Collin de Plancy's *Dictionnaire Infernal*, 1863.

by the de Plancy Azazel, and used as a flag staff, is a reference to this manufacture of arms.

It is something of a relief to turn away from the composite figure of Azazel to the slapstick AMDUSCIAS (*above*). For all his comic-book appearance, this unicorn–demon has a fearsome reputation as one of the dukes of hell. The grimoires tell us that he appears in the form of a unicorn, and that one of his feats, performed for the magician who has the power or cunning to command him, is to enchant the ears with the sound of sweet music, without requiring the presence of an orchestra. For once, almost every part of the de Plancy imagery may be related to the demonic tradition. The single horn of the unicorn, the coronet which befits one of the dukes (albeit of hell) and the musical instruments, are all part and parcel of the ancient grimoire tradition. In some ways, for all its intriguing beauty, this is probably the most unimaginative of all de Plancy's works!

MODERN OCCULTISM

Undoubtedly, the most important movement to have influenced the growth of occultism in the twentieth century has been the THEOSOPHICAL SOCIETY, founded in New York in 1875. The prime-mover in the exposition of THEOSOPHY was the remarkable Madame Blavatsky (*right*).

Blavatsky's ideas are expressed in her two major works, ISIS UNVEILED (1877) and THE SECRET DOCTRINE (1888). Both were vast works, derived partly from clairvoyant readings and contact with the Masters, and partly from her wide reading in occult and related fields. In these books she was among the first of a long line of occultists to open up for public scrutiny the secrets which had hitherto been reserved for initiates in the arcane fraternities. Indeed, in a sense, Blavatsky was one of the first to inform the general public of the existence of such things as ESOTERIC SCHOOLS – groups of men and women possessed of superior wisdom, initiated in such a way as to be familiar with both the material and the spiritual worlds.

Isis Unveiled was intended as master-key to the mysteries of science and theology, the modern forms of which Blavatsky viewed as being moribund. She argued forcefully that a soulless materialistic science was in danger of stultifying the human spirit, while theology had degenerated into mere dogma. In its place she formulated a return to the ancient wisdom – the lost knowledge of the initiates – in which science and religion were unified.

MADAME BLAVATSKY

Helena Petrovna Blavatsky (1831–1891) is portrayed here with the symbol of the Theosophical Society as a sort of halo above her head. A Russian of wide education, Blavatsky was the greatest female occultist of the nineteenth century. She possessed clairvoyant faculties of such refinement that she was able to make contact with the MASTERS, or secret adepts, whom she claimed as the guardians of sacred knowledge. Painting by Gordon Wain, commissioned by Charles Walker.

Her second work, *The Secret Doctrine*, expanded these occult ideas. It purported to be a commentary on an ancient, unpublished document, the *Book of Dyzan*. "Not many of this generation will understand it," she admitted to her followers (not without good reason), "but next century will see the beginnings of its acceptance and appreciation". Much of the text was concerned with justifying Oriental – especially Hindu – philosophy, and it introduced Eastern terms which have since been firmly established as occult terminology in the West.

THEOSOPHICAL SYMBOL

The symbol of the Theosophical Society, designed in collaboration with H.P. Blavatsky, is said to incorporate all numbers from zero to nine – which is to say that it encompasses all numerological combinations. On the outer periphery is Time, in the form of Ouroboros devouring its own tail. In the centre is the hexagon of the hexagram, which symbolizes the timeless etheric.

The esoteric emblem of the Theosophical Society (*left*) was designed with the help of Blavatsky and expresses the nature of the Society more pointedly than words may. The nine basic symbols from which this emblem is constructed are all from different occult traditions – for example, the swastika is Buddhist, the Ouroboros snake is Gnostic, the hexagram is Hebraic, and so on. The interesting thing is that this symbol, designed in the United States at the end of the nineteenth century, does not incorporate a specifically Christian element. Theosophy, in its inception at least, was essentially syncretic – an attempt to reconcile different traditions, especially those from Eastern culture. It was this very emphasis which so quickly led to schisms within the movement.

Some of the claims made by Blavatsky in her works were so extraordinary that few of her contemporaries were willing to accept them on trust. She insisted, for example, that the ancient culture of the Indus Valley knew the secrets of flight, and that they had access to weapons so destructive that they could wipe out whole armies in a few seconds. Blavatsky called the power known to the ancients as MASH-MAK, and said that it was the same as the mysterious VRIL described by the occult author Bulwer Lytton in his work THE COMING RACE. The name Vril may belong to fiction, she said, but the force itself may not be doubted: "When aimed at an army from an AGNI RATH fixed on a flying vessel ... [it] reduced to ashes 100,000 men and elephants, as easily as it would a dead rat."

These ideas, first set down in 1888, are not quite so astonishing in modern times: recent research has shown that the technology of ancient India did encompass a knowledge of flight, in the VIMANA crafts which are mentioned in many Sanscrit texts. In his remarkable work, *Vimana Aircraft of Ancient India and Atlantis*, David Childress reminds us that when the ancient city of Mohenjo Daro (in what is now Pakistan) was first excavated, human skeletons were found lying in the streets, many of them still holding hands. Thousands of years ago, huge crowds of people had died instantaneously, as though in some dreadful holocaust.

Among the important occult ideas popularized by Blavatsky was the notion of KARMA. The Oriental doctine of karma maintains that every thought, feeling and action on the physical plane has a consequence proportional to its original intention. The consequence of thought, feeling and action will be experienced at a later point – perhaps in a later life – by the one responsible for it. Karma is the fruits of action, and is radically different from the Western view of fate, which is not always connected with previous deeds, or with previous lives, but may be determined by the random fiat of the gods.

Karma, as one modern esotericist said, is like not making the bed in the morning: at night-time, when you want to lie down and rest, you find the bed is still unmade, and, because you are tired, it is somehow harder to make it at this point. The "making of the bed" is the adjusting of past karma.

The notion of karma was inseparable from the idea of REBIRTH, or REINCARNATION. Although the idea of reincarnation had been introduced into European occultism in the late seventeenth century, in the Rosicrucian school established by Franciscus van Helmont at Ragley (Worcestershire), it had not been widely promulgated in non-esoteric circles. Now, for the first time, the laws of reincarnation (at least, the laws as formulated in the East, and in predominantly Hindu literature) were made public in accessible literature. Blavatsky was one of the first esotericists to point out that in the coming twentieth century more and more people would be born with a distinct remembrance of former lifetimes. This realization would have a profound influence on the morality of such people.

Blavatsky adopted Hindu chronologies, and maintained that the incarnating ego of the individual human being experienced rebirth and death, rebirth and death, through extraordinarily long periods, through cultures and civilizations which have been entirely lost to exoteric history. Among such civilizations, which went back to an antiquity beyond the Indus civilizations, were the continents of LEMURIA (sited in what is now the Pacific Ocean) and ATLANTIS (sited in what is now the Atlantic Ocean).

One interesting element of the early Rosicrucian view of reincarnation (proposed by the great alchemist Van Helmont, and adopted by such modern occultists as Rudolf Steiner) is that the human ego incarnates alternately in male and female bodies. In contrast, Spencer Lewis, a former Imperator of the Rosicrucian Order for North and South America, maintained that the PERSONALITY (the incarnating ego or individuality) only occasionally enters a body of a different sex. All Modern Rosicrucians are united in the belief that the soul does not TRANSMIGRATE – that is, enter into the bodies of lower animals.

The more sophisticated theories behind reincarnation recognize that what is internalized in one incarnation becomes externalized in the next. For example, an immoral lifetime (that is, a lifetime in which the soul's inner activity is somehow deformed – through crime, dishonesty and so on) will result in a later lifetime in which the external form will be deformed. On the other hand, a lifetime spent in inner moral striving, and the cultivation of inner beauty or artistic talent, will result in a later life experience in which the physical form will be beautiful and attractive. As lifetimes

ILLVMINATIO

REINCARNATION IMAGE

Forbidden by the early Christian church, reincarnation was not discussed in Western literature until the Rosicrucian Franz Mercurius van Helmont reintroduced it in the seventeenth century. In previous centuries, its teachings were contained in arcane diagrams, such as those used in alchemical texts. In this image, from the 1550 edition of *Rosarium Philosophorum*, the incarnating or excarnating spirit is symbolized as a winged sun – an ancient emblem for the indestructible human soul. It is "hovering" over the sarcophagus – both entering and leaving it – which means that it symbolizes both rebirth and death. The alchemists recognized that the Greek word (*sarx*) from which we have taken our word sarcophagus means "flesh": this is the main reason the tomb is taken as a symbol of the body.

progress, the inner becomes the outer. Within the framework of such a belief we see that reincarnation, allied to karma, is a law of retribution.

One aspect of the theory of reincarnation which is not always taken into account in popular literature is the fact that lifetimes on earth are relatively short in comparison with the times spent in the spiritual world, during the intervals between lifetimes. Blavatsky called the non-corporeal worlds KAMALOCA and DEVACHAN, the former being the spiritual state equivalent to purgatory, and the latter being the spiritual state equivalent to heaven.

Blavatsky's follower, Annie Besant, attempted to represent her teacher's view of karma in a relatively simple form, and even published a book in which she revealed some of the more important lifetimes she herself had experienced – most notably as the heretic Giordano Bruno, who perished at the stake in Rome, in 1600. Besant noted that repeated thoughts in one life precipitate distinct tendencies in a later life. The will to do certain things will translate itself into an ability to do these things in a later lifetime. Because, what was heretical in the sixteenth century was no longer heretical in the twentieth century, it was possible for her to participate in the formulation of a new vision of the cosmos without being punished by the church.

It was left to another theosophist, Rudolf Steiner, to set out the laws of reincarnation in a way which was immediately accessible to modern thinking. Steiner indicated that karma was a creative formative force, by which the soul learned lessons and achieved life-aims, aided by mighty spiritual forces. In this work, the individual human was constantly attended by his or her personal angel.

The influence of theosophy was given a new direction when Steiner seceded, in 1912. In that year, Steiner participated in the formation of a new society consciously designed to remedy defects he perceived in theosopy. He and his followers attempted to expand and reform the theosophical outlook by uniting it with a new vision of esoteric Christianity, and with a new creative impulse which embraced art, literature, dance and music. Among its most important aims was to reformulate the goal of education as an artistic activity in its own right. This new movement was called ANTHROPOSOPHY.

Undoubtedly, anthroposophy is the most impressive of the modern esoteric movements, supporting a meaningful continuation of the occult tradition. Its members tend to trace their heritage in the stream of Rosicrucian thought which has permeated European occult life since the fifteenth century. There are, however, many elements in anthroposophy that owe a great deal to imported Oriental ideas – which is understandable since its roots lie in theosophy.

Anthroposophy is a society of like-minded people, with convictions which have grown out of the SPIRITUAL SCIENCE developed by Steiner. Steiner's legacy of writings and lectures has laid the foundation for a new appraisal of the rich stream of esotericism which forms the backbone of European occultism. Anthroposophy is not a religion, yet interwoven into the belief systems of its adherents is a deep awareness of the hidden wisdom behind Christianity, in the stream known as ESOTERIC CHRISTIANITY. Perhaps uniquely in the present age, this Christian impulse is harmoniously united with a living awareness of the reality of reincarnation.

As part of his programme of reform of theosophy, Rudolf Steiner left indications for research which have enabled his followers to discover many of the secrets inherent in occult lore, resulting in new appraisals of ancient beliefs. For example, Steiner's view of the cosmos has resulted in the development of a new cosmology, expressed in a form of astrology, sometimes called ASTROSOPHY, which is heliocentric (sun-centred) rather than geocentric (earth-centred). Astrosophists often use horoscopes related to the cosmic configuration at conception, called the PRENATAL CHART (or sometimes the CONCEPTION CHART) as well as a DEATH CHART – both of which are important within the framework of the notion of reincarnation.

The anthroposophical view of reincarnation is not directly derived from Hinduism, as was that of Madame Blavatsky. The formulation of the "rules" of continual rebirth into the physical plane is derived from Steiner's direct insight into the spiritual planes. He was an initiate of such a high order that he was capable of tracing through the AKASHIC CHRONICLES (occult history maintained in the higher planes as perceptible records) the sequences of lifetimes of important personalities, and thus accessing their contributions to world evolution.

For example, he would trace the connection between the great fourth-century Christian convert, Saint Augustine, and the Renaissance artist Leonardo da Vinci, pointing to those elements which were common to them, because the two represented incarnations of the same individuality. The symbols and images which were heretical in Leonardo's paintings could be traced back to heretical streams of thinking in Augustine,

ESOTERIC ARCHITECTURE

The Goetheanum at Dornach, near Basle, Switzerland, designed by Rudolf Steiner as a "fortress" replacement for the first wooden building, which had been destroyed by fire. Far ahead of its time as an architectural vision, the Goetheanum was founded on esoteric principles.

who had, to a large extent, repressed his inherited Manichean dualism – the belief that God and the Devil are of equal status, and fight for possession of the world – in favour of Christianity.

The periodicities of reincarnation have been carefully formulated by such anthroposophists as Waschmuth, who has shown that while periods between rebirths are getting shorter, the soul dwells in the spiritual realm for much longer periods between incarnations than is generally realized.

There are few realms of esotericism which have not been enlivened by anthroposophy, but probably the most important has been the approach to education, which is rooted in a spiritual conception of the child. The educational methods have been put to astonishing effect in the WALDORF SCHOOLS, which are now widely spread throughout Europe, and (to a lesser extent) the United States.

BIODYNAMIC FARMING – an agricultural method rooted in a spiritual conception of the earth's rhythms, linked especially with the observable rhythms of the Moon, and based on a SIDEREAL CALENDAR – has also flourished in anthroposophical groups. They were among the first people to be aware of the dangers inherent in modern chemical farming.

In the arcane realm of demonology (perhaps

STEINER AT WORK

The occultist Rudolf Steiner, in his studio by the old Goetheanum at Dornach, round about 1914, sculpting his great statue of Christ and the two Adversaries, *The Representative of Humanity.* This was intended to be set up in the middle of the first Goetheanum, which was built of wood. When it was burned down by supporters of the Nazis, the statuary was placed in a different position in the redesigned and rebuilt Goetheanum.

better described in an anthroposophical context as "angelology") Steiner has also been revolutionary. In place of the strict dualism which has been the bugbear of Christian dogma, he substituted a view of spiritual interpenetration of the realm of man by two beings, AHRIMAN and LUCIFER, who were fighting for possession of man's soul. In an enormous wooden sculpture, which is still displayed in the Goetheanum (*left*) at Dornach (designed by Steiner), these two figures are shown attempting to influence man into their own mode of thought. Lucifer is above the human, and Ahriman below, yet the two may be seen as spiritual balances, on either side of man – Ahriman being a creature of darkness, and Lucifer a creature of light. Steiner's view of Ahriman, while based on a direct apprehension of spiritual truths, is historically linked with Zoroastrianism, for this is the same "Prince of Lies" who was called ANGRA MAINU. In the present age, Ahriman works through human consciousness in such a way as to persuade mankind that the earthly values are the eternal verities, that materialism is itself a worthwhile creed, and that the physical appetites are of paramount importance. Through such persuasion, he seeks to deflect mankind from its spiritual destiny.

Lucifer, his antagonist, is also derived from the Zoroastrian cosmoconception, for he was the solar being AHURA MAZDA, a creature wholly concerned with light and spirituality. In the present age, Lucifer is visualized as attempting to draw man out of his physical condition, into the bliss of the body-free state. Behind all that is great in art, painting, music and poetry, the activity of Lucifer may be perceived. Just as Ahriman would carry the soul of man into the centre of the dense earth, so Lucifer would lose the human soul in the spaces of the astral realm, where responsibility for the earth would not be felt.

In this respect, therefore, the two beings are both seducers in their own way, each seeking to carry man away from his important destiny in the cosmos, which is to become a spiritual being committed to the growth of the earth. Steiner makes it an important part of his advice for spiritual development of man that he should seek to balance and harmonize the two urges in himself, and must develop a healthy respect for the workings of Ahriman and Lucifer.

MODERN ROSICRUCIANISM claims a direct descent from the late-medieval Rosicrucianism, which spread enlightenment through Europe in the seventeenth century (*see page 43*). However, it is usual for occultists to distinguish the later movement from the traditional Rosicrucianism by referring to it as Modern Rosicrucianism, or by using the ugly acronym AMORC, which stands for "Ancient and Mystical Order Rosae Crucis". Modern Rosicrucianism seems to have been established in North America gradually by Spencer Lewis, between 1909 and 1916. However, the official history of AMORC recognizes that European Rosicrucians did emigrate to America, "under Sir Francis Bacon's original plan", in 1694, to establish themselves first in Philadelphia, then at Ephrata, Pennsylvania.

The connection between the ancient and modern forms of Rosicrucianism may not be quite so tenuous. One of the founder members of the ROSICRUCIAN FELLOWSHIP, with headquarters at Mount Ecclesia, California, was Carl Louis Grasshoff, who wrote widely on modern Rosicrucian philosophy, occultism and astrology under the pseudonym Max Heindel. Heindel had studied under Rudolf Steiner, and this great initiate maintained, with good reason, that his anthroposophy was a continuation into the twentieth century of the old Rosicrucian principles. It is no accident that Steiner dedicated his GOETHEANUM at Dornach (*photograph, page 72*) with a ritual which was similar to a Rosicrucian rite, choosing the appropriate cosmic moment to unite heaven with earth.

The occult tenets to which Modern Rosicrucianism adheres involve an awareness of karma and reincarnation, and the need for a strictly moral and spiritually useful life. Indeed, the symbolic system of AMORC reads the ROSY-CROSS (Rose + Cross) as being combined images of moral and spiritual evolution (the growing rose) and karma (the heavy cross which one must bear, even though this is undoubtedly self-made).

The headquarters and Grand Lodge of AMORC are in San José, south of San Francisco, where the gardens and architecture offer an artistic feast for all those interested in arcane symbolism. In the well-kept gardens are a pyramid memorial tomb to Spencer Lewis and a number of beautifully designed buildings, including a working planetarium. Perhaps most impressive is the EGYPTIAN MUSEUM (*below*), with its remarkable exhibits from the ancient hermetic tradition.

The Russian mystic Gurdjieff (*illustration, page 76*) and his followers developed an esoteric group which was partly rooted in the SUFI (the esoteric branch of Islam) model of man and approach to spiritual development, and partly rooted in the ancient mystery wisdom of the Far-Eastern temples. The groups which formed around Gurdjieff were centred on his Institute for the HARMONIOUS DEVELOPMENT OF MAN, wherein were practised disciplines which are nowadays referred to as THE WORK – presumably short for "work on oneself".

Among the very many important contributions which Gurdjieff made to modern

EGYPT TRANSPLANTED

The facade of the Egyptian Museum in the Rosicrucian Park at San José, California, is an imitation of an Egyptian temple. The Egyptian hippopotamus–goddess on watchful guard is TAUERET. This museum houses some fascinating early Egyptian esoteric works, including a beautiful electrotype of the funerary mask of the initiate-Pharaoh, Tutankhamen, and a fine copy of the sacred zodiac in Denderah.

esoteric thought were the so-called MOVEMENTS, which were sacred and ritual dances, learned by Gurdjieff in various mystery centres and temples in the Middle East, China and Tibet. He taught these to his followers, not merely for the beauty of the art involved, but as difficult exercises in attention.

Gurdjieff's esoteric novel ALL AND EVERYTHING – probably his most important work – is an arcane space odyssey. It is set in the spacecraft "Karnak", which is under the control of BEELZEBUB, who (among other things) attempts to give his grandson an impartial account of the strange "bipeds" who dwell upon the remote planet earth, and who indulge in "periodic reciprocal destruction". Beelzebub is of the opinion that the only way these bipeds may be brought to their senses is for them to be made aware, at every moment of their existence, of the reality of their own death. This is an interesting proposition within the occult tradition, for one of the features distinguishing esoteric beliefs from ordinary beliefs is the tenet that death is by no means the end, and is in no way a cessation of consciousness.

G.I. GURDJIEFF

The esotericist George Ivanovitch Gurdjieff (1877–1949) preserved much of the Oriental temple wisdom from the ancient mystery sites, prior to the two periods of what he called "reciprocal destruction" by "terrestrial bipeds". This painting, by Gordon Wain, shows the spaceship "Karnak", which was the setting for Gurdjieff's esoteric novel *All and Everything*, a space odyssey.

Among the teachings of Gurdjieff are what he called the two great cosmic laws, the Law of Three and the Law of Seven. The LAW OF THREE denies the principle of dialectical materialism by insisting that all phenomena, from the sub-atomic to the cosmic, are a result of the meeting of three forces. Nothing results from the meeting of only two forces. This notion is derived from ancient occult lore, and is still preserved in the Hindu trinity of BRAHMA, VISHNU and SIVA – each different aspects of ISHWARA – as in other Oriental triplicities.

The LAW OF SEVEN, which Gurdjieff also called the LAW OF OCTAVES, was again somewhat opposed to scientific notion of things. Gurdjieff taught that vibrations of all frequencies were not continuous, but were subject to certain "breaks" or "discontinuities" which either accelerated or retarded the vibrations at quite distinctive points. The two breaks, corresponding to the INTERVALS in an octave, are found in each full schema of seven distinct states, or tones.

This septenary vibration was called the Law of Seven, and forms a link with the many septenaries of traditional occultism.

One especially interesting point which Gurdjieff made was that, while it was quite possible to conceive of the working of the cosmos (and everything in the cosmos) in terms of the Law of Three or the Law of Seven, it was never possible to understand the work of the two together. This was one reason why the human mind could not perceive – or, for that matter, conceive of – reality.

P.D. Ouspensky, a Russian journalist and writer (*right*), was among the most receptive and original interpreters of Gurdjieff's teachings or IDEAS. To a great extent, his writings popularized The Work, and in his attempt to make it more available to a larger public, he formulated another name to represent the inner search – the FOURTH WAY. This Fourth Way was the WAY OF THE CUNNING MAN, in some important respects different from the more traditional esoteric paths, or ways: those of the thinker, the saint and the artist.

Ouspensky's search for the miraculous was more obviously linked with the occult. He had many intuitions and insights which were later followed up by occultists to reveal the extent to which the esoteric permeated life in earlier

P.D. OUSPENSKY

The Russian journalist and writer P.D. Ouspensky (1878–1947) was the author of several esoteric texts, including *In Search of the Miraculous*, which tells of his meeting with Gurdjieff and gives some account of the esoteric background to The Work in the esoteric schools. Ouspensky was deeply interested in theories of recurrence. Painting by Gordon Wain, commissioned by Charles Walker.

days. For example, his intimation that many medieval cathedrals were repositories of secret lore – PHILOSOPHICAL MACHINES, built by initiates – was later confirmed by such occultists as Fulcanelli. The latter revealed in considerable detail some of the alchemical and astrological secrets contained in the sculptural programme of such buildings as CHARTRES and AMIENS cathedrals. Ouspensky's preoccupation with ideas of time, the fourth dimension, rebirth and – his pet subject – RECURRENCE also contributed to general modern esoteric thought.

The NEW AGE movement is essentially the result of a shift in human consciousness which is taking place in advanced societies. There is a widespread belief, fostered by many modern esoteric schools, that the old vision of society is outworn, and that a new vision –

CROWLEY'S DEATH CARD

The magician Aleister Crowley announced the imminence of a new "Age of Horus", and the design of his remarkable Tarot cards (painted by his associate, Lady Frieda Harris) partly reflected his view of this coming age. Although generally viewed as a "difficult" or "foreboding" card, this Death atout (picture card) is viewed by initiates as an image of initiation itself. It is symbolic of the fact that one must die to the ordinary world in order to enter into the new spiritual life beyond.

more appropriate in its feeling for spirit – is called for, and even being prepared. The coming of the New Age may well be heralded by disruption and change, yet it will mark a new era of peace and spiritual development. This new spirit of MILLENARISM (the belief in the significance of periodicities of a thousand years), culminating in the modern experience at the end of 2000 AD, has been highly commercialized in recent years, but it still remains an important tenet of modern occultism.

Many occultists maintain that the only way the wisdom of the past will survive the social fragmentation and collapse of civilization which is inevitable in the not too distant future, is for the seeds of esoteric teachings to be flung widely. After the holocaust, one or two seeds will survive, and grow to serve the esoteric requirements of the civilization which will follow.

There is much evidence to show that the need for this advance in spirit was foreseen by esoteric groups as early as the nineteenth century. Certain groups prepared special teachings to assist the birth of the new vision. Predictions of this coming new vision may be seen in the writings of the American, Andrew Jackson Davis, in the seminal books of Madame Blavatsky, as well as in the rituals of various magical orders. The announcement of, and preparations for, a New Age may also be seen in such widely diverse groups as the German ARIOSOPHISTS, the anthroposophical movement and the writings of Aleister Crowley (who thought that he would be the leader of the coming AGE OF HORUS).

The beginnings of such prophecies of a New Age may be traced to the MICHAELIC AGE which was forecasted to begin circa 1881. The prediction was made as early as the sixteenth century by the occultist Trimethius, and widely known in occult circles since that time. This periodicity of archangel rule, or SECUNDADEIAN periodicities, is divided into equal periods of 354 years, the nature of the periods being determined by the characteristics of the ruling archangel, or Secundadeian.

Among the astrological factors which have found a popular place in the mythology of the New Age is the imminence of the AGE OF AQUARIUS, which will replace the "2000-year period" of the AGE OF PISCES. These periods – in accurate terms, of 2160 years – are a popularized view of astrological PRECESSION. This phenomenon is linked with the dropping back of the vernal point in the zodiac, which occurs at the rate of one degree every seventy-two years, and is traditionally associated with the length of a human lifetime. The main problem with the literature and teachings that touch upon these Ages is that there is little or no agreement as to when they begin or end. Some specialists argue that the Age of Aquarius has already begun, while others see it beginning in the second or third century of the next millennium.

What is the new consciousness, in which the seeds of the New Age are being nurtured? According to Blavatsky and other modern occultists, such as Alice Bailey, the radical change in consciousness would be heralded by three important changes in human psyche. First there would be the growth of a new CLAIRVOYANCE which was no longer to be merely atavistic (like so much modern mediumship), but attained as a result of conscious meditative effort; by means of certain meditative disciplines many humans will learn to become clairvoyant. Second, there would be a marked tendency for children to be born with an awareness of, and even a specific memory for, PREVIOUS INCARNATIONS. This in turn would lead to an awareness that human life continues between birth and death, albeit in a different category of soul experiences. Third, there would be a HEIGHTENED CONSCIOUSNESS, sometimes called COSMIC CONSCIOUSNESS, in certain individuals – especially among those involved in a meditative life, or in some way involved with esoteric groups. Even in its most unadvanced stages, this heightened consciousness would enable people to perceive (literally see) the FIFTH ELEMENT, the QUINTESSENCE, a vision of which had been reserved in former times for initiates only.

This change of consciousness, even where it is not directly espoused by the New Age movement, and only dimly felt by the majority of people, has already led to revolutions in many fields of human endeavour.

WITCHCRAFT

Before they bring her to torture, others have the witch completely shaved, from the bottom of her feet to the crown of her head, because they believe she may hide a demon in the hairs of her head, or some other part of her body – he witch must be brought into the presence of her Judge with her face turned from him. This, because it is argued that if the witch can get a glance at him first, she may fill his mind with pity for her, or, otherwise, bewitch him ...

(Nicholas Remy, Demonolatry, 1595. Bk. III, chapter IX)

 woodcut of 1514, by the German artist Hans Baldung Grien, was highly topical in its day and is still worth close attention (*page 82*). Grien portrays five naked women indulging in a number of evil activities that were, in the early sixteenth century, associated with WITCHCRAFT. In the foreground, a pair of witches are playing around with magical ointments and spells, which are blasting small objects and frogs into the spiritual world. The dramatic upward rush of wave-like "air" is an artistic convention to show that the evil done on the earth is penetrating into the spiritual world, and polluting it.

In the air above, flying backwards, and carrying an evil concoction in a cleft stick, another witch is transvecting on the back of a he-goat (a conventional image of the Devil). In 1514, this was a standard means of indicating that the witch was on her way to the SABBAT, the demonic meeting-place of devils and their minion witches. To make this flight, the witch had merely to rub herself, or her flying stick, with a special UNGUENT (an ointment such as is being prepared by the witches below), and she would be carried through the skies to the sabbat by demons, or by the magical stick.

Curiously, in the same year that Grien published his woodcut, an Italian lawer, Andreas Alciatus, claimed that witches did not really attend sabbats. He suggested that they merely imagined that they made their way to these diabolical meetings, and fantasized about the events which befell them there. Alciatus insisted that these men and women took various

WICCAN RITUAL OBJECTS

(*Left*) Ritual objects used in a witchcraft coven in the 1940s. The objects include a demonic candle-holder, a scorpionic tripod for a crystal ball and a bird's foot amulet holder. Private collection.

drugs, or rubbed unguents on their bodies, which promoted the delusion of attending sabbats. Further, Alicatus maintained that such delusions could be cured by herbs.

Whether witchcraft was a delusion or a reality was still under discussion. Only four years before Grien designed this picture, an Italian monk, Bernard de Como, had written a book which insisted that sabbats really did take place, and that they were not imaginative delusions, as some scholars had previously suggested. He insisted that witches did meet together to worship the devil, and that they did plan their evil-doing, rounding off their meeting with orgiastic dances and lewd practices.

Unfortunately, the civil and ecclesiastical writers were more inclined to follow Bernard de Como, rather than Alciatus. Instead of offering herbs to those deluded men and women who had been tortured into confessing that they had attended sabbats, they had such victims burned.

Many of the recipes for the flying ointments of the witches have survived in grimoires and witch-books, but few have ever been tested. Quite possibly, this is because so many of them

PREPARING FOR A SABBAT

This woodcut of the early sixteenth century shows witches preparing and using a flying unguent, prior to making their way to the sabbat. In the foreground is a magic mirror. Coloured woodcut by Hans Baldung Grien, 1514.

required such ingredients as baby fat, and the poisonous herbs hemlock, aconite and belladonna – all of which would prove too much for modern digestions, not to mention morals.

There is one notable exception to this reluctance to test the old witchcraft recipes, however. In the twentieth century, Dr. Erich-Will Peuckert, of Gottingen University, is reported to have tested a medieval flying unguent upon himself and a friend. The recipe for this did not include baby fat, yet the poisonous herbs, BELLADONNA (once called WITCH'S BERRY) and HENBANE (once called DEVIL'S EYE) were in the ointment. After rubbing on the paste, the two men fell into a trance which lasted for twenty hours, during which time they had dreams of flying, and taking part in orgies with demons.

Are we to assume from this experiment that witchcraft was merely somnolent fantasy, born of memories derived from what occultists would later call ASTRAL TRAVEL? Perhaps

Hans Baldung Grien recognized this, for in the foreground of his print (*left*) is a curious object which is something of an enigma to the modern mind. What looks rather like a hat, with a filigree border around the brim, is actually a MAGIC MIRROR. This was a mirror used by occultists for SCRYING purposes (*see pages 123 and 168*): the magician would gaze into the polished surface of glass, and see within it images of events relating to the past or future. Grien seems to be implying in his print that the mirror is reflecting mere images, or illusions. The scene of witchcraft above is nothing more than a series of febrile images, which have no reality in the familiar world of experience.

Fantasy or not, those who professed witchcraft sought to bring evil into the world. Like Baldung Grien's naked women, they tried to pollute the atmosphere of the ordinary familiar world with their astral magic.

In the popular mind, the WITCH was an evil-worker. In legal definitions, however, a witch, and her male equivalent, the WARLOCK, were persons who had willingly entered into pact with the Devil. The term "warlock", which refers to a male witch, is from the Saxon word *warlogo*, which probably meant "deceiver". Nowadays, male and female witches are not usually distinguished by separate words. It was by means of pact that the Devil raised around him an army of evil people, who were intent on destroying social and religious life. This view, of witchcraft as being a sort of demonic religion, with the Devil as a dark papacy, was fostered by the Church itself, which built up a demonology and witchcraft in its own reversed image.

The excesses of the medieval witchhunts were a product of the paranoia and greed of the Church. Prior to the fifteenth century, there are comparatively few records of actual witchcraft. In those days, there were many village WISE-WOMEN and WISE-MEN, who would practise spells or incantations. They would attract good fortune and repel evil by means of spells, or make divinations, looking into the future by simple kitchen implements, such as shears and sieves (coscinomancy), by palmistry or by similar methods (*see Divination section*). These wise-persons performed a useful social function, however, and while they did sometimes fall foul of the law, they were rarely punished severely. In her monumental, eight-volume study of magic, Lynn Thorndike has to admit that, in the thirteenth century, she could find little trace of the witchcraft delusion which overpowered the populace of Europe in the following centuries.

In the pre-witchhunt period, there was a considerable literature, derived mainly from classical sources, relating to such diverse occult subjects as palmistry, astrology, magic-working and demon-lore. Among the last was an important book ascribed to Solomon the King, dealing with NOTARY ART, or the art of obtaining knowledge by means of invoked angels, mystical figures and magical prayers. This kind of literature was widespread in the monastic libraries, and therefore available to scholars, but there are few records of men or women being prosecuted for following Solomon's magical recipes.

During those early years, it was not just scholars and village magic-workers who used spells. The thirteenth-century visionary, Hildegarde, who became Abbess of the great monastery above Bingen, records large numbers of "medical" recipes chosen for their OCCULT VIRTUES, or hidden inner powers. For example, the reasons she gives for combining a number of different animals in an unguent against epilepsy have little do with pharmacopeia, and everything to do with magical beliefs. Hildegard explains that the mole's blood is included because, like the epilepsy itself, the mole sometimes shows itself, at other times hides. The powdered duck bill and the powdered claws of a goose are added because these parts of the birds' anatomies are the strongest.

To drive away diabolic PHANTASMS, or invasions from the astral plane, and all EVIL-WORDS (words intended merely to harm, as in a curse) she recommends the wearing of a belt made from the skins of a roebuck and the unidentified animal, the "helun", the former being "most pure", the latter "very brave" so that the belt and its wearer are thus repugnant to the dark spirits. The fastening of this magic belt must be made in accordance with occult practices. Four steel nails (perhaps recalling the four nails which, it was believed, nailed Christ to the cross) were to be used as fasteners, and as each was inserted, a special orison (prayer) should be chanted. In such a recipe, it is difficult to determine where Christian ritual ends and magic begins.

The later witch-hunters were careful to distinguish between forbidden magic – that of the witches and magicians – and LEGITIMATE MAGIC. The latter was, of course, the magic of the Christian religion – the rituals of the SPHRAGIS (the sign of the cross, made either invisibly in the air, or in a written form) and the rites of EXORCISM, by which the priests, following a prescribed ritual, would speak directly to the possessing demons, commanding them to leave their early habitation. In such practices, the borderline between priestcraft and magic is not clearly defined. The priest, protected by his fumigations, prayers and holy writ, addresses a demon occupying a human being. The magician, protected by his fumigated circle, itself reinforced with crosses and sigils, addresses a demon occupying a temporary semi-physical body or "appearance".

The borderline practices which Hildegard of Bingen recommends in her medical work *Causae and Curae* in the thirteenth century would almost certainly have led her to the stake in the following centuries. Both priest and magician claimed to make use of spiritual forces and angelic beings. Thus, while Hildegarde could fulminate against the MATHEMATICI, or astrologers, because they looked into the future, she herself made great use of astrological lore, which was at that time flooding into Europe from the great Arabic universities. She certainly used lunar phases as guides for the appropriate planting of her herbs, and recognized the influence of the planets on the earthly plane.

By the fourteenth century, most supposed heresies, such as the Catharians and the Templars, had been stamped out, or had gone underground, well beyond the reach of the Church. The vast ecclesiastical bureaucracy of the heretic-hunting machinery searched for new victims, and witchcraft was invented.

THE MEDIEVAL VIEW OF WITCHCRAFT

The late medieval view of witchcraft was very complex, and, as the anti-witchcraft machinery began to create witches and then destroy them, a large number of theological and judiciary books were written to define the witch. One thing most authorities agreed upon was that the witch was an evil-worker (indeed, one Latin term for sorcery was MALEFICIUM, which meant literally "evil-doing") who was working on behalf of the Devil. This notion was so deeply embedded in medieval thought that the Church authorities and judiciary frequently published details of precisely how the witch entered into agreement with the Devil, what powers the Devil gave his servants in return, and how this might be stamped out by the ecclesiastical authorities.

Behind most witchcraft lay the idea of a formal PACT, a formal agreement with the Devil. The pact need not be in writing, but the medieval witch-hunters claimed that the Devil preferred to have the agreement recorded, and they gave highly imaginative details of how a pact would be drawn up, and worded to the advantage of the Devil.

THE BLACK BOOK

To exercise power, the Devil was believed to have to reverse Christian traditions. This woodcut from the early seventeenth century shows the Devil exchanging the Christian "Book of Life" for the diabolical "Book of Death" (printed on black vellum) with his newly induced witches. In the book their future deeds would be recorded. From Francesco-Maria Guazzo, *Compendium Maleficarum*, 1626 edition.

The "ink" used by the Devil in the preparation of such pacts was usually the blood of the intended witch, but in some cases only the witch's signature was in blood. In those pacts signed by the Devil, or by his minions, his subordinate spirits, the demonic writing is sometimes scripted in mirror-writing. The reason for this inversion lay in the belief that the Devil had to reverse all the ordinary Christian virtues and activities in order to exercise his evil power. By similar inversion, the BOOK OF LIFE which was preserved by the angels (by the LIPIKA, in the secret tradition) became the black BOOK OF DEATH in popular witchcraft literature. In the woodcut from *Compendium Maleficarum* (*above*) the Devil is portrayed handing to his new converts the black book in which their future deeds will be recorded. Even the BLOOD-SIGNATURE of the pact was linked with this notion of reversal, for the giving of human blood to the Devil was seen as a parody or mockery of the sacrificial blood given by Christ to humanity.

Among several surviving pacts is one written for the priest Urbain Grandier, and signed by seven demons of high rank, some of whom drew their DEMON-SIGILS, or secret

GRANDIER'S PACT

This pact was said to have been signed at Loudun, France, in 1634 by the subsigned demons, for the soul of the monk Urbain Grandier. The mirror-written Latin, and its translation, are given in the main body of text. Note that six of the demons sign with sigils. The pact of allegiance, claimed to have been written in response in the same year, has also survived.

signs, alongside their names (*left*). This pact was introduced as evidence at his trial for witchcraft in 1634, and is almost certainly a forgery made by the ecclesiastical authorities to entrap the priest. The first three lines of this curious document read, in reversed, abbreviated dog-Latin:

mlE ntvL bbzlB ntS etmvui rfcL snetpp SON
eof tcp tpecca smebah eidH :qsila toratsA qta …
e sibon iuq rdnarG brU sired

When reversed, the Latin reads:

NOS pptens Lcfr iuvmte Stn Blzbb Lvtn Elm-
atq Astarot alisq: Hdie habems accept pct foe-
deris Urb Grandr qui nobis e …

When the abbreviations and short forms are taken into account, the first three lines of the pact may be translated as:

We, the powerful Lucifer, assisted by Satan, Beelzebub, Leviathan, Elim,
Astaroth and others, today have accepted the pact of treaty
with Urbain Grandier who is [present] with us …

The pact continues to offer the priest the love of women and the flowers among virgins (he will have the power to lie with women at least three times a day), worldly honours, pleasure and riches. In return, Urbain must offer the Devil an annual tribute of blood, trample the sacraments and offer prayers to the demons. After twenty happy years, he would enter into the realm of the devils, where he might curse God into eternity.

The pact was an obvious forgery. Urbain was no witch (though it does seem that he was a notorious womanizer): he had merely been foolish enough to upset the powerful French Cardinal, Richelieu. After a farcical trial, Grandier was publically tortured and burned alive as a witch at Loudun, in 1634, protesting to the last his innocence.

Grandier had been found guilty of having bewitched a group of nuns under his charge. There are many interesting sidelights to this dreadful injustice, not least of which is that two of the priests and the official witch-pricker who hounded him to his terrible end died insane within a short time of the execution. Exhibitions of DEMONIC POSSESSION were staged by the Loudun nuns for many years after Grandier's death. These worthy ladies contorted and cavorted in public to demonstrate how tightly the demons gripped their soul, for the ecclesiastical authorities realized that such exhibitions had become a money-making tourist attraction.

It is likely that few, if any, of the men and women who were condemned as witches during the late medieval period were witches in the sense that the Church defined witchcraft. Virtually all our knowledge of what witches were supposed to do, and of what powers they had to support their evil-doing, has come from ecclesiastical records, so the view is biased. However, the notorious official handbook of the witch-hunters, the MALLEUS MALEFICARUM ("The Hammer of Witches"), first published in 1486, set the main themes of the capability of witches.

This horrendous text maintains that since witches were persons who had entered into pact with the Devil, they might be tortured without mercy in order to reveal details of the alliance, and thus confirm their guilt. If the suspect continued to deny his involvement with the Devil, then he or she should be tortured until guilt was admitted.

The same book also sets out a list of the powers that the Devil invested in his witch, once a pact had been signed. Witches could copulate with devils, and by transferring stolen semen could generate a CAMBION, or child conceived by diabolic means. They could induce GLAMOUR or illusion to create phantasms (invasions from the astral plane); TRANSFIX, or hypnotize, and thus sway the minds of men and women to love or hatred; tie and bind men, by means of LIGATURES, in such a way as to obstruct or decrease the sexual powers; TRANSMUTE, or SHAPE-CHANGE, people into animals; offer newborn children in sacrifice; TRANSVECT, or transport themselves by aerial flight from place to place; raise storms; injure cattle, and so on.

It is surprising that witches, charged by their diabolic Master with such infinite powers, should ever be caught at all. The Church authorities, aware of this sentiment, argued that when the time was ripe, the Devil would betray his witch-slave, and delight in seeing them tortured and burned, bereft of the powers he had promised them. As the power of the machinery of witch-hunting grew, images of the sabbatic devil proliferated, with His Satanic Majesty sitting upon a throne with minion demons in respectful attendance. This crude imagery was taken to very sophisticated levels by the nineteenth-century French romantics (*illustration, page 88*).

The Italian monk Francesco-Maria Guazzo wrote a book on witchcraft which was intended to serve the judiciary of the seventeenth century, thus helping to reinforce the credulity in witchcraft. In this, it becomes clear that the Christian Church of the day could understand witchcraft only as an intentional rejection of its own beliefs – that is, in terms of heresy. The Church was comfortable in this view, for from the twelfth to the fourteenth century it had built a redoubtable machinery to extirpate heretics (people whose beliefs were opposed to those officially promulgated by the Church). The Inquisition, which by that time was pursuing witches with such vigour, had been established originally to fight such heresies as the Catharians, in the South of France. Indeed, one group of heretics was once so confused with witchcraft that the name VAUDOIS (one of the variants for Waldensians, a group of heretics) was used to designate a witch.

It is no accident that illuminations have survived which show such heretics as the Waldensians kissing the backside of a goat, or a demonic goat, for it was believed that this was one of their rituals. Guazzo did not hesitate to portray the ritual in his own work (*right*). Inevitably, this OSCULUM INFAME was transferred to the new social outcasts, the witches. Having largely stamped out the heresies of the Catharians and the Waldensians, the energies of the Church were directed towards ridding Christendom of the new

HIS SATANIC MAJESTY

The great "Sabbatic Goat", the devil, presiding over his vassals at a sabbat, the supposed meeting-place of devils and their minion witches. The goat was a standard image for the Devil. Design by Zuber, to M. Carron's *La Vie Execrable de Guillemette Babin, Sorcière*. Sadly, the story of Guillemette's downfall, though romanticized in this book, is true; it was told in Jean Bodin's *Demonomanie*, 1580. Bodin was responsible for the trial of Guillemette, who was condemned and burned to death at Poitiers in 1564.

dangers – which they themselves partly created, by legal definitions – perceived in witchcraft. This is one reason why the ecclesiastical writers, including Guazzo, portrayed many of the witchcraft rituals as mockeries of the Christian rituals.

Guazzo records that when a man or woman had decided to become a witch, the Devil would herd them together for a DEMONIC BAPTISM, which could take place only after they had denied Christ by jumping upon the cross. The Devil would scratch their forehead with his claw to remove the holy chrism which marked their Christian baptism. They would then reject their Christian name, and receive from the Devil a WITCH-NAME, along with new and more demonically suitable godparents, or DEMON-PARENTS. The final act in this part of the ritual was for the new witch to offer the Devil a piece of his or her clothing.

The only acts in this demonic baptism which were not parodies of the Christian practices were those towards the end. The witches would be required to swear allegiance to the Devil within a circle which had been traced upon the ground. Guazzo himself suggests that this was also an anti-Christian activity, for the circle was a symbol of divinity, which was therefore mocked by being included in such a ritual. However, it is more likely that this DEMON

CIRCLE was introduced by the witch-hunters because they wanted to make it clear that witchcraft was directly linked with black magic. The stamping on the holy cross was designed as a witchcraft ritual to ensure that the New Religion (that of Christ) was denied by the witches. Through this act of desecration, they accepted the supremacy of the Old Religion, or the rites of witchcraft, which predated Christianity by millennia (*illustration, page 90*).

It was widely recognized that, even in antiquity, magicians would use circles to protect themselves when they conjured demons. Guazzo missed the obvious point; that the baptismal fonts (which were originally designed to permit total immersion) were usually circular. By this inversion, the Christian would be baptised in a circle of water, while the witch was baptised in a circle of earth. As we shall see, the initiations of the modern wicca (*page 104*) take place in circles, but the symbolism is very far away from that proposed by the ecclesiastical writers.

MAKING OBEISANCE

The "Kiss of Shame", or obscene kiss on the Devil's posterior, as depicted in an early seventeenth-century woodcut. Also known as the *osculum infame*, this was (according to some) part of the ancient ritual of the sabbat. The kneeling woman, making obeisance, is carrying a torch, the better to see the object of her adoration. Woodcut from Francesco-Maria Guazzo's *Compendium Maleficarum*, 1626 edition.

Just as the newly christened child has his or her name entered in a registry of baptisms, so the demonic ritual required such a registration. The Devil struck out the name of the neophyte witches from the Book of Life, and entered their new names into his own Book of Death. In the previose woodcut (*page 85*) The Book of Life is written on white vellum, while the Book of Death is written on black parchment. Guazzo implied that he was familiar with at least one of these books, for he refers to a "black book" in which were recorded the names of the witches of Avignon.

The eighth stage of this initiation required the witch to undertake to sacrifice a child to the Devil – an act which must be repeated at least once a month. The ninth stage required their promise to make a DEVIL-GIFT to the Dark Master once a year. The witch-judge Nicolas Remy insisted that such gifts were acceptable only when they were black in colour. At the tenth stage, the new witch was branded, "as fugitive slaves are branded". Sometimes the DEVIL'S MARK was like the footprint of a hare, sometimes like the appearance of a toad, a spider, a dog, and so on. The brand was placed on the eyelids of men (or on the lips, shoulder or posterior), whereas on women it was burned into the breasts or privy parts. The eleventh stage marked the completion of the baptism, and at this point the witch made various promises to the Devil about how he or she would bring evil into the world.

STAMPING ON THE HOLY CROSS

Image of one of the rituals supposedly enacted during the induction of a witch. Trampling the Holy Cross, as shown in this picture, was a sign of allegiance to the Devil. Woodcut from Francesco-Maria Guazzo's *Compendium Maleficarum*, 1626 edition.

Looked at as an entire process of initiation, we see that the demonic baptism was really a systematic attempt to represent the idea of pact, of a conscious agreement to work evil on behalf of the Devil. Guazzo had maintained that there were two forms of pact: one which was written, and one which was tacit, and secret. The demonic baptism, which was enacted in secret places, was of the tacit kind and so did not require notarizing by means of a written treaty.

A witch who had entered such a tacit pact would require no document to remind him or her of the implications of what had been promised. Each stage was a step further towards making a more committed agreement with the Devil to be his slave. Emphasis was placed on the commitment made by the witch, and very little account given of what the Devil offered in return. Urbain Grandier was at least offered twenty years of unbridled sexual licence, wealth and power in return for signing his pact, but did not live to enjoy any of this. As Guazzo remarks, it is the height of folly to expect truth from the FATHER OF LIES, the Devil.

PERSECUTIONS

One reason the ferocity of witch-hunting persisted in many parts of Europe was that it proved to be a very lucrative business. When a man or woman was proved to be a witch, and was sentenced to death, they forfeited their goods. These goods were shared out among the lawyers, the local town or city council and the Church. Additionally, the victim was required to pay for their own torture, incarceration and execution. One interesting death warrant has survived. It is signed by Nicholas Remy, one of the most important of demonologists, the Attorney General of Lorraine, in France, who in his book on witchcraft boasted that he had burned no fewer than nine hundred witches in fifteen years.

This warrant, dated May 4th, condemns one George de Haut to be burned alive, "so that at least he will feel the flames keenly before being suffocated, his goods to be declared forfeit and confiscate to whom they belong, reasonable expenses for the trial first being deducted". So keen were the officials to lay their hands on the confiscation chattels that they sometimes raided a property before the suspect had been tried.

At SALEM, in Massachusetts (*below*), those acquitted of the charge of witchcraft had to pay for their stay in prison, as a result of which some unfortunates remained in jail

A SALEM WITCH-TRIAL

One of the hearings at Salem, Massachusetts (*main picture*), the most notorious of all American witch-trials. This lithograph, after the painting by Matteson, in the Essex Institute, Salem, shows the trial of George Jacobs, who was hanged in 1692 on the evidence of a child. Later, the girl confessed that she had falsely accused the man. (*Inset*) Cotton Mather (1662–1728) was the author of the semi-official and entirely credulous history of the Salem witch-trials, *The Wonders of the Invisible World,* 1862 ed.

because they could not afford the accrued fees. The black slave Tituba, who was one of the first to be pronounced a witch by the hysterical girls in 1692, was eventually declared innocent. However, by that time, she had been in prison for over a year, and was sold to pay her expenses.

In Offenburg, Germany, in 1628, the town council went out of its way to arrest wealthy individuals and condemn them as witches, offering a substantial reward for each witch handed in for trial. Many wealthy people were arrested and burned, until the clergy complained that their share of the confiscated goods and money was unfair. The burnings were stopped for a couple of months while negotiations with the clergy were brought to a satisfactory conclusion, and then resumed with despatch. By the end of 1629, no fewer than seventy-nine of the richer citizens had been burned. The evidence for their involvement in witchcraft was, by modern standards, dubious since all the confessions had been obtained by savage torture. It is instructive that when, in certain areas of Germany, confiscations of property were made illegal, the business of witch-hunting ceased.

One or two courageous individuals did speak out against the belief in witchcraft, and in particular against the atrocities such beliefs encouraged. In the sixteenth century, Johan Weyer, who had been a private student of the great occultist Cornelius Agrippa, questioned the validity of the witchhunts and tried to distinguish between the activities of the harmless village wise-women and those who had entered into pact with the Devil.

Weyer claimed that the whole realm of magic was invented by the demons, and that man could accomplish nothing by means of its practice. Additionally, seeing that it was the belief in sorcery itself which was causing so much mistrust, enmity and slaughter, he made the novel proposal that the majority of evil-workers were hallucinating. Surely, Weyer argued, the Devil was powerful enough to work evil without the help of human slaves? He saw quite clearly how the savage torture, which drove most suspects to dementia, was itself the cause of their confessions. Even the German judge Peter Binsfeld, who was a firm believer in witchcraft and was quite convinced that witches should be tortured and burned, recorded that under torture some had confessed to the murder of men who were later found alive. However, had Weyer not been afforded the protection of Duke William of Cleves, he would probably have been drawn into the hunts, and burned as a witch himself.

Witchcraft trials finally began to die out not because the law changed, but because people began more and more to doubt the efficacy of magic. Judges and juries became reluctant to convict in cases where they perceived the prosecutors and the prosecuted to be suffering more from delusion than any demonism.

The last persons to be charged with witchcraft in England were Jane Clerk and her son and daughter. They were brought to trial in 1717, but the jury rejected the indictments. Although the English law seemed to have washed its hands of the witchcraft delusion, the ordinary man in the street had not; as late as 1751 a suspect witch, Ruth Osborne, was beaten to death by a mob. In this case, however, justice prevailed, and the ringleader was hanged for murder. More than a century later, in 1865, a mob ducked a suspected warlock in the dam at Rawlinson's Mill, Sible Hedingham, Essex; he died of exposure, and those guilty were arrested for his murder.

The last execution for witchcraft in Scotland was in 1727, when Janet Horne was burned in a barrel of pitch at Dornoch (Ross-shire), allegedly for shape-changing her daughter to the form of a pony, and riding her to the sabbat. A witch-stone, in Littletown, Dornoch, marked with the earlier date, 1722, is regarded nowadays as being the memorial to Horne.

In Sweden, the end of witchcraft was dramatic. Between 1674 and 1676, seventy-one people were beheaded or burned, and in the latter year Stockholm became the centre of the witch mania, with accusations being thrown from all quarters. Eventually, it was discovered that some young informers were acting out of mercenary interest, and the Swedish King, Charles XI, banned further prosecutions.

In Germany, where the witchhunts had been the most extensive and bloody, the last burning was in 1775. The final executions for witchcraft in France had been thirty years earlier, in 1745. Three years previously, Father Guillaudot had been burned alive at Dijon for divining for treasure after entering into pact with the Devil. His confessions under torture led to the arrest of many accomplices. After long trials at Lyons (ending in 1745), five were sentenced to death, and the others were banished or condemned to serve in the galleys. A priest, Father Debaraz, who is supposed to have held sacrilegious masses to help find the treasure, was burned alive – the last to die for witchcraft in France.

In the United States, the judicial murders which followed the Salem case of 1692 hung like a spectre over the area for many years. Ten years after the last executions, a judge officially confessed the guilt of the Court, desiring the pardon of men. In 1711, many of those who had been convicted and hanged were cleared. (However, it was argued by some, with good grounds, that this was a whitewash to protect the Salem judiciary and officialdom from civil suits.) Finally, as late as 1957, the Commonwealth of Massachusetts reversed the findings against all those not already cleared. In the words of the historian of witchcraft, George Burr, writing in 1890, "Salem was the last bright flicker of the ghastly glare which had so long made hideous the European night."

WITCH MEMORIAL

The most impressive memorial to a witch-burning is the dramatic pile of stones, surmounted by a stone cross, at Dunning (Tayside) in Scotland. It was here that Maggie Wall was burned alive in 1657. Memorial witch-stones still exist in several parts of Scotland. In some cases, they mark the places where the barrels of lighted pitch, in which the unfortunate victim had been rolled, came to a stop.

SABBATS AND OTHER SUPERSTITIONS

Some of the curious ideas which emerged during the period of the witch-craze are worth recording, if only because they reveal the deep superstitions to which the belief in demonic activity leads.

Of all the notions of witchcraft that were invented by the ecclesiastical authorities, the most pernicious was that of the SABBAT. According to writers of the late fourteenth century – which is when the idea of the sabbat first enters the literature of witchcraft – this was a convention of witches, intent on paying homage to their demons. It occurred weekly, and the word itself is probably a corruption of Sabbath. Later accounts turn the sabbat into ritualistic adoration of Lucifer or Satan, who would appear in the form of a horned man, or a goat. The witches and warlocks would offer him the OSCULUM INFAME, or KISS OF SHAME (the backside kiss), and sacrifice young babes. As the idea of the sabbat grew – mainly through the leading questions put to suspects under excruciating torture the view of the sabbat as a lewd homage to demons and unbridled sexuality developed.

To find their way to the sabbats, witches would prepare special magical flying salves, or unguents which would give them the power to fly or transvect to the meeting, usually on the backs of demons or on sticks *(left)*.

The idea of the sabbat as a place where witches might marry (again in inverted rituals), and where they could plan with the demons their future iniquities, soon followed, and became an accepted superstition. By the seventeenth century, we find witches confessing (under torture, of course) that the sabbats were held not weekly, as the name would suggest, but once a day, during the WITCHING HOURS on either side of midnight. The notion that sabbats were attended by COVENS or organized groups of witches, and that such covens always consisted of thirteen persons, is an entirely modern idea, proposed by Margaret Murray. Although

TRANSVECTION TO THE SABBAT

Among the remarkable series of lithographs by Zuber depicting romantic notions of witchcraft (in which the nineteenth century excelled) is a plate depicting witches transvecting on sticks and goats over a sleeping French town – perhaps Poitiers, where the naked goat-rider was burned, in 1564. Lithograph by Zuber, to M. Carron's *La Vie Execrable de Guillemette Babin, Sorcière.*

this idea is now widely accepted, there is absolutely no evidence for it in the historical documents.

A further development of the sabbat mythology has certain types of witch carrying to the meeting the exhumed bodies of children, or of those hanged on gallows, from whose remains powders and ointments could be made to aid evil-working. In a much later phase of witchcraft literature, which developed when the witchhunts had given way to a literature of popular occultism, the sabbat rituals were transformed in the BLACK MASS, the true inverted parody of the Christian Mass, in which diabolical rituals were held over the body of a naked woman.

The Black Mass, viewed as the sabbat worship taken to extremes of diabolic parody, is really something which belongs to occult literature rather than to the history of witchcraft (*right*). Its most famous graphic description is from the book JUSTINE by the Marquis de Sade, in which the young virgin, Florette, is made to strip and lie face down upon a big table: the diabolical Mass was celebrated on her buttocks. Descriptions given by a young girl who was being tortured into confession in 1594 were less dramatic, though damning for herself. The sabbat she confessed to attending included the usual signing of pacts and intercourse with the goat, followed by a travesty of the Mass, with the host parodied by a segment of black turnip, and a chalice filled with water rather than wine. A vast quantity of ink has been spilt on the nature of these sabbats, even though the evidence suggests that they existed only in the minds of theologians set to root out the witchcraft heresy, and in the demented minds of their tortured victims. Whatever the roots of the sabbat, they were not diabolic. The gatherings of "witches" may be traced to more-or-less innocent rural festivities, designed to ensure good crops and animal fertility.

It was believed that those witches who sought to bring evil to the world had recourse to many strange methods and implements. Among these were the WITCH KNOTS, sometimes called "WITCH LADDERS", which were cords tied by witches into elaborate loops, sometimes with feathers set into the fibre-strands. The idea was that the knots bound into the rope certain diabolical powers, which could be untied and released at the convenience of the witch. The occultist Olaus Magnus called them NODI MAGICI, magic knots, and recorded that witches would use them to bind winds, which could be released to cause gales.

Another important witch implement was the POPPET or WITCH-DOLL. The word poppet

THE BLACK MASS

This anonymous coloured drawing shows a sabbatic ritual, with mock altar and naked suppliants. Found inside a grimoire used by a coven in the North of England in the 1930s, it was intended as an illustration for Huysmans's classic satanist novel, *Là-Bas*, published in 1891. It may be a copy after the Belgian artist Felicien Rops (1833–1898).

is from the French for doll (*poupée*), and denotes a doll made in the image of a living person, who is the intended victim of the witch.

Poppets were used by witches and magicians in what is often called SYMPATHETIC MAGIC. This form of magic is based on the notion that a model, or a drawing, has a sympathy with the thing which it represents. Thus, a doll which in some way resembles a living person, by facial appearance, or by clothing, was believed to have a sympathy with that person. It was believed that if the doll was damaged in some way – perhaps by pricking it with a needle, or by mutilating its features – then the person it represented would also be harmed. One way in which magicians ensured that a poppet was a convincing copy of the person they intended to harm was to name the doll, either by literally christening it with the same name as the intended victim, or by pinning to it a piece of paper on which the name had been written.

Poppets designed for named spells were also called CURSE DOLLS, for it was a common practice for the magician to pin to a named doll a written curse. Since poppet heads were often made from wax, the curse dolls were sometimes called WAX IMAGES, or even simply IMAGES, and a whole section of sympathetic witchcraft, called IMAGE MAGIC, was devoted to the lore of making such poppets, and constructing appropriate spells and curses.

One woman who had been arrested as a witch in Lancashire, in 1612, and who died in prison during her trial, explained that if you wanted to hurt a particular part of a person, then you should stick a thorn or pin into the corresponding part of the image. If you wanted a part of the body to be consumed away, then the appropriate part should be melted, or burned away. Interestingly, her testimony suggests that crude drawings were regarded as being as effective in such evil-working as poppets.

CURSE DOLL

A curse doll with the curse or spell tucked into the belt, in its hardwood box. In former times, such images were buried under crossing points such as doorsteps, or in chimneys – places from which they could exude their influence in secret.

Since it was a common practice for curse dolls to be placed in hidden crevices, walled in behind partitions, or hidden in chimneys, where they could work their evil undisturbed, a few examples have survived. On some of these the names or curses are still legible, their burial jars, boxes or coffins still intact (*left*).

The DEVIL'S MARK, or STIGMATA DIABOLI, was a scar, birthmark or malformation on the surface of the skin that the witch-hunters took to be a sign that the person had entered into pact with the Devil. There are cases in which men and women were burned merely because such malformations were found on parts of their skin. Such marks were supposed to be incised by the Devil's claw as a sign of thralldom – a sort of brand of ownership. Some writers insisted that it would remain unhealed, until the next sabbat, at which time the area would become insensitive.

This belief – that witches had areas insensitive to pain – led to the idea of pricking a suspect, to prove that he or she had had contact with the Devil. Undoubtedly, many WITCH-PRICKERS, those hired to seek out such scars, made a fine living discovering witches by means of fraudulent bodkins or pins, pretending to prick the skins of their victims, who showed no sign of pain. The victim would later be burned or hanged, and the witch-pricker would receive a considerable fee.

Often confused with the Devil's Mark (even in the trial records) was the so-called WITCH-MARK. This was a protuberance, such as a wen or a supernumerary nipple, from which the demonic imps were supposed to suck the blood of the witch. Any suspect who had the slightest hint of such a protuberance on any part of the body – even inside the sexual areas – was taken to be a witch.

The Devil was said to give each witch and warlock an IMP, or FAMILIAR, at their first sabbat. This creature would accompany the witch for the rest of their natural lives, presumably acting partly as a demonic helper, and partly as a spy, to ensure the bad conduct of the witch.

GUILT BY ASSOCIATION

The self-proclaimed "Witchfinder General", Matthew Hopkins, with two of his female victims. The woman to the right is Elizabeth Clark, naming her imps, or familiars, which Hopkins claimed under oath that he had seen in her cell. Clark was hanged on this evidence. Although the canine-like creature named Vinegar Tom, in the foreground, has horns, the presence of an ordinary dog would have been sufficient to hang the women.

The French judge and writer against witchcraft, Jean Bodin, complained that witches used "unnatural remedies", such as the brain of a cat, the head of a raven. However, such gruesome and unpleasant remedies were part and parcel of the herbalist's repertoire from very early times, and really had little to do with witchcraft. A thirteenth-century manuscript, now in Bruges, uses a similar magic when it recommends the roasting of a fat goose, stuffed with chopped cat, as a remedy against quartan fever.

It was generally believed that witchcraft could be hereditary – indeed, Bodin insisted that the child of a witch was almost certain to become a witch or warlock in later life. As we shall see, some modern witches claim to be able to trace their ancestry back to late medieval times through a succession of witchcraft initiates. For example, the influential modern witch Gerald Gardner traced his descent from a witch named Gairdner, who was supposed to have been burned at Newburgh, in Scotland, in 1640. Several modern witches have collections of regalia which can be traced back through several generations.

MODERN WITCHCRAFT

THE KNOWLEDGE

The word KNOWLEDGE above Aleister Crowley's signature in the endpapers of a grimoire formerly in the possession of David Murgatroyd, a friend of Crowley's. The word refers to the Knowledge acquired by initiates into the Craft of wicca.

The modern movement, which is only loosely associated with the ancient practices of witchcraft, is often called WICCA. Technically, this is an inaccurate use of the term as it is the Old English word meaning "a male magician, or wizard". The original term for witchcraft was WICCECRAFT, and, properly speaking, wicca should be wicce.

Many of the adherents of this modern art prefer to call it the CRAFT, which is not so much an abbreviation for witchcraft as for wisecraft, a term which has its origin in the Germanic *wissen*, meaning "to know". Thus, the Craft is the CRAFT OF KNOWING. The initiated witch has been given KNOWLEDGE, and this word is found in more than one of the personal record books of modern witches (*left*). The term suggests that the wise-men and wise-women of former days, who were so frequently accused of diabolical practices and were persecuted as witches, are the real ancestors of the modern Craft.

Another name for the practitioners of the Craft is PAGANS. This name, which originally meant merely "those who live in the country", and which was later applied to non-Christians as well as to those who did not believe in one God, is misleading, for very many who practise the Craft do believe in one God – often alongside a plurality of other demiurges (heavenly beings subordinate to God). Indeed, very many modern pagans who are opposed to the repressive element and power-structure of the organized Church recognize the spiritual pre-eminence of Christ, and would describe themselves as being Christians. A more satisfactory term, which is rapidly gaining popularity in the United States, is NEO-PAGAN.

The roots of modern witchcraft may be traced to romantic notions of what the old pre-Christian and medieval wise-men and wise-women believed, which is why wicca is sometimes called the OLD RELIGION. The truth is, however, that the old religion (by which is meant pre-Christian religions) was rooted in mystery schools which worshipped a plurality of gods, while it seems to be a fundamental teaching in wicca that, for all the multiplicity of names in the rites and lore, there is only one ultimate Goddess-God. The non-monotheistic and dualistic teachings of the ancient mystery schools have survived, through Gnostic and Manichean streams of thought, into modern esoteric and arcane schools, yet are rarely found in the beliefs or rituals of wicca.

What, then, are the distinctive beliefs of wicca? Some of these beliefs were formulated (not very accurately, as it turned out) by Margaret Murray, in her book *The Witch-Cult in Western Europe*. Murray believed that witchcraft was a survival of an organized cult which had its origins in the fertility cult. She proposed that the witch groups were organized into covens, and that covens numbered thirteen members. There was no genuine evidence for this last idea, but modern researches have shown the existence of medieval FERTILITY CULTS, which led a shadowy and uneasy existence alongside organized religion throughout the medieval period. This pantheistic fertility imagery has deeply influenced modern wiccan groups, and it is partly this which explains the popularity of images of the great god Pan, in their artwork and ritual objects (*below*).

However, the rites and beliefs of the ancient groups remain a mystery, and while it is tempting to find in these the roots of modern paganism, there is no real evidence for this. It is more likely that the origins of wicca may be traced in the country lore of the wise-men and wise-women, in oral traditions relating to plant-craft, herbalism, snakelore, healing, and so on.

THE GREAT GOD PAN

The great god Pan, with his pipes, is a popular subject for wiccan art and ritual objects. This is a bronze cast of a sculpture by Graham Fenn-Edwards, whose main speciality is the sculpting and casting of magical ritual objects.

A later book, published in 1954, carried the view of the influence of witchcraft to absurd levels. In *The Divine King in England*, Murray proposed that English royalty, from the Conquest to the seventeenth century, were involved in witchcraft. Perhaps this was a result of a misreading of the undeniable fact that many of the rulers and heads of dynastic houses of Europe were initiates, and aware of the esoteric tradition – but this is far from the notion that the Kings of England were witches.

Murray's first book was published in 1921, by which time there was already a ground swell of interest in what she called the DIANIC CULT, or the Old Religion (*see page 98*). For all its historical deficiencies, the work did have the effect of popularizing the notion that witchcraft was an organized cult, practised in secret, and prosecuted by the Church. Unfortunately, this view of the history of witchcraft is certainly erroneous: as we have seen, witchcraft was more of a legalistic definition than an actual practice. If medieval witchcraft had not existed, the Inquisition, by virtue of its own momentum, would have had to invent it.

The modern development of wicca lore, and the adoption of certain magical rituals designed to attract beneficent spirits, coincided with a new urge towards emancipation among women. As a result, there was a pronounced emphasis on the feminine nature of the old religion. The old paternalistic image of God and god-figures was overshadowed by the espousal of feminine deities and goddess-figures. Thus, there emerged, in early forms of wicca, a romantic notion of the EARTH GODDESS, the LUNAR GODDESS, the DARK GODDESS (because she borrowed light from the Sun), or sometimes ISIS (in reference to the ancient Egyptian lunar goddess) or FREYA (by those who favoured the ancient northern mystery lore). This link with the lunar goddesses partly explains why there are so many different names in the goddess-lists of those who practise the old religion. The Jesuit priest Kircher was in no way sympathetic to witchcraft in the seventeenth century, yet when he investigated the classical roots of the many names of Isis, the pre-eminently lunar goddess, he produced a list of no fewer than fifteen goddesses who were her equivalent.

The modern wicca lists appear to have trebled this number – an indication of just how the movement is involved with the much-needed recognition of the feminine powers in men and women. This emphasis on the feminine was no doubt a necessary reaction to the deeply entrenched masculinity of the Christian religion. Though it pays lip-service to the Madonna figure (alone of all her sex), it emphasizes the suffering Christ, proposes a severe, judgmental Father, and, until recently, has been organized mainly by men, with male interests at heart.

The argument that there is, or was, an organized Craft, with roots in the pre-Christian religious life, who worshipped the HORNED GOD, is not historically sound, unless one defines witchcraft rather superficially, in terms of a sort of "developed psychicism and clairvoyance". The village wise-woman, who had an innate knowledge of the hidden workings of nature, along with a facility for clairvoyance and a working knowledge of elementary spells, weather-working and simple divinatory practices, seems to have existed in virtually all communities, and in all ages. If such a person may be seen as a true witch, then there was indeed a historical Craft, passed on from generation to generation (though not always in terms of family lines). However, there is little evidence that such "true witchcraft" was organized.

Furthermore, in comparison with the shamanistic practices of the professional magicians, such agrarian and rural witchcraft is distinctly amateur. The true shamans, who are probably the closest one may come to the genuine antique witchcraft tradition, have acquired either through initiation or through inheritance an uninterrupted vision of, and communication with, the spiritual world. They have a precise knowledge of how this world may be used to operate human wishes on the material plane – which is a far cry from the village witch.

WICCAN ALTAR

Ritual in front of a magical altar. Among the ritual objects is a grimoire, a sigillated candle holder, a skull and various chalices.

This important distinction has led many commentators on witchcraft to term the amateur spell-working of the village wicca as LOW MAGIC and the more sophisticated wicca which makes use of ceremonials and shamanistic practices as HIGH MAGIC. However, both forms are designed to contact the spiritual world, and call down into the physical realm potent spiritual powers to serve the human will. Both are therefore rooted in the occult, and it is often difficult to distinguish the two.

The modern interest in SHAMANISTIC WITCHCRAFT, with its ritual use of drum-rhythms, trance states, dance movements and SPIRIT-FRIENDS, or invisible disincarnate helpers, is almost certainly a result of the unconscious wish on the part of many wicca adherents to deepen the traditional rural element of ordinary witchcraft. Indeed, certain of the witchcraft ritual paraphernalia used in modern wicca – the ritual daggers, or ATHAME, the SCRYING GLASSES, magic candles, skulls and human THIGH-BONE TRUMPETS or horns (*photograph, page 105*) – are remarkably similar to the implements used by traditional shamans in parts of North America, particularly Alaska, and in the Far East.

THE MOTHER GODDESS

Among the many important wicca goddesses is ARADIA, the MOTHER GODDESS or Great Mother, who is identified with a mysterious HERODIAS (from which name the word Aradia is said to have derived) mentioned in certain fourteenth-century Italian witchcraft trials as an object of worship, and said in such trials to be one of the names of DIANA, the moon-goddess. A modern study of a medieval Italian agrarian white-witchcraft practised by the BENANDANTI, or "good walkers" (who battled in a spiritual and bodiless state against the dark witches), records that Herodias was called "mistress of the game".

The "derived" name, Aradia, was popularized by Charles Leland, an American student of folklore, in his book *Aradia: the Gospel of the Witches,* which was essentially a collection of North Italian spells and gipsy lore, "a delightful grab-bag of odd learning, full of demons, devils, dances, songs, sex, toad-lore, egg-lore and such-all", that did not live up to

RITUAL DANCE

This group of witches is performing a ritual dance in a pentagram, at the centre of which is a seated figure who is playing on a shaman's drum. All the members of the group are wearing masks.

the promise of its title. This is perhaps curious, for Leland records that he was nursed as a child by a Dutch sorceress, who performed magical rites over him that he might develop into a scholar and wizard. The curious name he bequeathed wicca may not have been derived from Herodias, for the name does not seem to appear in the older records of witchcraft. It is probably modern – a result of yoking together the Latin words *ara* (altar) and *dea* (goddess).

According to Leland, Aradia was the daughter of Diana and Lucifer (that is, she was born of the Moon and the Sun, since the name Lucifer means "light-bearer" and the being is therefore sometimes associated with the Sun), and charged with the mission of teaching the Old Religion to humanity. Because Aradia is born of the Moon goddess, Diana, and the emphasis in the cult is on the female principle, the practices and rituals of modern wicca are sometimes called MOON MAGIC, in deference to the mother. Many of the modern wiccan rituals involve the Moon.

Among the spells recorded by Leland was one which has been amended slightly to form part of the wiccan rite of "THE CHARGE OF THE GODDESS". This

RITUAL SWORD

Magical ritual with a sword, conducted in front of the full moon. The symbolism here relates partly to the fact that the sword is essentially a rigid line (the equivalent of the runic Is), while the Moon is a receptive circle. These two forms mark the graphic and spiritual extremes between matter and spirit, and have their intellectual roots in Aristotelian cosmological notions.

spell requires the adherents of the Craft to meet naked at the full moon in a desert place or forest, and adore the "potent spirit" of Aradia's mother, Diana – in other words, worship the spirit hidden behind the outer appearance of the earth's satellite. It is possible that Leland invented this mythology, and, as with so many other of his ideas, garnished it with eclectic occultism, yet it has had a profound influence on the modern view of the origin and purpose of wicca.

The nakedness favoured by so many of the modern practitioners of the Craft is explained in this spell as a sign that they are "truly free". However, many of the wicca groups refer to the state of nakedness as being "SKY-CLAD", which means "clothed in the stars" or "in an astral state" (since *aster* is the Latin for "star"). Thus, while the uninitiated see merely naked bodies, the wicca groups themselves strive to see the hidden inner being, the astral form, or STARRY BODY.

WICCA BELIEFS

So individualistic is wicca, so given to eclectic practices, that it is difficult to generalize about the nature, or even the purpose, of the WICCAN RITUALS. Generally, the rituals take place in a 2.75 metre (9 foot) diameter circle (marked by chalk, paint or rope, or sometimes marked invisibly with the point of the knife or sword). The priestess carries two athame, or magical knives, and wears a necklace and tiara. While some covens work sky-clad, others wear special ceremonial robes, and even masks. Some covens supplement their orisons (prayers) and chants with music, drumming and dance (*right*).

The ritual of DRAWING DOWN THE MOON is widely believed to have been derived from witchcraft practices of antiquity, and is among the most beautiful of the wicca supplications. Unfortunately, the ritual has been confused with an ancient divinatory process (*see page 204*), the aim of which is to evoke a demon; this has lent the ritual associations it does not deserve. The modern ritual is designed to INCARNATE, or draw down to a physical body, the powers of the Mother Goddess, in one or other of her many names. The masculine variation of this ritual is called DRAWING DOWN THE HORNED GOD.

WICCAN GROUP IN RITUAL

The idea that witches always celebrate their rituals naked is not quite true, as some covens wear ceremonial robes. Undoubtedly, though, many wiccans prefer to be "clothed in the stars" or "sky-clad" because their rituals are dedicated to astral powers. Other groups give quite different accounts for this urge to worship naked, but at root the idea is linked with the wish to return to basics, and divest oneself of the external trappings of everyday life.

Gestures derived from the ritual forms recorded by Crowley (in, for example, *Magick in Theory and Practice*) are employed. The gestures are designed to heighten the consciousness of the participants, and externalize psychological events and aspirations. These range from the ritual of Osiris Risen, sometimes called the gesture of the Pentagram, to the upward stretch of the Trident gesture, with arms stretched upwards and outwards, a posture linked with the Egyptian Typhon, and intended to symbolize rebirth. There may also be movement around the circle, from specific points symbolizing death to the section symbolizing birth. By means of such gestures, the priestess invites the lunar force into her own physical body, and may even be invested with an extraordinary wisdom, expressed in words, poetry and song.

Since wicca strives to be dogma-free, it is not fenced in by an official creed. This means that it is left up to the personal responsibility and inclinations of the witch member as to what beliefs are held. However, there is no doubt that the modern wicca movement was rooted in a degree of political rebelliousness, with the fortunate result that a certain independence of thought is one of the most endearing and enduring qualities of those in the Craft.

In spite of this independence of thought, however, it is possible to trace in the wiccan groups a certain conformity of beliefs. Generally speaking, the initiated witch believes in – has no doubt about – the reality of the spiritual world. He or she is convinced that it is possible to make contact with that world (wherever it is located), and utilize its energies for their own good.

Among the wicca groups there is usually a deep feeling for REINCARNATION – the general idea of rebirth, and the connected notion of KARMA, the spiritual system of adjustment by which personal achievements are rewarded and personal mistakes made good during a progression of lifetimes. These ideas point to the origins of modern wicca, for, although the notion of reincarnation was introduced into the Western culture in the seventeenth century by the Rosicrucians (*see page 69*), it did not become exoteric (non-secret) until the end of the nineteenth century, with the theosophical publications of Madame Blavatsky. It was the witch Gerald Gardner (*see page 108*) who, in his eclectic fashion, adopted this idea (and the notion of karma) from the writings of Blavatsky and Steiner, and gave the ideas a place in wicca.

To this day, however, many members of the Craft remain convinced that their belief in rebirth is derived by direct succession from the ancient Druids. Nevertheless, not only is there no known direct succession from ancient Druidic lore, but there is little evidence that the Druids themselves believed in reincarnation – or, if they did, what form of reincarnation they accepted.

The wiccan member generally has no doubt about the healing power of nature, and usually this means that there is a lively interest in herbalism, homoeopathic medicine, massage, and such oriental techniques as acupuncture, feng shui and t'ai chi.

As a corollary to this acceptance of the healing power of nature, the wiccan usually believes in the sanctity of the earth, which is perceived as a living organism. He or she makes serious attempts to understand the nature of this organism, and to live in harmony with its rhythms. Since the earth is part of the planetary system, and this system is in turn part of the cosmos, the wicca member often finds himself interested in astrology, in biorhythms, and in the sacred numerology which reflects the nature of the living earth. Such ideas are reflected in the timing of the wiccan rituals and celebrations, which correspond to the twelve-fold cycle of lunations, the so-called LUNAR FESTIVALS, as well

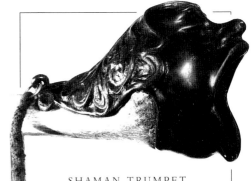

SHAMAN TRUMPET

Bowl of a shaman trumpet in the form of a face. The bronze head is mounted upon a human thigh-bone, with a grotesque mouthpiece. It was designed and cast by Graham Fenn-Edwards, who has modelled and cast some of the most interesting of all ritual gear, such as shaman trumpets, scrying bowls, pipes and incense burners.

as the four or eight main SOLAR FESTIVALS, related to the solstitial points. Love for the earth – a transformation of the agrarian cultus of the older forms of witchcraft – is paralleled by a love for all created things. "For my Law," ends the rite of *The Charge of the Goddess,* "is love unto all beings."

In fact, an alliance of witches, brought together in 1973 by the publisher, Carl Weschcke, of St. Paul, Minnesota, as the COUNCIL OF AMERICAN WITCHES, did make a serious attempt to discover what principles were held in common by members of diverse wicca groups. Among the principles recognized by the Council were the practice of rites to attune themselves to life-forces (specifically, lunar forces), and a deep awareness of responsibility for the well-being of the environment. The council also recognized the existence of the spiritual world, deeper powers than those usually apparent in the average person, and the existence of a Creative Power which lies both in the universe and within each individual. A witch was visualized as a person who seeks to control the forces within her/himself, in order to live wisely and well, without harm to others, and in harmony with nature. There is nothing in any of this which would be rejected by an occultist, alive to the exigencies of the esoteric tradition.

One other important aspect of modern wicca is its commitment to creativity. There is a general belief that all human actions should be rooted in creativity, and should spring from love. This explains why so much of the writing and artistic work published in wicca magazines is of such a high quality. Among the most notable modern wicca artists is the American Allen Holub, the most impressive American voodoo-master Michael Bertiaux, the English artist Steffi Grant and the English sculptor Graham Fenn-Edwards (*photographs, pages 99, 105, 123, 177*).

The influence has not been restricted to wicca artists: some of the finest modern illustrators have found a harmonious relationship in providing pictures for important texts on witchcraft, in which the deep-seated yearning for pagan oneness with nature has acted as an inspiration.

It is significant that, for all the personal styles and visions developed by such artists, each of them has, in his or her own way, been influenced by the work of Austin Osman

DEMON LOVER

Wood engraving illustration by Robert Gibbings for Esther Forbes's *A Mirror for Witches,* 1928, which tells the story of the perverse Doll Bilby, who preferred a demon lover to a mortal. The designs cut by Robert Gibbings for this book are among his best work.

Spare (*right*). Spare was the greatest British occult artist since William Blake (of whom he considered himself to be a reincarnation), and like this genius he combined a great talent for drawing and painting with a profound talent for writing. His interest in magic led him to develop a theory of sigil-making which is already revolutionizing modern magic.

According to Spare, his initiation into the Craft early in his life came from a Mrs. Paterson, a female HEREDITARY WITCH — one whose line of powers and lore could be traced back through the generations. She could trace her ancestry back to a witch of Salem, Massachusetts (*see page 91*). It was only after this initiation that Aleister Crowley began to play an important role in Spare's life, as a teacher and as a source of commissions for paintings and illustrations.

Spare developed a highly personal art of "AUTOMATIC DRAWING" involving contacting the unconscious. This specialized form of ritual, frequently combined with sex-magic, so intrigued the witch Gerald Gardner that he commissioned many talismanic sigils for use in the rituals conducted in his own coven. SIGIL MAGIC, as it is called nowadays, is one of the most rapidly developing forms of personal creative magic of modern times.

SIGIL-MAKING

Austin Osman Spare (1886–1956) is shown painting sigils upon his own picture in this portrait by Gordon Wain, commissioned by Charles Walker. The picture in the background was one of Spare's last pastels, entitled "Blood on the Moon".

In essence, Spare believed that the activity of making sigils was a legitimate and wholesome way of approaching the personal unconscious. He evolved a method of expressing a wish (it may be a wish for some personal possession, for money, and so on) in writing, and then subjecting the written phases to a special coding. Usually, this coding simply involved the reduction of the sentence to the primal consonants. For example, the phrase

"I wish to become very rich"

would be reduced to

"wsh tbc mvry".

These three groups of consonants would then be subjected to combinations, shape-changed, overdrawn, played with (doodled with, perhaps) in order to change their shape completely (*illustration, page 108*).

The aim of this reduction is to remove all conscious elements from the phrase, so that the subconscious (which forgets nothing) will hold the wish, while the conscious mind, which usually interferes with the operation of the will, forgets it. A degree of ritual is involved in this sigil magic, yet its very simplicity as a device for releasing the will is

v ry   nt   l c s M g

vry

ntl

cs

SIGILLIC REDUCTION

An example of sigil technique is shown here, where a phrase from Crowley, *Every intentional act is a Magical Act*, is subjected to stages of sigillic reduction, in order to communicate with the subconscious directly. This stage-by-stage demolition of the sentence involves the ejection of the vowels, the rejection of all repetitions of consonants, and the grouping of the remaining letters into convenient sets of two or three (*top*). The groups are subjected to artistic interpretation individually, and are then yoked together to make a single design (*above left*). It is possible to trace the original forms of the sigillated *cs* on the bottom right and the *vry* on the extreme right. The artist may subject this pattern of sigils to further distortion by uniting the various elements. Although the original thought is lost in this sigillic reduction, its energy remains intact within the image.

attested to in the large number of magical groups which have developed their own personal approach to the system.

In an article on sigil magic, Spare called the repressed element in man ("that which is at the back of your mind") the DREAM-MAN, and offered sigil magic, or automatic drawing, as a means of giving expression to this creature. Deeply conversant with occult traditions, he recognized that this dream-man was the "DWELLER ON THE THRESHOLD" – the spiritual being who stands guardian between the familiar world of experience and the spiritual realm beyond, in which the uninitiated would meet forms which he or she would not comprehend and which might even unbalance his or her mind. This is why Spare could announce that "automatic drawing is a cure for insanity", a release for obsessions.

A large number of different WICCA GROUPS are found in the United States and Europe. Among the most well-established are those which trace their origins to such early writers as Murray and Gardner. For example, the DIANIC WICCA is that based (somewhat eclectically) on the system hinted at by Margaret Murray (*see page 100*), and lays emphasis on the power of the goddess. The so-called ALEXANDRIAN WICCA is a reformed Gardnerian system promulgated by Alex Saunders, who claims to have been initiated into the Craft at the age of seven by his grandmother. There is also the SEAX WICCA, or Saxon Wicca, of Raymond Buckland, and the CHAOS MAGIC which is now so popular in England and Germany.

Gerald Gardner (*right*) had a seminal, if much disputed, influence on wicca. As we have noted, he claimed to be a descendant of a practising witch of the seventeenth century. However, his early witchcraft lore seems to have come from Aleister Crowley, who initiated him into the esoteric group Ordo Templis Orientalis, the English section of which Crowley headed. Later, in 1939, through his contacts in Christchurch, Dorset, where he had retired, Gardner participated in a group of New Forest practitioners of the Craft, who were familiar with certain forms of ritual magic. His experiences in this realm were eventually published in his novel *High Magic's Aid*, which was followed by witchcraft manuals described by some as being the first accounts (albeit partisan and inaccurate) of modern wiccan lore.

It was Gardner's conscious attempt to break with the tradition of silence and secrecy (an attempt seen by some as ill-advised, by others as reflecting the New Age view that the old form of elitist esotericism was no longer permissible) that publicized his particular form of modern witchcraft. Gardner had a facility for writing simply about witchcraft, while hinting at deeper secrets which he was forbidden to reveal, and this undoubtedly attracted many to take an interest in the Craft.

The MUSEUM OF WITCHCRAFT at Castletown, on the Isle of Man, had been established by Cecil Williamson in 1951, as though to reflect the repeal of the last remnants of the old witchcraft Acts. There was in fact no law against witchcraft in England at that time, but the Fraudulent Mediums Act (which had its origin in the 1604 Acts of James I, repealed in 1736) had left a legacy of legal restrictions which construed the practice of such things as fortune-telling, palmistry and wicca as illegal. After 1951, when these last remnants of legal restriction were removed, wicca – as well as many other occult arts – could be practised openly. In spite of this, however, the legalized pursuit of fortune-tellers, clairvoyants and mediums (all, by definition and popular tradition, linked with witchcraft and wicca practices) persisted well into the middle of the twentieth century.

Aware of the sea changes which the repeal of the Acts would bring, Gardner, after adding a few of his own articles to the collection, purchased the museum and the mill in which it was housed. When the museum was closed, after Gardner's death, in 1964, most of the exhibits found their way to Canada, and items were sold to the Ripley Museum in Toronto, after which some were transferred to a branch of this museum in San Francisco. Fortunately, some of the more important items are still cared for by members of the Craft.

Gardner felt an urge to reinstate the feminine element into rituals, as into the life of mankind, and future historians may see this as his most important contribution to occult thought. In a sense, he attempted to feminize and reform what he took to be a traditional witchcraft, yet succeeded, almost inadvertently, in creating a new form. His writings attracted a numerous following, and many of the covens which have been formed as a result are still active. In order to distinguish this form of wicca from other types, the line of succession has been called GARDNERIAN WICCA.

GERALD GARDNER

Gerald Brosseau Gardner (1884–1964) had a profound influence on modern wicca. It is said that most of the various groups which now exist in Europe and the United States owe their origins, if not their rituals and present beliefs, to Gardner's enthusiastic espousal of paganism.

MAGIC

Astrology was scarcely discouraged, and if the alchemist was occasionally tortured, it was only to extract his secret. There was no danger in these things, and hence there was no judgment against them, except by imputation from their company: but Magic, but dealing with spirits, was that which made even the peasant tremble, and when the peasant shakes at his hearth, the king is not secure in his palace nor the Pope at St. Peter's, unless both can protect their own. Moreover, in the very claim of Ceremonial Magic there was an implied competition with the essential claim of the Church.

(A.E. WAITE, *THE BOOK OF CEREMONIAL MAGIC*, 1911)

ll magic is easy: it is nothing more than the ritual ordering of the will. At times, MAGIC may degenerate into the psychic manipulation of other people, aimed at suborning their will to that of the magician, yet, in its real purpose, magic is merely a set of procedures designed to intensify a natural human faculty. "Every intentional act," Aleister Crowley said famously, "is a Magical Act."

The magician who sets out to lend emphasis to his will does so with the aid of special, age-old rituals, and with a paraphernalia of consecrated objects and symbols, used in a formal prescribed order usually called CEREMONIAL MAGIC. This form of ritual magic is an attempt to concentrate the will by calling to its service the aid of spiritual beings. If the spiritual beings evoked through such rituals are angelic, then the magic is called white, and it is termed magic of the RIGHT-HAND PATH. If the spiritual beings evoked are demonic, then it is BLACK MAGIC, of the LEFT-HAND PATH.

The extreme form of black magic is that in which the magician, by an exercise of will, kills another human. The DEATH PRAYER of the Hawaiian KAHUNAS, Polynesian magicians, is an example of this kind of magic of the Left-hand Path, in which they literally "pray to

---

MAGICAL RITUAL

(*Left*) Ritual gesture with an athame during an act of magic. The point of the dagger is aimed at a chalice, near the stomach of the magician. The dual symbolism transforms the gesture into an outer expression of a creative act, the alchemical union of the rod (knife) and the receptive circle (the ritual bowl, not visible in the picture but immediately below the knife).

AFRICAN NAIL-FETISH

This nail fetish is a *Nikishi*, from the Bakongo people of the lower Congo. The wooden carving is set with hundreds of magical nails. The Horniman Museum, London.

death" their victim. Western commentators imply that the death prayer works by suggestion – that the victim is literally frightened to death by the power he supposes the magician has. However, the victim does not need to know that he has been prayed to death, and he will weaken very rapidly before dying. The kahunas claim that they merely instruct lower spirits to suck from the unsuspecting victim his or her vital spirits. Those who have witnessed such attacks say that it begins as pins and needles, which are overtaken by a pricking numbness starting in the feet, before paralysis of the entire body sets in.

The kahunas call the death prayer ANA-ANA, a doubling of the Polynesian root which expresses the idea of being "satiated" or "filled with food". The magic of ana-ana implies that the evil spirit set against the victim becomes satiated with the vital forces which, following the instructions of the kahuna, it sucks from the dying person.

There is also a counterbalance to such a death prayer, in the magical rituals designed by the kahuna magicians to impart *mana* – a spiritual energy – to objects, so that there may be healing, and energy available to those who know how to touch these objects in the right way. The genuine kahunas are a dying race, but to this day, on the island of Maui, in Hawaii, there is a huge natural phallic rock which has been charged with just such a *mana*, and which is used in modern times as a source of magical energy (*right*).

However, the more common use of magical energies lies in the destructive urge. Many museums in Europe and the United States display effigies of FETISHES, which are used in killing rituals similar to the death prayer. Usually, these are stuck with knives or nails (*above*), the driving in of each sharp edge or point imagined as an attack on the person which the wooden figure represents. Another kahuna death-dealing is known as KUNI, or burning. This black magic involves burning (again with rituals) a portion of the intended victim, such as a lock of hair, and destroying the ashes.

Whenever the magician seeks to intensify his will, for whatever purpose – whether to satisfy some mere whim of ego or to improve the condition of the human race – he or she stands in the midst of three worlds. To the right is the angelic, to the left is the demonic, and in the centre, where the magician stands, is the human.

Occultists have always insisted that there are THREE WORLDS. There is the world of nature, of which man is a part. There is the higher spiritual world, properly the realm of angels, and there is the lower demonic plane, ruled over by the demon-king, LUCIFER. In occultism, as in most theologies, man was visualized as balanced between the angels and the demons, susceptible to the persuasion of both, yet free (within certain limits) to determine his own course through life.

Because he was at a fulcrum between the two spiritual entities, man felt the need to propitiate them, or even use their secret powers to his advantage. Simple prayer and worship were usually reserved for the angels, and the formulae for these acts of white magic were largely in the hands of the Church. Indeed, the supreme practitioners of white magic are priests, which is why so many practioners of the black art imitate or mock the priestly rituals. It was inevitable that those men who sought to make contact

SET IN STONE

The phallic stone of Molokai, Ka-ule-o-nanahoa, in Hawaii, is said to have been formed when Nanahoa was petrified for having abused his wife. There is no doubt that the stone was once used as a ritual focus-point by kahuna magicians, and it is still visited by women who seek to become pregnant.

ALL THE FROLICS
OF THE SABBAT

In the top left of this eighteenth-century engraving a witch falls (seemingly with some pleasure to herself and those below) from her transvecting goat to her rightful place at the sabbat. Incendiary demons lead the witting and unwitting around the summit of the Brocken towards the sabbatic goat, which is having its posterior kissed by a new convert. In the foreground, a devil embraces an unwilling maiden, while a huge winged demon uses his chamber pot.

with the lower realms of demons should choose to imitate the rituals of the white magicians, the priests. The early texts on medieval witchcraft and black magic are at pains to show how the sabbats and unholy Masses in service of the Devils were inversions of the religious rituals favoured by the Church. Woodcuts specially printed in the service of this ecclesiastical attempt to eradicate witchcraft depict the witches trampling on the cross, for example in mock ritual baptisms. Later, the concept of the Satanic Mass as a parody of the Christian Mass was developed to high levels of sophistication, along with suitably lewd and demonic imagery (*illustration, left*).

One fifteenth-century account of black magic, the SCOURGE OF SORCERERS by Petrus Marmoris, records how certain thieves carried with them the hand of a corpse, to which the sacraments had been applied to give it power. With this macabre relic, they made the sign of the cross, in reversed fashion, over some sleeping householder, thereby causing him to fall into a stupor for twenty-four hours, during which time they could rob his house at their leisure. This magic of the DEAD HAND is a variety of the famous HAND OF GLORY (cut from the body of a hanged felon, and used as a mount for a lighted candle) which plays an important part in late medieval witchcraft. Superstitions of this kind take on a new poignancy when we find the same Petrus Marmoris recording that his friend had seen a woman burned at the stake with a dead hand tied around her neck. It was claimed that she had been using this dead hand to keep men sleeping while she worked her evil. We note that the power or secret virtue of this relic was not so much in the hand, but in the demoted or reversed white magic of the sacraments and the cross.

In the traditional magical texts, a variety of names were given to the three regions of nature, angels and demons, and they were traced as triplicities in all living things. In man, for example, the three worlds were the INTELLECTUAL (angelic, linked with the mind), the EMOTIONAL (natural, linked with memory and feeling) and the WILL (demonic, linked with the elemental world), each with corresponding operative centres in the head, the heart and the sexual parts. The spiritual activities of these three centres were often described in alchemical terms, as the THREE PRINCIPLES of Salt, Mercury and Sulphur. This important triplicity is examined on page 34.

NATURAL AND ARTIFICIAL MAGIC

Magicians believed that it was possible to work magic by using each of these three worlds. As a result, a variety of rituals were evolved to contact the relevant powers in each. The form of magic used in the familiar physical world – the human realm – was called NATURAL MAGIC. It was believed that all physical things had OCCULT VIRTUES, hidden seminal powers, which were secret to ordinary people but of great practical value to the occultists and magicians who knew these secrets.

At one extreme of natural magic was the interest in such occult properties as gravity, secret virtues, optics and magnets. Anyone who has watched with awe as iron filings are attracted to a magnet has felt something of the fascination of the occult realm of natural magic, and may grasp what the occultists meant by the term virtue. The power of the magnet was invisible, beyond understanding, and occulted to the mind.

In the view of the medieval magicians, the entire world was a living organism. It is difficult for us now to realize that the first astronomers to gaze through telescopes genuinely believed they were looking into living spiritual mechanisms driven by angels – literally by the MOVOTORI, or by the INTELLIGENCES, who directed this stellar motion.

The first men to look through microscopes believed they were looking into the realm of demons. It is no accident that William Blake based his drawing of a demon on the enlarged head of a flea, which the scientist Robert Hooke had sketched through his microscope and published in his entirely scientific work, *Micrographia*, in 1665 (*right*).

At the other extreme of natural magic lay pure superstitions, rooted in the notion that there was no universal law underlying natural phenomena. It is most curious that this lawless magical world is one from which modern science evolved.

The seventeenth-century Frenchman Jean Leurechon, (remembered, if at all, as the first person to use the word "thermometer") is typical of the advanced

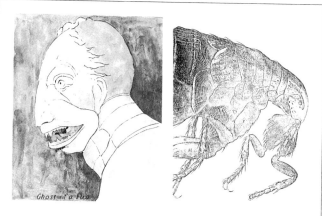

Ghost of a Flea

THE GHOST OF A FLEA?

Engraving (*above left*) of the Ghost of a Flea, circa 1820, by the artist-astrologer John Varley, in *A Treatise on Zodiacal Physiognomy*, after a drawing by William Blake. Blake maintained that he actually saw this "ghost", or manifestation, during a seance. Was he, however, influenced by Robert Hooke's drawing of the head of a flea seen under a microscope? Shown here (*above right*) is an engraving of the Hooke drawing, from Hooke's *Micrographia* of 1665.

thinkers of his time in his experiments relating to natural magic. He proposed building a bridge around the earth, and knocking away its supports, fully expecting it to remain suspended in the air under the force of gravity. This "wonder of gravity" was a fine example of natural magic. One of his later editors, presenting a more up-to-date version of Leurechon's book, strayed from natural magic into superstition, however. This man, Caspar Ens, claimed that if one dangled a GEM-PENDULUM – a diamond or emerald ring – by a thread over water in a glass, the ring would strike the sides of the glass as many times as there are hours. He did not explain whether this was due to the operation of angels or demons or some secret natural virtue in the stones.

Whereas natural magic made use of secret powers known to exist in nature, yet which were not understood, the use of such powers often verged on mere stage conjuration. There is no doubt that in ancient times tricks, sometimes called ARTIFICIAL MAGIC, were used to cause mechanical statues to move, temple doors to open, and ghosts to appear.

An innovative example of such magic might have been used by the ancient Egyptian priests who caused the colossal statues at Thebes (*left*) – the so-called COLOSSI OF MEMNON – to sing, "to welcome the dawn". It is said that, secretly, the priests left the head of each statue untied to the lower blocks from which the chest of the figure had been made. The bottom of the neck joint was especially roughened. When the first rays of the rising sun appeared over the temples to the east, the upper block expanded in the heat. This expansion-movement, against the cold block below, meant that its rough surface grated, and the resultant friction against the lower block caused the hum or singing for which the statue was famous. The statues would probably sing to this day, had not the Roman Emperor Septimus Severus attempted to find out how the magic worked, and dislodged the stones.

GREETING THE DAWN

The two great Colossi of Memnon, on the western banks of the Nile at Karnak (ancient Thebes). These are the last remnants of a huge temple, for which they were the portal guardians. Until the Roman Emperor Septimus Severus investigated the legend, by moving the upper blocks of stone, the statues were reported to sing to greet the dawn.

Undoubtedly, demonic magicians – those of the dark schools which follow the path of the VARMA MARG (the tantric equivalent of the Left-hand Path of black magic) would have attempted to vitalize an inanimate statue in a different way. It was believed that, under normal conditions, demons and angels could not live in animate physical bodies, and considerable effort was made by magicians to ensure that a suitable receptacle was at hand for these entities to "materialize". Many of the more reputable magicians were said to have TALKING HEADS, usually manufactured from bronze, which would move realistically, and answer questions put to them. The most famous of the speaking AUTOMATA was that of Albertus Magnus, an established theologian whose name is incorrectly linked with several demonic grimoires.

People who listened to such rasping voices had no doubt that they were hearing an infernal speech, and many legends developed around those magicians who owned such diabolic contraptions. So widespread was this notion of a severed talking head that stage magicians used mirrors to create illusions of such heads, which appeared to be resting bodiless on plates or on tables.

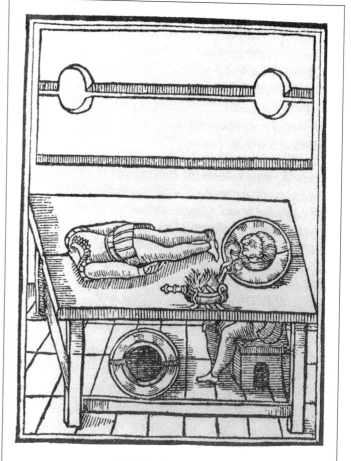

ALL IS REVEALED

In the sixteenth century Reginald Scot, one of the first Englishmen to write about how certain magic tricks were done, reproduced a plate which explained one way in which the stage magician creates the illusion of the beheading of John the Baptist. The head on the plate is pushed through a hole in the table top. The audience cannot see the man seated below, as a cloth is draped over the entire table. Plate from Reginald Scot, *The Discoverie of Witchcraft*, 1665 edition.

The Scottish magician Michael Scot is said to have had his own speaking bronze head buried with him at Melrose Abbey – though neither the head nor the fabled perpetual lamp was in the grave when it was excavated. In his INFERNO, Dante tells us that his contemporary, the magician–astrologer, Guido Bonatti, was consigned to the eighth circle of hell. Along with all the other sorcerers (including Michael Scot), he had his head twisted behind him, thus being compelled to see only behind, into the past – a suitable punishment for men who had dared to usurp the previsionary power of God. Bonatti was supposed to have owned a talking head, which he kept in the Italian city of Forli, and this may have been part of the reason Dante chose to name specifically these condemned spirits with "twisted heads".

Not all "talking heads" appear to have been automata. One amusing record, taken at an unconventional hearing before the King's Bench in 1371, tells of a magician who had been arrested carrying a Saracen's head in a bag. The magician explained that he had acquired the head in Toledo (then a hotbed of magical practices) with the intention of persuading into it a spirit which would answer questions. Such a practice, openly involved with the use of spirits, is closely linked with the divinatory practice of necromancy (*see page 204*).

Just as mechanical heads could be galvanized into speech by demons, so people in a trance might be overshadowed by angels. This belief is not very different from that widely held in modern times by mediums who claim they are overshadowed by beneficent spiritual beings when they indulge in CHANNELLING, acting as willing recipients for supposed disincarnate spirits. In earlier days, those possessed by demons or spirits were exorcized, and little or no credence was paid to the words they issued. However, since it was considered dangerous for humans to act as receptacles for demons or spirits, it was believed that it was morally legitimate to persuade spiritual beings to descend into the specially constructed physical models, or ARTIFICIALS.

The most enduring story of an artificial creature is of the GOLEM. The golem belongs to medieval Hebraic lore, yet the concept of a magical artificial creature is found in almost every culture and period. The sixteenth-century Swiss occultist Paracelsus is supposed to have bred a HOMUNCULUS, or little man, by chemical means in an alchemical retort (glass vessel).

The story of the golem which threatens the life or well-being of its own creator has been linked with Mary Shelley's modern Prometheus story of FRANKENSTEIN. The monster, made from bones and flesh of mortuaries and charnel-houses, takes on a life which cannot be controlled by its creator, and eventually causes the death of Dr. Frankenstein. Since the story was told, a surfeit of Frankenstein films have changed the monster even more, giving him a name. The monster has most cleverly adopted its creator's name as its own: in the popular mind, Frankenstein has become the monster. The scientist, Dr. Frankenstein, has merged with his own creation to become a talking humanoid, bereft of all hope of being loved – a terrible symbol of modern alienation.

The approach to natural magic led to a crossroads. To the left lay a descent into mere superstition and stage magic. To the right lay the invitation to make pact with the demons. Straight ahead, the road continued into modern science. This is one reason that, in modern times, the traditions of natural magic have been largely forgotten, and magic is designated as being either demonic or angelic.

ANGEL MAGIC

In the past, it was widely believed that the angels possessed enormous spiritual powers, and were anxious to help those who approached them through prayer or rituals, or because they had elected to aid a human being during a particular trial (*right*). The personal, or GUARDIAN ANGEL, might be approached most easily by prayer, but the service of many other angels might be called up by means of special rituals. To tap their benign and endless power and attract the angels to the service of man, a complex system of magical rituals was designed. In some circles, this type of angel magic was called WHITE MAGIC, on the grounds that it did not resort to the darker realms of the demons. In later times, those who practised such magic, and rejected the approach to power by way of the demons, followed the Right-hand Path.

ANGEL MAGIC is one of the most enduring of all ritual magical practices. It is rooted in the notion that through the correct performance of ceremonial magic, by means of certain rituals

DANTE AND THE ANGELS

Dante, Virgil and the angels are shown in this illustration by Gustav Doré, circa 1865, for the *Commedia* of Dante Alighieri.

involving perfumes, special magical patterns, arcane sigils, sacred secret sounds (including music), and occult postures, angels may be induced to make their presence known, and offer their services to the magicians. The finest literature of angel magic contains detailed instructions as to how these rituals are to be performed in order to call special angels to the service of the magician. Indeed, a vast literature has been constructed around this need to contact the higher and lower intelligences, ranging from the low-grade demonic pulp of the grimoire type to the sophisticated (and, in the hands of the uniformed, perhaps no less potentially dangerous) texts of the magician, Aleister Crowley.

One of the best known of the so-called ANGEL BOOKS is that ascribed to Honorius. This is the "HOLY BOOK" (*Liber Sacer*), or "BOOK OF THE ANGELS" which promises the world – even the cosmos – to those readers who follow its instructions in the magical art. It is the book by which one may see God, while yet in this life. In its pages one may learn how to visit hell and purgatory without dying. From it one will learn how to subjugate all creatures, other than the angels, and converse with beings of the invisible realms ...

Unfortunately, the contents scarcely live up to these promises, yet the collection of strange words, prayers, alphabets and spirit-names affords a rich quarry for those who seek out MAGICAL SYMBOLS and amuletic number magic. Most of these are still used in modern magical practices, and one at least deserves a brief mention.

The PENTAGRAM is the "allegorical star of the magi", as the French occultist Eliphas Levi puts it, adding that it exercises a great influence upon spirits and terrifies phantoms. Poetics and histrionics aside, the secret symbolism of the pentagram is considerable. The ratios of the lines which make up a pentagram are in the sacred proportion – what Leonardo da Vinci called "the Divine Proportion". It is said to represent the ETHERIC BODY of man, that superessential invisible body which occultists maintain is made of the stuff of the stars (*see page 24*).

Occultists versed in the esoteric stream of symbolism represented this notion of the etheric force by drawing man inside the pentagram, with his sexual parts at the centre (*far right*), and his four limbs and head distributed to show the relationship between the pentagram and the human form.

The pentagram, with an encircled dot in the centre, was one of the Egyptian HIEROGLYPHICS, or sacred writings. It was the SBA-STAR, which represented the idea of God, Time, and the Spiritual Essence (*near right*). There is little wonder that magicians made use of this physically perfect astral symbol to communicate with the spiritual world. Levi, who knew far less about magic than he pretended, was right, for once, when he called it the sign of the MICROCOSM – of man, the LITTLE WORLD – for in man is focused the power of the entire cosmos (the larger world, or MACROCOSM).

In the "Holy Book" of Honorius, the name of God is discussed in terms of the seventy-two names of his angels. Since this number is among the most esoteric of all occult numerations (*see page 38*), we must assume that the "Holy Book" was derived from sources which were linked with true arcane magic. One chapter is devoted to teaching the reader how to determine the hour of his or her death, while another explains how to learn about hidden events in the past, present and future. Later chapters tell how to control spirits by words, seals, sigils and incarcerations (imprisionment of spirits by magical means); how to bring about thunder and lightning, snow, storms, etc.; how to become invisible; how to wage war and destroy whole towns by means of mirror magic; how to sow discord and produce apparitions. It would seem from this array of dark promises that only the title of the "Holy Book" is on the side of the angels.

In former times, it was claimed that one feature that distinguished the two forms of Black and White lay in SACRIFICE. In those rituals where an animal or bird was sacrificed, the aim was contact with the demonic realm. But even this division is no longer so clear, for in recent centuries sacrifices have been conducted in circles who seek to contact angels. In general, however, animal sacrifice implies black magic, or the conjuration of demons, rather than angels. Some magicians who were nominally White, such as Eliphas

Levi, would sacrifice animals to promote his THEURGY (personal system of magic).

Certain of the black-book grimoires insist that animals be slaughtered as an essential part of the evocation of the so-called angels (which must, of course, have been demons to be attracted to the blood and suffering of the sacrificial victim). For example, the GRIMOIRE VERUM instructs the magician to cut the throat of a kid, after placing it on a block so that the neck may be severed in one slice. As the blade cuts through the throat, the KARCIST, or magical operator, must announce the name of the spirit he seeks to invoke.

One of the difficulties in distinguishing between black and white magic is that their rituals often appear to the uninitiated to be very similar. In strict terminology, the conjurer of spiritual beings will seek to BIND or ADJURE demons to service (as though they

THE PENTAGRAM

The sba-star (*above left*), or five-rayed star with solar centre, of the ancient Egyptian hieroglyphics is one of the most remarkable of all Egyptian sacred images, and is the determinative for such things as Time and the Deity. The pentagram of Western magic is undoubtedly linked with this hieroglyphic. Detail from the walls of the funerary temple of Queen Hatshepsut, ancient Thebes.

This figure of cosmic man in the pentagram (*above right*), with his sexual parts at the centre (marked by the sigil for the Moon), is from Agrippa's *De Occulta Philosophia*, 1534. The planetary sigils in the outer band do not appear to have any significance other than to mark the ancient order (in clockwise direction) of the planetary spheres, omitting the Sun.

were slaves or domestics), and stand in greater spiritual awe of the angels. While the demons would be commanded, the angels would be implored.

Some books on magical conjuration use the word DAEMON to refer to the beings which are to be raised in the magic circles. The seventeenth-century manuscript *A Treatise on Angel Magic*, now in the British Library, defines the spirits to be conjured as "a substance intelligible, free from all gross putrefying mass of body, Immortal, insensible, influencing all things". This sounds a convincing enough definition of the daemons and demons, until one realizes that not all daemons are invisible and immortal, after all. We are told that "in Denmark and Norway there are Daemons of a divers kind that are subject to the service of men, some of them are corporeal and mortal". The bodies of these eventually perish – even though they are reputed to have a long life.

However, the text is careful to note that "Daemons are not those which we call Devils", for they are intelligent and wise, and under the power of God. A lower class of such daemons is permitted to influence the course of man's destiny by way of a "certain invisible virtue, which none can behold, which directs our Journeys and business". They determine the outcome of battles, bring success or prosperity or inflict adversity, as the karcist (the name for one who seeks to raise demons) pleases. This description of a daemon's work seems to be very little different from that promised by the devils. In most grimoires, we find details not only of the demon's names, attributes, appearance and magical sigils, but also of the special powers for which he, she or it is sought out for service. This same Treatise describes four types of the lower daemons, each linked with one of the four ELEMENTS – Earth, Air, Fire and Water. The AERIALS (air daemons) serve the active life of the magician, following the rational powers. The WATERY DAEMONS, the demonic equivalent of the undines, follow imagination, sensitivity and the "voluptuous life", and will serve the magicians best in these areas. Earthy daemons, or the SUBTERRANEANS, follow nature (by which is meant the lower inclinations). Surprisingly, the fiery daemons, sometimes called AETHNICI, follow the contemplative life, and are most usually contacted to serve aspirations in this spiritual direction.

In this classification of the ELEMENTAL DAEMONS, we find a close correspondence with the so-called elementals – the sylphs of the Air, the undines of Water, the gnomes of Earth, and the salamanders, or fire-beings. These invisible elementals, or ELEMENTARIES, are sometimes called FAIRIES, and are said to be prepared to help men, or sometimes trouble men, depending upon how they are treated.

Although many modern groups of occultists and secret fraternities still practise ceremonial angel magic, or WORKINGS, one development is linked with the widespread use of the Sanscrit name DEVAS. The devas are those spiritual beings, invisible to ordinary sight, who are the lesser gods. In a very real sense, the devas are the equivalent of the Western angels, but the classification (see page 52) into nine orders is not the same. The Sanskrit word DIV means "to shine", and explains the term well, since the devas do appear to be beings of light. There are records of the temporary blinding of people who have accidentally perceived the devas, so bright is the spiritual light in which these creatures dwell.

One complication with the modern use of the word "devas" is the fact that, in certain New Age circles (which really grew out of various occult trends established at the end of the last century), the word has been used to denote the elementals, or NATURE SPIRITS.

In all the occult traditions, we find that the good spirits of one culture are demoted to demon rank by the culture which takes over. The devas are no exception. In the early Vedic religions, the devas were regarded as being spirits of light, who were helpful to man. However, in the later Zoroastrian cult, the devas were demoted, and were viewed as demons, under the control of the Spirit of Darkness, AHRIMAN. This demotion explains why the Sanskrit term "div" may be traced in such seemingly contradictory words as "divine" and "devil".

In occultism, the word DEVACHAN, which originally meant "the way of the gods", or "the way of the devas", is now used to mean HEAVEN – the place where the human spirits may mingle with the lesser gods and angels. The modern development of the deva consciousness has meant that some occult schools now concentrate on rituals directed towards serving and attracting devas.

BLACK MAGIC

In contrast to angel magic, BLACK MAGIC is ritual involving the conjuration of demons. As one might expect, the demons are no fools and, ever anxious to seize their human prey, have made use of this distinction. As a result, many of the books dealing with angel magic contain the names of demons disguised as beings of light. Only when the magician makes some error in his ritual is the pretended angel revealed as a being of darkness … to the cost of that magician's soul. Many of the old books, which carry such titles as "The Art of THAUMATURGY" (the art of miracle-working, or magic), contain the names of demons masquerading as angels.

The study of the demons raised by means of black magic really carries us into the realm of demonology (*see page 57*); but in the present context of black magic, we may as well ask, just what power do the evil spirits possess?

The fifteenth-century Florentine William de Bechis was constrained to write a detailed criticism of occultists because of their unholy approach to the spiritual world. In particular, he was worried by the fact that so many of the French, among whom he had lived, resorted to astrology and other divinations, used magical characters and SCRYING MIRRORS (reflective surfaces in which clairvoyants might see images of the past, present and future) and consorted with demons. Such "mirrors" were often constructed from shallow dishes, in which was poured an ink-blackened liquid to act as a reflector. The dishes were frequently of ornate and bizarre construction.

In his fulminations against such practices, William de Bechis left us a description of the imagined power of demons which became standard in later times. He records that, according to some, the magicians were enabled by demons to TRANSVECT, or fly through the air, travelling great distances at night, and that they could pass through closed doors, have sexual relations with demons, transmit diseases and storms, and practise SHAPE-CHANGING (transforming themselves into animals and other forms). William de Bechis himself expresses the opinion that this power of the demons is really a delusion, that the powers granted to magicians are nothing more than dreams or fantasies. He agrees, however, that spirits are incorporeal and can neither assume

SCRYING DISH

This modern scrying mirror, designed by Graham Fenn-Edwards, is set upon a mount of three skulls. The shallow bowl is filled with black ink, to offer a reflective surface for the scryer.

physical bodies nor manipulate on the physical plane – except by way of their slaves, the witches, warlocks and magicians.

One interesting modern working (as certain modern wicca members call their rituals – the term is related both to "work on oneself" and "work in magic") throws some light on the esoteric view of demons. This ritual, recorded by the historian of esotericism Kenneth Grant in his book *Outside the Circles of Time*, took place a couple of decades ago in Ohio. During this working, a number of demons were raised and imprisoned during a ceremony practised by ANDAHADNA, a priestess serving the CHILDREN OF MAAT, which is an order that works through meditation, ritual magic and channelling.

In a lone working, conducted in a desolate region of the Red River Gorge, Andahadna was directed by spiritual agencies to prepare seven pyramids. During the rituals that followed, many visions arose, all of a terrifying nature. A whirlwind, which kept returning, was announced by the image of a red-and-white candy-striped dog, and at the end of each session, a demon remained imprisoned inside one of the pyramids. Andahadna later described these seven demons, which included an albino woman with triple breasts and head antennae, a brass-copper serpent, a "headless" white spacesuit with red gauntlets, and three formless shapes relating to the fear of Death, Life and the Void.

It is not clear from the available records whether the demons were offshoots of what the Children of Maat call the FORGOTTEN ONES. These are described by Andahadna as those forces which have been labelled as Satanic by our Western Christian society. By virtue of being suppressed, they have taken on a formidable power, which is presently threatening disaster for humanity. The Forgotten Ones seem to be linked with the OLD ONES of H.P. Lovecraft, whose imaginative writings have become a source of inspiration for many wiccan members, esotericists and artists.

WHISPERER IN DARKNESS

One of many modern artists who have been influenced by H. P. Lovecraft, Dave Carson has illustrated the Lovecraftian horrors with profound insight. This drawing is to Lovecraft's *The Whisperer in Darkness*, from the limited edition of Carson's drawings, *Haunters of the Dark, and Other Lovecraftian Horrors*, 1987.

ENOCHIAN MAGIC

From the foregoing accounts, it will be clear that, although in theory the three different forms of magic were clearly defined, in actual practice the dividing lines between them were blurred. Some of the ancient texts which set out the rituals and names of spiritual helpers do so under the guise of being tracts on angel magic, yet among the lists of beings who may be evoked are many demons. This merging of the White and Black proclaims the existence of a fourth category of magic (the other three being natural magic, of which artificial magic is a type; angel magic; and black magic). It may be called, somewhat misleadingly, GREY MAGIC, because it uses both angelic and demonic forces.

Among the more interesting and intellectual of the modern evocation systems, in which the White and the Black have merged to a grey, is that linked with ENOCHIA, sometimes called the magic of the THIRTY AETHYRS. This ENOCHIAN MAGIC was introduced into the stream of history by the great Rosicrucian John Dee in the sixteenth century. Dee's system, which evolved during seances held with the clairvoyant–conman Edward Kelly, involves the calling of angelic beings by means of a series of mantras in a strange language, called the ENOCHIAN LANGUAGE. By such converse with the angels, Dee was able to discover the alphabetical base for this language, and a series of fascinating sacred letters has been preserved (*above*).

Dee has preserved thirty evocations known as CALLS or AIRES. By the substitution of thirty named beings, or AETHYRS, it is possible to evoke a range of angels. Dee and Kelly published the Aires, and translated them with the aid of the angels Kelly channelled. They also provided a list of the aethyrs that might be evoked by the Enochian system.

In modern times, mainly because of the interest shown in Enochian by Aleister Crowley, several magicians make use of the language, the alphabet and the system of calls, to evoke mighty spirits.

Those who have studied the language insist that its extraordinary sounds and forms belong to a complete system of thought. It is suggested that this Enochian language is named after the Biblical Enoch, the son of Jared, and seventh in the chosen line from Adam, who "walked with God". Enoch had intimate converse with the highest spiritual

ENOCHIAN LETTERS

Some of the letters of the secret Enochian language, used in Elizabethan times. The sigillic group, from which this artwork was made, was the centre of a magical table used by the occultist John Dee and his partners in raising Enochian spirits to their bidding. This table was illustrated in Meric Casaubon's *A True and Faithful Relation* of what passed for many years between Dr. John Dee ... and some spirits, 1657.

planes. We have seen that Enoch is also linked with a whole chain of demons – the so-called ENOCHIAN DEMONS – and this should remind us that in occultism there is a practice of establishing what are called "OCCULT BLINDS" to mislead the uninitiated. In this case, a link with demonic lore will deflect the superficial researcher away from the more serious "angelic" lore of the universal language associated with Enoch. The occult blind is designed to lead the superficial researcher up blind alleys, and thus preserve the higher truths from the profane.

Some modern occultists who have studied Dee's bequest claim that it is the language spoken in Atlantean times, while others suggest that it is one of the main languages of initiates, a sort of pre-Babel universal speech. Whatever its origin, almost all those who study it, and practise it for communing with spirits, remind us that it is extremely powerful, and that misuse leads to incredible dangers. The name ENOCH means "dedicated" and serves to remind us that only those who are prepared to dedicate themselves to a study of the Enochian system should meddle with it.

A recent ENOCHIAN DICTIONARY, compiled by Leo Vinci, points out that the dangers in the evocatory system arise from the fact that the spiritual beings evoked are not from the lower elemental plane (that plane which is most usually contacted by such evocationary systems as the OUIJA board) but from higher, extremely powerful planes. He emphasizes that the dangers in the malpractice of the system may be devastating. The title of Leo Vinci's book is GMICALZOMA, an Enochian phrase which points to the main requirement to avert danger when using the system. The title, pronounced as Ge-Mi-Ca-El-Zood-Oh-Ma, means approximately "With a Power of Understanding".

One historically interesting account of the use of the Enochian Aires, or calls, is that recorded by Aleister Crowley (*illustration, page 78*) with his companion, the poet Victor Neuburg. Crowley had a profound knowledge of magical ritual, and had come to the conclusion that the system recorded by Dee afforded a method for reaching into the highest levels from which angels may descend at the command, or request, of the magician. He was perhaps persuaded into this favourable view of the Enochian system by the fact that he believed himself to have been Edward Kelly in a previous incarnation.

During a stay in Algeria in 1909 Crowley and Neuburg had experimented with most of the calls of the Enochian system, evoking various named angels. Then, on December 6th, in the desert near Bou Saada, Crowley dropped any pretence that he would be evoking good spirits. He expressed his intention of calling the mighty DEMON OF THE ABYSS, named CHORONZON, "the most deadly of the powers of evil".

He and Neuburg constructed a circle of rocks in the sand, and consecrated these. Around this unconventional circle they wrote protective power-names (presumably in the Enochian alphabet). Outside the circle they drew a large triangle, wherein, according to the tradition of ceremonial magic, the demon was to manifest. Through the calling of the Aires, mingled in Crowley's highly characteristic manner with sexual magic involving his companion Neuburg, the pair were led to the ceremonial evocation of Choronzon. It appears that this ritual magical act was performed with the aid of the Tenth Aire of Dee's Enochian system. Surprisingly, Crowley broke with the magical tradition, and remained within the triangle, where he sacrificed three pigeons by cutting their throats. Neuburg sat within the circle, clutching a notebook, into which he was to make a record of the call and its manifestations.

According to Neuburg, Choronzon manifested in several guises: first as a French prostitute, who attempted to seduce Neuburg into letting her into the circle; next, as an old man, then as a snake, and finally in the form of Crowley himself. All were devices by which it would be permitted access to the circle, where it might do its worst damage. Neuburg perceived these stratagems, however, and kept the demon back.

After blasphemies and arguments, Choronzon managed to throw sand over the outline of the protective circle, and thus found legitimate

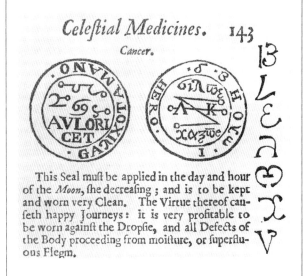

Celestial Medicines. 143

Cancer.

This Seal must be applied in the day and hour of the *Moon*, she decreasing; and is to be kept and worn very Clean. The Virtue thereof causeth happy Journeys: it is very profitable to be worn against the Dropsie, and all Defects of the Body proceeding from moisture, or superfluous Flegm.

ENOCHIAN IN USE

The two circles containing sigils are talismanic "seals" linked with the magical power of the sign Cancer. These are given by the occultist Paracelsus in his book, *The Archidoxes of Magic*, 1656, as part of his treatment of Celestial Medicines. An occultist has drawn several manuscript Enochian letters in the margin, alongside the seals. It is clear from the forms of these that he or she was interested in their similarity to the arcane sigils and letters on the Paracelsian seals, which belong to a tradition far more ancient than that of the Enochian language.

entry. In the form of a naked man, it threw itself into the circle, and tried to kill Neuburg by tearing his throat with its teeth. After a fierce struggle, Neuburg pushed the demon out of the circle, and repaired it with the ATHAME or magical dagger with which he had defended himself.

Stripped of its drama and esoteric overtones, what this story appears to be is an account of simple POSSESSION. The naked man who conned his way into the circle appears to have been Crowley, in a state of deep trance. Occultists would claim that Crowley, in opening himself in such a reckless way to the lower world of demons, had invited Choronzon, or some other invading entity, to possess him. His physical body had been taken over by the disincarnate being, and used by it as an instrument in an attempt to murder Neuburg. Whatever the truth, Neuburg afterwards remained convinced that he had fought with a demon, and the experience remained deeply etched in his soul.

Typically, it was Crowley who took the success of this struggle upon himself, and read in the "repulsion" of Choronzon a sign that he had been promoted to a higher (even the highest) level of initiation.

CURSE MAGIC

Among the areas of magic which do not fall conveniently into the realms of either angelology or demonology is CURSE MAGIC, which sets out the rules and rituals for bringing harm to humans or creatures.

Curse magic and curse-making are among the oldest forms of popular magic: many examples are found among ancient Egyptian papyri. It has even been argued with some conviction that the weapon marks on animals, painted in prehistoric times in such caves as Trois Frères in France or Altamira in Spain, are relics of curse magicians who sought the death of such creatures by ritually slaying images of them. Some historians claim that the arrow-like lines above the body of the cave-painting of a horse (*below*) are a relic of such KILLING MAGIC; to the prehistoric mind, the image of an arrow hitting a horse would encourage the real arrows of the hunter to find their targets. This kind of magic is a sort of pictorial wishful thinking, designed to empower the hunter. The superstition – if it be superstition – is not merely confined to prehistoric times: a whole realm of magic has survived into the modern age, rooted in the idea that it is possible to harm a person, creatures or things by means of drawings, pictures and acts of the imagination.

Curse magic seems to have been used to great effect in ancient China, though the tendency was for the State curse to be somewhat over-dramatic. According to Tso Chuan, the ruler of a certain Chinese state decided to avenge the murder of one of his main political supporters. He therefore ordered every centain of his many thousands of soldiers to contribute a pig, and each group of twenty-five soldiers to provide a fowl and a dog. This huge number of animals were sacrificed, and every soldier in the army cursed the one who had done the murder over the blood of the slaughtered creatures.

The word CHARM is derived from the Latin *carmen*, meaning "song", and reminds us that certain charms were chants intended to bring evil on the head of a named individual. Although the power of the cursing was believed to be derived from the energy of the hatred contained in the voice, the whole secret of curse-making soon evolved into a written form – especially into the art of making magical images, or strange alphabets. In former times, so few people knew how to write that a scribe was often regarded as

KILLING MAGIC

Prehistoric cave painting of a running horse, with arrow directed towards its back, from Lascaux, France. Many of the cave paintings in prehistoric Europe appear to have had a magical purpose: some are quite certainly involved with the "ritual killing" of the image, as a part of hunt magic. Such magic is rooted in the notion that for an event to occur on the earth plane, it must already have been enacted on the astral plane.

being a magician. Indeed, all too frequently even the art of reading was interpreted as a magical or diabolical art by the unlearned.

One important book of magic – indeed, some would insist, the most important medieval book of magic – the PIXATRIX, records many curses and magical invectives, but emphasizes that the executive power resides not so much in the words of the spells as in the IMAGES and CHARACTERS made from lines of geometrical figures, sigils and constellations. There seems to be no end to their magical power: special images were designed to throw down buildings, enable men or women to walk on water, bring rains, induce the stars to fall down from the heavens. The magician who knew how to use the appropriate image could fly through the air like a falling star, speak with the dead, travel vast distances in the twinkling of an eye, cause water to burn. It is not surprising that with such a power at his command, the IMAGE-WORKER was regarded as the doyen of the evil curse.

In comparison with the power of invective in a spoken curse, the written curse was seen as being more magically potent, presumably because papyrus, paper or a waxen tablet would usually endure for so much longer than sound. This notion of endurance must have played a part in the Romans choosing to scratch their curses on leaden tablets.

Many LEAD CURSES which have survived from Roman times can be seen in modern museums. One, now in the London Museum, is a scratched curse against T. Egnatius Tyranus and P. Cicereius Felix, which (to judge from the nail-hole) had once been affixed to a shrine. Lead may have had another magical connotation, however, for not only was it an enduring substance, but it was under the rule of the dour planet SATURN. By sympathetic association, a curse written on lead would carry a far more malevolent charge of dark Saturnine brooding than one written on papyrus, relegated to the rule of the more benign Mercury. Perhaps the act of nailing was itself involved with this notion of fixing, of setting down permanently.

The archaeologist Ralph Merrifield has suggested that one reason why Welsh CUNNING MEN or WISE-MEN (as those who practised magic were called) so frequently used slate for curses is not because of its availability in Wales but because of its resemblance to lead. This would certainly explain part of a curse which was discovered buried in a bank near Holyhead in the last century, and reported in 1872. Beneath a slate, on which had been written the name of the accursed, "Nanney Roberts", were the remains of a frog which had been pierced, or STUCK, by a number of large pins. This sacrificial creature was intended as a substitute for the named victim. The slate is now in the Museum of Welsh Antiquities, Bangor.

Of course, the leaden curse is not uniquely Roman. In the Gloucester Museum, England, is a fine example of a seventeenth-century curse on a lead tablet, on which the name of the person cursed is written backwards (such reversal, or negative, magic is popular in simple magical spells – *see page 134*). Below the name are some crude sigils linked with the Moon and the lunar spirits – probably taken from a book by the German occultist Agrippa, who popularized a series of magical squares (*see page 137*) and magical sigils for each of the seven planets. There follows the name of the lunar daemon, HASMODAI, with his magical number, 369, along with a fairly illiterate BANISHING CURSE: "make this person to Banish away from this place and countery amen to my desier amen."

This mixing of Christian, pagan and occult terms and images is typical of curse magic from peasant sources, and the influence of Agrippa (probably by way of cheap grimoires) seems to have been widespread.

The Romans used the word DEFIXIO for such curses. The idea in this name is that the curse was intended to fix or bind the cursed person to the fate ordained in the curse. A similar word has come down to us from medieval times, for a LIGATURE was a binding practised by witches and black figure magicians intent on limiting or harming a victim in some way. The true ligature was a knot, but sometimes the word was used of a magical potion which would limit the victim, or even kill and maim.

According to the seventeenth-century Italian monk Guazzo, the ligature was used mainly to establish impotency – that is, to tie and inhibit the generative faculty. Such ligatures would inevitably induce hate between lovers, and prevent ejaculation, conception and all forms of sexual activity. Guazzo gives a dramatic description of a woman who has been fixed against her husband by such a curse. As a result of this evil-working, although the woman loved her husband, she could not bear his presence. She agreed to be tied down on her bed, that he might approach her:

> but when he came in, never was seen such terrible fury. No wild beast was ever so
> fierce or so filled with madness and rage as that woman. She foamed at the mouth,
> gnashed her teeth and rolled her eyes, whilst her whole body seemed to be shaken and
> possessed with demons. The women who were present said that when they touched
> her belly, which was twisting under the ropes, it appeared to be stuffed full, and all
> her skin was covered with weals as if she had been beaten.

The woman's torment lasted until her husband left the bedroom.

For all such dramatic results, the making of a ligature was one of the most simple forms of curse magic. The magician obtained a strip of leather or cord – preferably from among the possessions of those to be cursed – and tied this up while pronouncing or chanting the formal curse. Since the magic would remain operative until the knot was discovered and untied, the usual practice was to hide it in some inaccessible place: buried beneath the floor, sealed in a hollow tree, or up a chimney, where so many magical items have been preserved.

Although this operation seems simple enough, there were a number of ligature-makers, with their own specialisms. One suspect witch, arrested in 1567, told the French judge Jean Bodin that she knew of more than fifty ways of knotting the AIGUILLETTE (the

KNOTTING THE WIND

The belief in ligatures probably arose from the ancient notion that magicians had the power to tie up winds in knots, to release them at an appropriate time. Here a warlock is preparing ligatured winds for sailors, whose ship seems to be becalmed. In the days of wind sail, it was widely believed that witches had the power to control the elements. From Olaus Magnus, *Historia de Gentibus Septentrionalibus*, 1555.

French equivalent of the ligature), depending upon what sort of restriction or illness was to be doled out to the victim.

Ligature magic is often little more than ordinary evil-working, as may be seen from the following curse story, related in 1608 by Guazzo. In San Gimignano, Tuscany, a married man fell so deeply in love with a local witch that he left his beautiful wife and family, to take her as mistress. His wife, convinced that this behaviour was due to ligature, sought out the charm which had caused it. Eventually she found, beneath her own bed, a jar in which was incarcerated a toad which had its eyes stitched up. She unstitched the eyes and then burned the unfortunate creature. The husband promptly returned to her, face glazed, as though awakening from a trance. The sewing-up of the eyes had been the ligature which restrained his own vision. This example of black magic, however, is of a different order to that usually linked with curse magic.

In former times, ligature magic was taken very seriously, and was even recognized as a just cause for the dissolution of a marriage. In a famous book on EXORCISM, or the driving out of evil spirits, the seventeenth-century Franciscan friar Brognolus gives a special prayer aimed at releasing a victim from impotence brought about by this form of curse magic – an interesting example of white magic versus black magic.

AMULETS AND TALISMANS

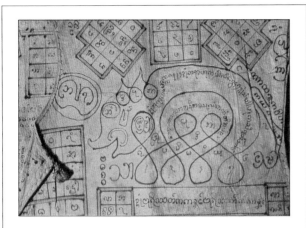

AMULETIC SHIRT

A good example of the talismanic art is the Lan Nal, or amuletic shirt, which was designed to go under the armour of a Burmese soldier, to protect him while he fought in battle. The magical squares, images and spells are believed to protect the wearer during journeys or warfare. Amuletic shirts were often worn by soldiers beneath their armour – a sign that they placed just as much faith in magic as in steel. Like this one, some of these shirts have survived without sign of sword-thrust or bullet holes, which may be a signal of the effectiveness of paper in comparison with metal. From the collection of the Gordon Reece Gallery, Knaresborough.

T he power of curses invites us to look at the measures magicians may take to counter such dark magic. Generally, magicians fight curses, maledictions and general ill-fortune with amulets and talismans.

AMULETS, widely used in both white and black magic, are protective symbols. The word is from the Latin *amuletum*, meaning "a preservative against illness". Since, in former times, illness was believed to be caused by demons, the amuletic symbols were indeed intended to drive away the devils and restore the victim to health.

In modern times, the amulet is often confused with the TALISMAN. Properly speaking, the amulet always contains an image, whereas the talisman carries a sigil or seal in an abstract design, letters of an alphabet, and so on. However, the word talisman is from the Arabian word *tilism*, which means "magic image", so at one time the amulet and the talisman must have been more or less the same thing. It is probably best to think of a talisman as a surface – stone, metal, wood or parchment – on which have been inscribed characters, sigils or symbols.

Some of the most interesting occult symbols from the medieval world are those which were intended to serve the purpose of TALISMANIC MAGIC. These are portable charms, set with astrological figures, magical squares (*see page 137*), and symbols from the occult repertoire. The most popular talismans incorporate the sigils for angels, such as the planetary angels, or the zodiacal angels.

The artist who practises the art of making talismans is not concerned merely with the accuracy and aesthetics of his designs, however: it is of paramount importance, if the talismans are to work with undiluted power, that they be made with the appropriate material and at the right time. This "right time" is usually a precisely determined astrological time, calculated in advance by consulting an EPHEMERIS, or table of planetary and zodiacal positions. To serve the purposes of the talismanic manufacturer, a series of PLANETARY HOURS has been worked out, indicating the rulerships of the planets over specific hours of day and night. The right material would be a substance ruled by the appropriate planet. Again, the books on talismanic magic set out lists of substances under their planetary rulers. A talisman for Saturn, for example, would have to be manufactured under the appropriate hour of Saturn, and drawn or inscribed on lead, the "metal of Saturn". The art of talismanic manufacture has been reintroduced in recent times, with very satisfactory results.

Some amulets are well established in the occult tradition, and many are now worn for decorative purposes by those who know nothing of the spiritual background to these forms. Among these amulets is the Egyptian ANKH, which, on its simplest level, is a symbol of spiritual life. Before the advent of Nazism, the SWASTIKA, one of the sacred Buddhist symbols, was a popular amulet, its four arms a symbol of solar movement, of cyclical change, and of recurrence or reincarnation, which is one reason it is sometimes found on Buddhist graves.

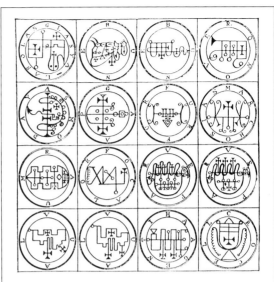

DEMONIC SIGILS

An arrangement of sixteen talismans of encircled demonic sigils, each charged with the energy to repel, or attract, the demon it represents. All the sigils are derived from one or other of the manuscripts known as *The Lesser Key of Solomon the King,* but were assembled in this form by William de Laurence, in his 1916 edition of the grimoire. The amulets of the top row (starting at the left) give the sigils for Glasyalabolas (who appears in the form of a dog), two variants for Bune (who appears as a dragon with three heads, only one of which is human) and Ronwe (who appears as a humanoid monster). This is not a jolly crew from which to seek protection.

Another popular amulet is the CROSS – though few Christians who wear it would recognize its magical connotation or appreciate that the cross is a symbol far older than Christianity.

THOR'S HAMMER, or the MJOLLNIR, was the most popular of Teutonic amulets. It was in the form of a short-handled hammer (*page 134, top*), and was supposed to represent the throwing-hammer owned by the god Thor. The original was said to have been manufactured by the earth elementals, the DWARFS, and was so designed that it would hit anything at which it was aimed, then return to the thrower. The magical quality in this amulet rests partly in the TAU form (reminiscent of the Egyptian sacred T, on the back of the resurrection-beetle, the sacred SCARAB) and partly in the decorations, which, in the example (*overleaf*), include pictorial reference to the World Serpent. More important, however, is the boomerang quality, for it is this which lifts the amulet from being purely protective into a special realm where its facility for PSYCHIC DEFENCE (the spiritual ability to drive back evil entities) is unique.

THOR'S HAMMER

The most popular of all the Teutonic amulets was Thor's hammer, or the Mjollnir. The Midgard serpent swirls upon the head of this hammer. There was a seal of destiny in the sound of Thor's hammer, and at one time burials and many civil contracts were "struck" by the blacksmith's hammer, in imitation.

The underlying idea is that the Mjollnir protects the wearer from witchcraft and evil-working because it prevents the person from being overlooked by the JETTATURA, or EVIL EYE which is thrown from the eyes of witches. As the beams from the eyes of the witch strike towards the victim, the hammer hits back, deflecting the current of the evil eye, before returning, its virtue unsullied, to the wearer. It is possibly some unconscious memory of this protective quality of the Mjollnir which explains why, in modern times, so many young people wear amulets of tau form.

One of the notions behind the manufacture of amulets was that the virtue supposed to be in the object used would remain effective on the ASTRAL plane, that mysterious invisible realm of spirituality in which man dwells. Thus, the poison in the fangs of a snake could be used in an amuletic form to protect the wearer from snake-bites, or poisons. The abbess Hildegarde of Bingen preserves a recipe for such an amulet: one is advised to kill a venomous snake, remove its heart and dry this in the sun. The desiccated organ is placed in a thin metal cover, which makes it serviceable as an amulet. Anyone who holds this amulet in the hand will be immune from poisons, and will be relieved of all feelings of gloom or sorrow. The "occult virtue" to dispel gloom is an example of REVERSAL MAGIC – an idea that everything in the spiritual world is a reversal, or mirror-image of its counterpart on the earth. In this case, the live snake (which sought out the dark places in the earth) now being dead, will work in the opposite direction, and reject the dark crevices of the soul, wherein depression is found.

Another abbess, Hilda of Whitby, is associated with a curious SNAKE AMULET. Legend has it that before St. Hilda built her abbey on the clifftop above Whitby, on the north-eastern coast of England, the grass was quick with adders. Using magical spells, she drove the adders over the cliff top, and they all fell to their deaths on the pebbled beach below. The legend may be a pretty tale to explain the ammonites which were found in such profusion on the Whitby beaches. Even today, the ammonites are worked by locals into what they call ADDER-STONES, with the spiral of the ammonite deftly transformed into a curled snake by

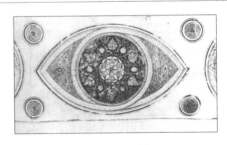

MAGIC EYE

Designed to counteract the evil eye, this Arabic amuletic eye, drawn with a never-ending band, has a "pupil" and "iris" made of magical flowers. It is from a magical scroll, probably from fifteenth-century Egypt, in the Dar al Athar al Islammiyyah, Kuwait.

the addition of a serpent's head. These snake-stones are believed to have a protective magical virtue.

The medieval Arabs excelled in the manufacture of amulets linked with eye-forms. Many fine examples are found distributed throughout the museums of the world (*left, below*) while even more are still worn in Arabic countries in modern times. The idea behind such a form is that the eye may receive the EYE-BEAMS (projected sight) of the evil-worker, and throw this back towards him or her. This eye-beam magic is closely linked with the notion of FASCINATION, the idea that the eye of an evil-worker can hypnotize, and superimpose his or her will on a victim. The ancients believed that certain people had such a strong power of imagination that their eye-beams could discharge corruption into the atmosphere, spreading evil contagion. By the power of reversal magic, the image of a eye could repel this contagious power of the evil eye: this explains why so many amulets contain images of the eye (*right*).

On the southern coastlines of Portugal and Spain, as in certain Greek islands, the fishermen still paint or carve crude eyes on the prows of their boats. The sailors themselves insist that the eyes also keep back the MALOCCHIO, or evil eye, and protect their boats from witchcraft.

The most popular of Arabic devices is the BASMALLAH, a pious Koranic formula, which translates:

PROTECTIVE MAGIC CHARM

Many of the horse-brasses which were so widely used up to the beginning of the twentieth century had magical eye devices, intended to keep the horse wearing it from harm. This superb early nineteenth-century example has a painted boss to repel the evil eye. Besides resembling the eye, this also calls to mind the sun, for the thirty holes act as a radiant. The number thirty is also a lunar figure: thus, the cosmos is evoked in order to protect the animal. In the collection of Cliffe Castle Museum, Keighley, West Yorkshire, England.

In the name of God, the Compassionate, the Merciful.

Clearly, we are in the realm of white magic with this amulet, and the inscription is found engraved, written and printed on a wide variety of gems, amulets, formulae and spells, in a bewildering variety of styles and forms, sometimes interlaced with Koranic inscriptions. The magical potency of the Basmallah is highly appreciated because it is widely believed to offer a recapitulation of the entire Holy Koran. In the Romanized transliteration, the formula reads:

Bismillaahir al-Rahmaanir al-Rahiim

The sound of the first three words explains the name, Basmallah. When this is shorn of its vowellic markings (quite acceptable in the Arabic calligraphic style), the transliteration gives nineteen letters: *BSM ALLH AL-RHMN AL-RHIM*

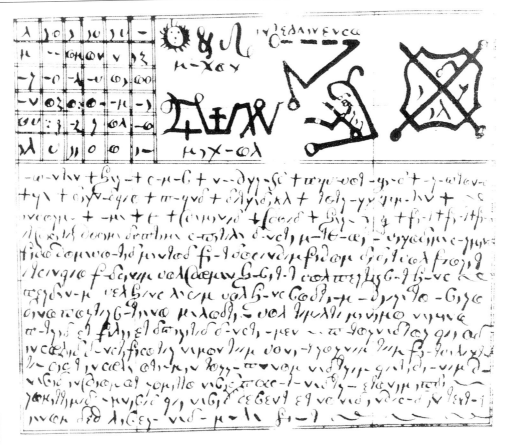

PAPER MAGIC

A muletic charm, written in the eighteenth century, and found in a barn at West Bradford, Lancashire, in 1825. The charm includes (*top left*) the magical square for the Sun and also sigils for the daemons of the Sun and for the archangel of the Sun, Michael. Crude as they are, most of these symbols and sigils appear to have been derived from Agrippa, the sixteenth-century occultist. The mixture of Greek and Roman letters is, for the most part, easily decoded, and forms an adjuration to keep evil spirits and hauntings away from a certain person, from a particular place and from cattle. From *The Proceedings of the Historical Society of Lancashire and Cheshire*, 1852.

In the Arabic magical system, this number has profound significance, for at one level it connotes the seven planets and the twelve zodiacal signs, thus calling into its virtue the realms of the cosmos. An insight into the Arabic approach to magical exegesis (the scholarly explanation of magic) may be seen in the comment of the first imam, who wrote specifically about the initial letter of the Basmallah, saying, "I call God to witness that, if I wished, I could produce a commentary on the letter ba of the Basmallah equal to the load of seventy camels." One Islamic justification for regarding the Basmallah as a protective device is supported in the words of the Prophet: "He who desires immunity against the nineteen henchmen of Hell needs to recite the Basmallah."

Not all amulets were especially manufactured. Certain small objects, especially coins or medals, were sometimes regarded as being possessed of a special virtue, which gave them a protective aura. A well-known COIN-AMULET is a Noble (gold coin) of the fourteenth-century English King, Edward III; it had a Latin biblical inscription regarded as offering immunity to travellers. Coin-amulets were often carried by those undertaking a long voyage. In 1597, Queen Elizabeth presented one to the Earl of Essex, to protect him on his expedition to the Azores.

Much of the GEM LORE of the amuletic tradition was learned by medieval Europe from the Arabs, in the tenth and eleventh centuries. According to the gemsection in the grimoire known as "The GRAND ALBERT" (which is supposed to be one of two angel-books written by Albertus Magnus, in the thirteenth century), light-coloured EMERALDS are the most powerul talismanic gems. These were supposed to be obtained with great difficulty from the nests of griffons. The effort of retrieving such a gem was worthwhile, for it was believed that its virtue was so powerful that no magician or evil-worker could weave spells in the neighbourhood of the stone. This belief seems to stem from a much older tradition which maintains that demons cannot bear the sight of emeralds. An even earlier belief is that serpents who gaze upon the gem become blind.

As a DEMONIFUGE, or demon-repellent, the emerald acquired a reputation for preserving love in human relationships, which is one reason it is often incorporated into engagement or marriage

MAGICAL SQUARE

MAGICAL SQUARES are squares divided into specific grids, each smaller square of which contains a number. The seven planets are all associated with particular grid systems. The simplest is that of Saturn, which has a nine grid system, and the most complex is the Moon, which has an eighty-one grid system. Midway between these two extremes is the twenty-five grid system for the planet Mars, shown here.

The numbers of each square, in any vertical or horizontal division, always add up to the same sum, which is the MAGICAL NUMBER of the daemon or spirit associated with the planet. For example, the daemon of Saturn is ZAZEL, who has the number 45. The daemon of the Moon has the number 3321, but with a Hebraic appellation too long to record. In this magical square for Mars, there are sigils for the daemonic rulers, Graphiel and Barzabel, and also sigils for the associated signs (of the sixteenth century), Aries and Scorpio. The number of this square is 325, and the sum along the line 65. From Cornelius Agrippa's *De Occulta Philosophia*, 1534.

rings. In an Italian manuscript, "De Mineralibus", there is an account of how an emerald, set in a ring on the finger of King Bela IV of Hungary, was fractured when he caressed his wife. The text is not specific: one wonders who was being unfaithful to whom.

The greater number of more recently constructed amulets are written on paper, as the cheapest available writing material. One eighteenth-century protective charm, written on paper in a crude code of Greek and Roman letters, was found tucked in the roofbeams of a barn at West Bradford, Lancashire, in 1825 *(photograph, page 136)*. The fact that almost all the symbols and sigils relate to the "benefic" and supportive Sun suggests that the charm is intended to protect the barn. In fact, a decoding of the text, by Richard Garnett, has shown that the magic seeks specifically to protect the place from enchantment, evil spirits and hauntings. Among the crudely drawn symbols is the sigil for MICHAEL (the archangel of the Sun) and the magical square of the Sun, which had been popularized in the sixteenth century by the German occultist Agrippa.

Among the codes of the West Bradford charm are two of the most common of all magical conjuration words – Agla and Tetragrammaton. The AGLA is widely used in talismanic magic as a POWER WORD, or term charged with occult virtue. Some occultists claim that it is an acronym for the Hebrew phrase, *Atha Gibor Leolam Adonai,* which translates, "Thou art mighty for ever, O Lord", and which is of magical numerological significance in the cabbalistic system. Some amulets and gems have nothing but this word inscribed upon them, and are usually called Aglas.

The TETRAGRAMMATON is another power word of Hebraic origin, though the word itself is of Greek origin, meaning "four letters". It is the name of God, in four letters: in the English version IHVH, and in the Hebrew, Yod, He, Vau, He. Tradition insists that the true pronunciation of the name of God is unknown, but the word is usually read as Jehovah. Sometimes, the English equivalent of this Hebrew is used for magical purposes, as in this pentacle (*left*).

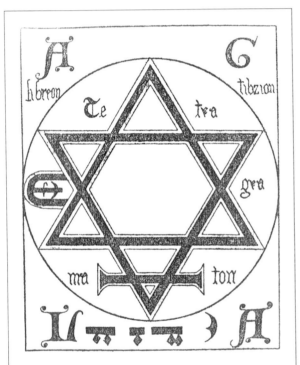

TETRAGRAMMATON

The magical symbols of this fourteenth-century invocation circle include an encircled magical HEXAGRAM. On the outside of the circles, in each of the four corners of the retaining square, are the four letters making up the magical word "AGLA". The name of God, the Tetragrammaton, is inside the circle in five units: Te tra gra ma ton. The historian C.J.S. Thompson claims that this pentacle, designed to evoke angels, is the earliest of its kind.

Few magical documents, grimoires or angel books exist which do not make use of either the Agla or the Tetragrammaton in symbolic form.

Much of the magical ritual of the past rested secure in the knowledge that man lives immersed in pictures – in what is nowadays called the imaginative life. Sometimes, these pictures are internally derived, and sometimes they are externally derived, but in general mankind cannot escape the destiny of living within images. Knowing this, magicians reasoned that, since we spend all our soul-life (intellectual and spiritual life) immersed in pictures, then our human power must be somehow involved in images. They came to the conclusion that it would be possible – and quite permissable in the eyes of God – to control and manipulate the external world by means of IMAGES.

This explains the extraordinary power of the belief in image-making in earlier times, and, incidentally, accounts for the profound importance of amulets, talismans and charms in the occult tradition. A story told of Alexander the Great, by the medieval English-man Neckham, tells how monsters would destroy the walls of Alexandria, even while they were being constructed. The monsters would emerge from the sea each dark night and pull down all that had been built in the previous day. In order to see the monsters, Alexander had a submarine tank made, and lowered this to the sea bed. There he saw the monsters, with fiercesome bestial heads and human bodies, and sketched them on a papyrus. He then ordered his craftsmen to make images from these sketches and display them in different parts of the city. The magical images worked – presumably because the monsters recognized that Alexander now knew what they looked like and therefore had power over them. When, later,

"THE PENTAGRAM OF FAUST"

A rather crude symbol, invented by the French occultist Eliphas Levi, represents the Tetragrammaton (in Roman characters) around the magical pentagram interlace. Wrongly called by Levi "The Pentagram of Faust", it is entirely typical of his syncretic approach to symbolism – that is to say, derived from a wide and discordant set of traditions of symbolism. In the centre is a curious sigil which combines Mercury with the earth, and on the band of the pentagram are numerous other sigils from the popular occult lore. None of the extraneous symbols has anything to do with the pentacle, which is essentially a symbol of the Venus principle. From Levi's *Transcendental Magic*, 1896.

the monsters began to return, Alexander had new images cut into wood and constructed talismans to stop them devouring the inhabitants of the city.

This profound belief in the power of images is somewhat difficult for us to understand nowadays, for we live in a plethora of moving imagery which confuses our souls. In earlier days, images had a sanctity about them, and a knowledge of the appearance of a thing was on the same level as having knowledge of its name or symbol.

The belief in the power of images was of considerable importance in sympathetic magic. It was widely held that the image of an object or person was linked to that object or person by an invisible virtue. This is why the making of waxen images, or POPPETS, was such big business for magicians and witches (*see page 95*). When an image of Queen

Elizabeth I was found in London, the great magician Dr. John Dee was called in as consultant, to give his opinion on what magical purposes were afoot. Such image-making was illegal in those days.

The great alchemist Van Helmont denied that there was any black magic (by which he meant "diabolical magic") involved when a magician stuck needles into an image of his or her victim. He traced the undeniable power of such image magic to the imagination of the witch – the operation of magic intensifying the evil current, giving it sufficient power and direction to achieve its purpose. In a sense, therefore, Van Helmont was reducing image magic to the level of natural magic.

Just as images were seen to have a magical power, so were a special group of artificial images (specially constructed symbols) known as SIGILS. A sigil is a written character which contains within its form a representation of a spiritual truth.

Good examples of sigils are the manuscript forms for Mars and Venus, the archetypal Male and Female symbols. THE MARS-SIGIL was originally a circle, surmounted by a cross.

THE VOODOO LOA

The possession of a member of a voodoo group (*above left*) by a loa, or god-form, is part of the serpent-cult wisdom of the voodoo stream derived from Africa (mainly, it seems, from the original Whydah, later Dahomey). The possessed sometimes channel the wisdom of the loa. In the modern voodoo rituals, the vevers, or secret sigils (*above right*), are drawn on the ground (though they may also decorate ritual objects, in a more permanent form) and are shaped by pouring cornmeal or any convenient powder through the fingers. This vever is being prepared prior to a ritual of healing. It is the sigil for Agwe, the loa of the seas, and in some respects resembles a boat led by the stars, trailing its anchor.

The idea contained in the sigil was that in the Male principle matter predominated. The circle of spirit was weighed down by the four elements (the four arms of the cross):

The VENUS-SIGIL is the spiritual opposite, for the circle of spirit is lifting the cross of matter, proclaiming that in the Feminine principle spirituality predominates. In each case, the sigils do more than denote the planets – they also describe, in graphic form, something of the principle in the planetary action. Sigils are more than symbols, for their forms reflect spiritual realities.

VOODOO is among the most misunderstood of modern magical systems. In its modern forms, it is a cult of mysticism and ecstasy, in which those practising the cult may permit god-forms, divine archetypes known as LOA, to OVERSHADOW, or possess them on a temporary basis, while they are in a trance. Voodoo is a trance-cult which was originally derived from Africa (especially from Dahomey), but which has been enriched by native Carib influences, as well as certain beliefs taught by the Catholic Church. Perhaps the unfortunate reputation which voodoo has acquired is a result of the public displays of the cult, often staged for touristic purposes, in which black pigs or white hens are sacrificed. It is true that voodoo does involve itself with sacrifices, yet behind the crude-seeming ceremonials lies a profound view of the nature of mankind and man's relationship to the gods. Undoubtedly the cruellest sacrifices are those which take place during the secret initiation of the servants of the loa, when chickens and other birds are torn to bits while still alive.

Among the many preparatory voodoo rituals, which culminate in the trances and possessions that are the outward form of the cult, is the drawing of special sigils (*photograph, page 140, right*) called VEVERS. Inevitably, in a cult which traces many of its rituals to the pre-slave cultures of Africa, snake-forms tend to predominate, yet many of the vevers are strangely reminiscent of the demon-sigils which abound in Western grimoires.

Generally, a vever symbolizes the loa which is to be evoked during the forthcoming ritual, and is of a traditional design. Melta Denning and Osborne Phillips, who have studied Haitian voodoo in depth, have published an interesting account of certain vevers, and have shown that, rather than being merely decorative, they are graphic portrayals of spiritual activities.

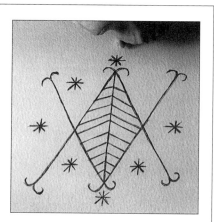

VEVER

The vever for AYIZAN, the archetypal Mother-goddess, the patron goddess of initiation, has a graphic form which denotes her special function as a combiner of the two sexes. The two inter-locking Vs of the vever represent sexual congress, the meeting of the dual sexuality as one. The stars of the vever, like the stars in Egyptian symbolism, indicate that this merging of the male and female principles is taking place on the astral, or star-world, level. The distinctive linear shading within the inner lozenge is undoubtedly a reference to the principal veins of the palm-leaf, as the palm tree is one of the worldly attributes or symbols of Ayizan.

DIVINATION

The fortune-tellers are the moralists, as well as the consolers of the lower classes. They supply a want that society either cannot or will not do.

(THE BOOK OF DAYS, EDITED BY R. CHAMBERS, 1863. QUOTED BY KEITH THOMAS, RELIGION AND THE DECLINE OF MAGIC, 1971.)

n ancient times, at the Temple of Ceres in Patras, Greece, there was a fountain which housed an oracle intended to be consulted only by the sick. The sick person, after offering incense and praying to the gods, would let down to the surface of the water a mirror upon a string, so that its base touched the water. He or she would then look into the mirror: if the reflection was of a healthy face, then recovery was sure, but if it was of a ghastly aspect, the end was near.

This example of CATOPTROMANCY (*see page 207*) expresses some of the staple beliefs about divination. It is believed that, in looking into the future, one is to some extent entering into the realm of the gods (who must therefore be propitiated). Furthermore, the diviner works through images, or pictures which he sees projected on the outer world, yet which are probably derived from his own mind's eye. This is one reason why the diviner is often called a SEER, for he sees beyond the familiar world of experience; his perception reaches into that other world, proper to the gods.

There are many of these DIVINATORY ARTS, and a survey of the more frequently used terms which cover these arts begins on page 175. This lists well over a hundred interesting methods of looking into futurity. Meanwhile, we may examine five of the important popular methods of PREDICTION which are still in wide use in the West – palmistry, the Tarot, runes, the Chinese Book of Changes (better known as the "I Ching") and crystal-gazing or crystallomancy.

Each of these five general methods of prediction is coloured by astrological lore. This

---

AIDS TO DIVINATION

(*Left*) Paraphernalia used in various techniques of prediction. Among the objects is a palmistry hand, crystal ball, sticks for the I Ching, crystals and crystal ball, rune stones, playing cards (for cartomancy) and Tarot cards.

is interesting, because while almost all predictive arts have been banned or forbidden by either Church or governments in the past centuries, astrology has remained relatively free of such embargoes. Perhaps this reluctance to extirpate the art of the stars was connected with the fact that, by the eleventh and twelfth centuries, astrological imagery was an intimate part of church architecture and design. The eleventh century had seen the Arabs pass on to the West their wealth of astrological knowledge, and these Eastern-derived symbols were incorporated into many cathedrals, churches and abbeys.

Among the earliest of the European churches influenced by Arabic astrological designs is the SACRA DI SAN MICHELE, in the Val di Susa, Italy. The remains of eleventh-century zodiacal and constellational roundels are still incorporated into the door at the top of the Staircase of the Dead, in the main part of the monastery. Three of the constellational images are shown here (*opposite, top*). Some of these images closely resemble the ones used today, but a couple would not be recognised by a modern astrologer – for example, the image of Capricorn as a dragon. The names for the constellations are carved above these delightful roundels; next to Capricornus is the more recognisable Sagittarius, the horseman, shooting his bow and arrow over his back.Scorpius grasps in his claws the sign for Libra, an image which is a throwback to the time when Scorpius and Libra were described as being one constellation.

More remarkably, one Florentine church, built in 1207, has been shown by Fred Gettings to have been constructed almost entirely around medieval astrological theory. This basilica, SAN MINIATO AL MONTE, still retains the original enigmatic marble zodiac, as part of its ornate nave pavimento (*opposite, right*). Taurus is rearing on its hind legs against a background of ornate floral interlace designed to indicate that the bull is not a "real" bull, but one from the starry realm. (In medieval art, the floral interlace is commonly used to represent the idea of the invisible ETHERIC realm, which occultists maintain exists behind the physical realm.)

In the next century, zodiac imagery became a standard requirement in the programme of church design. At AMIENS Cathedral for example, the twelve images of the zodiacal signs are still preserved in the northernmost of the three western portals. The image of Pisces (*opposite, bottom left*) has the two fishes with their mouths conjoined by the SILVER CORD, which in the days when this was carved, would have been called the NODUS. Such symbols for planets and zodiacs proliferated in European art until well into the seventeenth century, and did not belong to a tradition of forbidden sciences.

The fact that astrology was never officially "forbidden" does not mean that it plays no part in the occult realm of forbidden arts. On the contrary, as we have seen from the Introduction and the chapter on alchemy, astrological terminology finds its way into virtually all the divinatory arts; and few of these are more deeply marked by astrological notions and terms than palmistry.

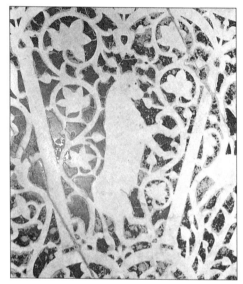

MEDIEVAL ASTROLOGY IN CHURCHES

Three of the constellational images (*top*) from the so-called "zodiacal arch" at the top of the Staircase of the Dead, in the Sacra di San Michele, Val di Susa (Italy). To the left is the image for Capricornus, as a curl-tailed winged dragon. Next is Sagittarius, shooting his bow and arrow over his back, and follows Scorpius, grasping the constellation Libra in his claws. Twelfth century.

Early fourteenth-century zodiacal quatrefoil from the porch of Amiens Cathedral (*above left*), displaying the image for Pisces. Note how the fishes are joined at the mouths by the distinctive cord. Later called the silver cord, it was seen as the invisible link which unites spirit to body. There may be a constellational explanation for this cord, however.

This zodiacal image for Taurus (*above right*) is from the early thirteenth-century marble zodiac in the nave of the basilican church of San Miniato al Monte, in Florence. Set down in 1207, the zodiac is so orientalizing in design that until comparatively recently it was believed that it had been brought to Florence from Constantinople, after the sack of this city by the Christians, in 1204.

PALMISTRY

THE PALMIST LE NORMAND

Marie-Anne Le Normand, the French female chiromancer and cartomancer (*see page 147*) – some would say charlatan – reading cards in dramatic mode to the Empress Josephine. Le Normand was able to predict the premature death at the guillotine of Josephine's first husband, Alexandre de Beauharnais, and certain future events for Josephine's next husband, Napoleon – including their divorce. The great man was so impressed by Le Normand's prevision that he insisted that the complete record of these predictions be deposited with the prefecture of police. Suspicious that his wife's confidante might warn Josephine, he also took the precaution of having the unfortunate palmist arrested until the scandalous divorce had been completed. Under this drawing by Jean Ribault is printed some of Le Normand's previsioning. From M.A. Le Normand's semi-official *Memoires historiques et secrets de l'Imperatrice Josephine*, 1827.

PALMISTRY is probably the most popular divinatory method in the West. The term is actually rather misleading, for it suggests an art which is concerned with the study of the palm. In fact, genuine palmistry is the study of all elements pertaining to the hand – from fingers and palm, through to fingerprint patterns, hand flexions, gestures, malformations on the skin, and even photographic records left by electrical discharges from the hands.

Palmistry is concerned mainly with portraying character from the study of the hand, but in some cases palmists have the ability to predict future life directions, and even specific events, from an examination of the hand.

Modern palmistry differs from the ancient methods in concentrating on what is called CHIROGNOMY at the expense of CHIROMANCY. Chirognomy is the study of the form of the hand, and involves such aspects as general proportions, shapes of the fingers and mounts, and the classification according to hand-types. Chiromancy is the study of the lines of the hand, and is not much concerned with the form.

We may assume from the books and illustrations the early palmists left us that almost all the medieval palmists were chiromancers, and that chirognomy did not greatly interest them. They appear to have been more concerned with interpreting the meaning of lines, or special signs, on the palms than in studying the shapes of the palm and fingers, and the general form of the hand on which such signs were found.

The chiromantic form of palmistry was much interested in prediction – in attempting to determine the future events in the life of the person concerned – with the result that many of the old diagrams and texts deduce cataclysmic results from extremely simple forms and symbols traced within the palm lines.

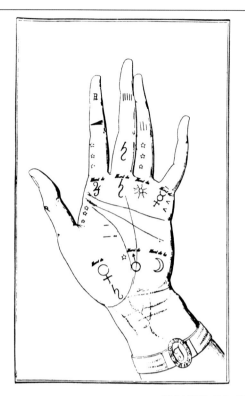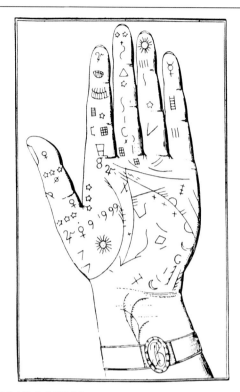

HANDS OF GREAT LOVERS

To judge from the engravings that the chiromancer Le Normand left of the hands of Napoleon (*above right*) and Josephine (*above left*), she must have made her predictions about Josephine's life (see page 146) on intuitive or clairvoyant grounds, for there is nothing in the diagrams she provides which would lead to such interpretations by the rational application of the rules of palmistry. Of Napoleon's hand, Le Normand wrote in 1827, in her *Memoires historiques et secrets de l'Imperatrice Josephine*: "There was revealed everything, even those marks which proclaimed him as hero and conqueror." It is clear from Le Normand's text that she knew little about palmistry. While we might reasonably imagine that the sigils and stars on the hand are meant to reveal the relevant planetary rulerships, Le Normand was convinced that she could actually see these, marked on the hand. For example, because she saw the sigil for Jupiter on the tip of the finger for Jupiter, she saw this as a sign that Napoleon would obtain great honours. The two stars on the tip of the middle finger (the finger of Saturn) she saw as a sign that he would be "crowned in a cathedral built by islanders in France". Prediction after the event, of course.

In contrast, modern chirognomy is generally interested in determining the general character, the psychological type and the inclinations of the person, and is only peripherally interested in predicting the future. The general idea is that the "future" or "destiny" of an individual is very much an outcome of his or her own character.

Although it is a relatively modern science, chirognomy is nevertheless rooted in certain traditional forms. For example, it recognizes the age-old classification of the fingers, according to planetary associations, which interprets them as indicators of particular energies or life directions.

THE PALMIST COCLES

The Italian palmist Barthelemy Cocles is depicted in this woodcut from his *Ciromantia* of 1532. It was a sign of Cocles's deep belief in the validity of palmistry that he seriously proposed that a judge, prior to torturing the accused at the commencement of a witchcraft hearing (*see page 91*), should examine the witch's hands – presumably in the certainty that this would reveal indications of guilt.

One of the most interesting palmists of the late fifteenth century was Bartolommeo della Rocca, who lectured and wrote under the name Barthelemy Cocles (*left*). Cocles was especially famed for his personal predictions relating to famous people, and for his interest in the exact prediction of dates and types of death. The popularity, and hence the survival, of many of Cocles's predictions from the hand is probably due to his interest in palmistic signs of death, which some modern commentators see as prefiguring his own destiny. The mathematician and occultist Jerome Cardan records that Cocles left a list of no fewer than forty-five men who would die violent deaths. By the time Cardan wrote, all but two of the predictions had been fulfilled. Cocles even foretold accurately the time and manner of his own death. He was murdered, on September 24th, 1504, by Antonio Capponi, on the orders of the son of one of Cocles's former patrons to whom, ironically, he had once presented a copy of his book on the violent deaths of great men.

It is evident that Cocles combined astrology with hand-reading, in a form which was later called ASTROPALMISTRY. In the ANASTASIS, Cocles traces the introduction of syphilis into Europe to stellar events. As an Italian doctor, he frequently came across the disease, which was believed to have begun among the French in Naples, and which was already devastating Europe. Cocles agreed with earlier astrologers that its commencement was due to the GREAT CONJUNCTION of Jupiter and Saturn in 1484, and to subsequent malign ASPECTS (planetary angular relationships) affecting these major planets.

Due to his interest in chiromancy, Cocles observed that those who had the disease revealed similar characteristics in their palms. He traced these to a weak HEPATIC LINE (*linea epatica*, or *hepatica*), which later chiromancers called the HEALTH LINE. When well marked and long (and therefore an indicator of good health) the HEPATICA runs across the hand, crossing the beginning of the LIFE LINE, terminating on the Mount of Mercury.

There may be little doubt that this line is directly related to health, and several palmists point to this as the most reliable indicator that lines do change with the passage of time, and are not mere FLEXION LINES. The nineteenth-century palmist Heron-Allen records that he has seen this line on a fresh young hand; initially as clear as any of the other lines, it proceeded to break up and practically disappear in only a few years. That Heron-Allen recognized that the line was linked with the sexual parts is evident from footnotes in his book, set out in Latin to limit its readership: these indicate that a star near the junction between the headline and the hepatica suggests sterility in a woman.

THE TAROT

The original TAROT pack was a set of cards designed to aid the practice of CARTOMANCY, or divination by means of cards. In fact, since the end of the last World War, Tarot cards have become the most popular modern form of divination by occult means. In the past two decades alone, over 230 different Tarot packs, in designs intended for cartomantic use, have been published. Unfortunately, with this proliferation a great deal of the original symbolism, upon which the divinatory strength of the Tarot rested, has been weakened or lost.

In modern times, the majority of Tarot packs consist of two separate sets of cards. One set, called the MAJOR ARCANA, is made up of twenty-two picture cards, each with an image full of symbolic detail, and usually linked with the tradition of secret symbolism. A pair of sample cards from the traditional "MARSEILLES DECK" are the FOOL and the WHEEL OF FORTUNE (*page 150, top*). The major arcana images follow a traditional numerical order and are linked with an ancient symbolism. Although several modern pack designs have changed the traditional names to serve their own specialist purposes, the numerical order and names of the major set, in English, French and Italian, are:

1	JUGGLER	LE BATELEUR	ILBAGATTO
2	LADY POPE	LA PAPESSE	LA PAPESSA
3	EMPRESS	L'IMPERATRICE	LA IMPERATRICE
4	EMPEROR	L'EMPEREUR	L'IMPERATORE
5	POPE	LA PAPE	IL PAPA
6	LOVERS	L'AMOUREUX	L'AMORE
7	CHARIOT	LE CHARIOT	LA CAROZZA
8	JUSTICE	LA JUSTICE	GUISTIZIA
9	HERMIT	L'HERMITE	L'EREMITA
10	WHEEL OF FORTUNE	LA ROUE DE FORTUNE	LA RUOTA
11	STRENGTH	LA FORCE	LA FORZA
12	HANGING MAN	LE PENDU	L'IMPICATO
13	(An untitled image of a skeleton called the DEATH card)		
14	TEMPERANCE	LA TEMPERANCE	LA TEMPERANZA
15	DEVIL	LE DIABLE	IL DIAVOLO
16	HOUSE OF GOD	LA MAISON DIEU	LA TORRE
17	STAR	L'ETOILE	LA STELLA
18	MOON	LA LUNE	LA LUNA
19	SUN	LE SOLEIL	IL SOLE
20	JUDGEMENT	LA JUGEMENT	IL GIUDIZIO
21	WORLD	LE MONDE	IL MONDO
22	THE FOOL	LE MAT	IL PAZZO

TWO MAJOR ARCANA

These two ATOUT, or picture cards, are from the traditional Marseilles deck of Tarot cards. The Fool is in the guise of an itinerant beggar, pursued by a dog. The tenth card is the Wheel of Fortune in the medieval manner, with the Ape of Life (symbolic of the creative man, who imitates nature) rising and falling in turn.

TWO MINOR ARCANA

The minor arcana of the Tarot are closely related in their number symbolism to ordinary playing cards. These two are eight of Swords, and five of Cups. After a French nineteenth-century deck.

The complementary set (*below left*), called the MINOR ARCANA, usually consists of fifty-six cards which closely resemble (in their number symbolism) the pip cards of ordinary playing cards. As with traditional playing cards, the minor arcana are grouped into four distinct suits, each of which bears a specific meaning:

Sceptres Cups Swords Pentacles

In turn, these are given a numerical and/or pictorial symbolism, in which each card has a divinatory significance.

Although some clairvoyants use the entire set of seventy-eight cards for the purpose of divining the future, many mediums use only the major arcana, insisting that the combinations of the twenty-two symbol cards are sufficient to answer most questions about the future.

Usually, the Tarot pack is consulted as a means of resolving a question. The question may be about the future or the past. In order to answer such a question, the clairvoyant will have the client shuffle the selected pack, cut this several times, and then lay out the cards, in sequence, into one or other of a number of formal patterns (*right*).

The popularity of the Tarot stems from the fact that anyone may learn to use it effectively after only a few weeks of study; it is unique as a divinatory tool. This contrasts strongly with the divinatory methods of the Chinese Book of Changes or European astrology, which takes many years of deep study.

So accustomed are we to thinking of the Tarot cards as being "occult" and ancient that it is difficult for us to grasp that this notion was not introduced until the eighteenth century. This is perhaps a disturbing thought, for nowadays it is all too easy to assume that the Tarot is rooted in

FORMAL PATTERN

In this modern reading of the Tarot cards, the girl is using a modern printing of the Wirth deck (*see page 156*), which she lays out in a formal pattern of great simplicity. Some Tarot readers prefer to evolve their own systems of formal pattern, but the most popular is the so-called Celtic Pattern, which is essentially a crossed circle.

DEATH AND THE JUGGLER

Two cards from the Tarot designs preserved by Court de Gebelin: the thirteen card, the unnamed Death, which in fact pertains to regeneration rather than death; and the first numbered card, the Juggler (Le Bateleur), with one hand pointing to the heavens and the other to the earth, showing the initiate's mastery of the two planes. Despite de Gebelin's claims of Egyptian origins, the cards belong to the French cartomantic tradition.

astrological and esoteric symbolism, with a background of Hebraic esoteric lore (CABBALISM) thrown in – and indeed many modern cards have designs based entirely on symbols derived from precisely such sources.

In fact, it was a Frenchman, Court de Gebelin, who somewhat dramatically announced the connection between the Tarot and the occult, in 1772, in his remarkable and quite unlearned bestseller, *Le Monde Primitif*. In this book, de Gebelin claims that the Tarot has existed for 3,757 years, and was designed by ancient Egyptians to represent a synthesis of all knowledge. The card designs reproduced by de Gebelin are traditional, and cannot be traced back beyond the late sixteenth century, while the numbers he accords the images are even later associations (*left*).

Even though there is not one iota of truth in what Court de Gebelin says about the Tarot, or indeed about the primitive world at large, his book about the Tarot entitled the BOOK OF THOT (so named after the Egyptian mystery god THOTH) became wildly popular in France and spawned many erroneous notions about the Tarot. Despite de Gebelin's high-flown sentiments, the truth is that the cards were originally used mainly for playing games. The literary evidence suggests that the Tarot was not used for the purpose of divination, as a form of cartomancy, until as late as 1527.

For all his inventive account of history, Court de Gebelin has had a profound influence on the development of the Tarot as a predictive tool, if only in introducing a nominal link with Egypt. The extraordinary personal symbolism proposed for his own Tarot pack by the self-styled "GREAT BEAST", Aleister Crowley, has little to do with Tarot symbolism, and everything to do with syncretic ocultism – yet, even so, he chose to extend Gebelin's concept and name his own set "The Book of Thot Tarot". The designs for these cards are among the most original and evocative of all modern packs; yet some mediums find them too "dark", too charged with energy of a questionable sort, to use in divination (*photograph, page 78*).

The Book of Thot may never have seen the Egyptian sun, yet it is now widely believed that the Tarot has something to do with the arcane wisdom of the Egyptians – which is, of course, iconographically impossible.

If the Tarot cards really were not designed or used in ancient times for the purpose of divination, is there any basis for such use now? The simple answer is that the Tarot qualifies for divinatory status because it may be legitimately regarded as a useful AUTOSCOPE. The word "autoscope" was probably first used in a divinatory context by Carl Gustav Jung. This great psychologist believed that certain formal patterns and symbols provide a sort of doorway between the human mind and the realm of archetypes, which reside (as creative potential) within the unconscious. Such a view implies that the Tarot cards, regarded either singly or within a formal pattern, should not be seen as having anything like fixed meanings (as so many of the popular "cook-book" texts on the Tarot imply). Instead, they should be treated as so many pegs on which to hang the creative and intuitive working of the unconscious, which has access to realms of knowledge denied the more analytical mind.

This does not imply, however, that we should approach the symbols in a spirit of ingenuous ignorance. On the contrary, it has been shown that the more a human being is consciously prepared regarding the matter of the hidden meanings of symbols, and the more extensive his or her iconographic and historical awareness, then the more alert he or she will be to the symbolism of line, colour and structure – and the more meaningful will be the interpretation.

The Tarot itself is such a complex system, with a rich history and intriguing substratum of symbols, that it would be difficult to give a precise example of just how important a well-informed knowledge of symbols may be to the interpretation of a given card.

Even were we to deal with one card, such as the enigmatic LADY POPE, or La Papesse

MINCHIATE SET

Sets of cards with symbols derived from the esoteric and occult repertoire were in existence before Court de Gebelin invented an ancient history for the Tarot. Especially noteworthy is the MINCHIATE SET, designed in Florence in the early part of the eighteenth century. This incorporated cards more or less corresponding to the standard twenty-two major arcana, but added a further nineteen images, consisting of zodical signs, and other cards corresponding to the four elements.

Six cards from the Minchiate design are shown here. These are the first six zodiacal cards (*from top left to bottom right*): Aries, Taurus, Gemini, Cancer, Leo and Virgo. Their numbers do not, however, correspond to their sequence in the pack.

Even earlier, a Venetian, Andrea Ghisi, had invented a game reminiscent of the Tarot symbolism, which he called the LABYRINTH. The images for this pack consist of crude personifications of such subjects as the Pope, the Emperor, the seven planets, the virtues, the Muses, astrology, theology, and so on. The rules of the game are unknown.

CENTURIES OF ACCRUED MYTHOLOGY

The Lady Pope (La Papesse), sometimes called Pope Joan, from an eighteenth-century Marseilles deck (*above left*). The notion of a lady pope had been dreamed up nine hundred years earlier. It was further enbellished in the twelfth century, as shown in this woodcut (*above right*) of Pope Joan with her child, hanged from a gibbet in front of the jaws of hell.

in the French set, or Pope Joan (*above*), we would be taken into ninth-century mythology, where the notion of the female pope (who had no actual existence) was dreamed up. From there, we would be carried into the twelfth century, where the mythology was embellished with details of Joan's supposed child, and her death, by hanging, in Rome (*above right*).

On a different level, a more profound knowledge of this same card will also take us into a more historically reliable link with the image of Isis, which was introduced in a similar iconographic figure structure in the seventeenth century (*right*) by the Jesuit Athanasius Kircher. An association between Isis and the Lady Pope is quite valid, on iconographic grounds, and means there is virtually no end to the symbolic nuances one may sense in this single card. Isis represents the eternal feminine – the Virgin, the Night, the Black Madonna and the White Madonna, the mysteries of the ancient world, and the Feminine in all, which seeks to reconstitute the dismembered body of the male consort Osiris.

From another point of view, we might be inclined to examine the graphic significance of the card. For example, we might recognize a secret graphic symbolism, with a geometry of lines linking the mystic triangle with the earthly quaternary of the four elements (*illustration, page 156*).

The list of possible approaches to this single card is almost endless, and serves to indicate how the more information one has about a symbol, then the more potential one may sense in it and the more confidently one may reach into the hidden recesses of one's own richness. As a divinatory technique, the Tarot seems to offer a method by which this

ISIDIS
Magnæ Deorum Matris
APVLEIANA DESCRIPTIO.

Nomina varia Ifidis.

Ifis
Minerua
Venus
Iuno
Proferpina
Ceres
Diana
Rhea feu
    Tellus
Peffinuncia
Rhramnufia
Bellona
Hecate
Luna
Polymor-
    phus dæ-
    mon.

Expl cationes fymbolorum Ifidis.

A Diuinitatem, mun-
dum, orbes cceleftes
BB Iter Lunæ flexuo-
fum, & vim fœcun-
datiuam notat.
CC Tutulus, vim Lu-
næ in herbas, &
plantas.
D Cereris fymbolum,
Ifis enim fpicas in-
nenit.
E Byffina veftis mul-
ticolor, multifor-
mem Lunæ faciem.
F Innentio frumenti.
G Dominium in om-
nia vegetabilia.
H Radios lunares.
I Genius Nili malo-
rum auerruncus.
K Incrementa & de-
crementa Lunæ.
L Humeĉtat, vis Lunę
M Lunæ vis viĉtrix, &
vis diuinandi.
N Dominium in hu-
mores & mare.
O Terræ fymbolũ, &
Medicinæ inuentrix.
P Fœcunditas, quæ fe-
quitur terram irri-
gatam.
Q Aftrorum Domina.
R Omnium nutrix.
S } Terræ marifque
M } Domina.

MOTHER OF THE GODS

Isis, the mother of the gods, with her various name-guises, one foot on the water, one on the earth, in the same symbolic posture as Fludd's ANIMA (*page 52*). This plate, based on the description of the Isidic mysteries by Lucius Apuleius, is from Kircher's *Oedipus Aegyptiacus*, 1652/55. It records fifteen of the many names of her related spiritual femininity, and lists the symbolic meanings of her clothing and attributes.

GRAPHIC ANALYSIS

The Lady Pope card with its graphic analysis, which is of a triangle resting upon a square. The triangle represents spirituality, which is here firmly balanced upon the square of the four elements. Graphically, the card announces that all is right with the world. The open book, itself a "doubled rectangle" of the four elements, has the curious cross (formed by the hem of the internal regalia) attached to it. This is another graphic symbol of the cross of materiality resting firmly upon the enclosed quaternary of the elements.

inner iconographic richness may be explored without danger.

A number of interesting hand-painted Tarot decks have come down to us from the late fifteenth century. Because they have been published in sound academic restorations or TAROT FACSIMILES, some of these sets are still used by modern TAROMANCERS.

Among the most useful of these restored decks is the original hand-painted VISCONTI-SFORZA DECK, produced in Milan in the middle of the fifteenth century. A completed facsimile edition of this set, based on the surviving nineteen cards, was published in 1983 by Luigi Scarpini, and is sometimes called the SCARPINI PACK. Facsimiles of the Bergamo Visconti-Sforza deck (probably created by Butinone and Zenale in the fifteenth century) were published in 1975, with the two missing arcana (THE DEVIL and THE TOWER) carefully recreated. The main problem with these interesting sets is that the symbolism does not correspond to that which traditional cartomancy and Tarot-users are accustomed to. Fortunately, this deficiency in the Italian packs is remedied in some slightly later French decks.

The oldest surviving French deck was made by Catelin Geofroy, in Lyons, probably in 1557. Curiously, there is a reference to the Tarot (in fact, to *tarau*) in Rabelais's arcane text, *Gargantua*, of 1534, and several later mentions of the "game" in other French sources. This means that decks must have been available in France for at least a quarter of a century before this surviving pack. Thirty-eight cards have survived, with unconventional suits such as parrots, peacocks and lions. Interestingly enough, the surviving twelve major arcana follow the classical French tradition (the so-called MARSEILLES DECK) suggesting a remarkable antiquity and supporting the occult tradition that the Marseilles deck was the one first used for predicting the future.

A most useful facsimile of an old French pack (probably the oldest surviving complete set) was made available by André Dimanche in 1984. The originals were coloured by means of stencils. The seventy-eight cards have been dated to the early seventeenth century, and are commercially available as the PARIS TAROT.

The WIRTH DECK is a pack which has gained great popularity in modern times. This is the nineteenth-century design of the occultist and specialist in arcane symbolism Oswald Wirth, who wrote an analysis of the meanings of the cards which is still widely accepted by cartomancers. The symbolisms of the individual cards are interrelated, and he has followed the nineteenth-century esoteric tradition and linked each of the major arcana with the twenty-two letters of the Hebrew alphabet.

If we take two of the major atout (picture cards) – the Juggler (*near right*) and the Hanging Man (*far right*) – we may follow Wirth's intimations and see the "arcane structure" within the two cards. The four-sided table top of *Le Bateleur* is an enclosed symbol of the fourfold elements, upon which rest the four sacred symbols of the minor arcana. By contrast, in *Le Pendu*, this fourfoldness is thrown into "open space" (that is, it is no longer enclosed or confined) in the space determined by the fourfold structure around the hanging man – formed from the earth, the two tree-uprights and the curious lintel. This enclosing of space in the first card, and the opening or "exploding" of space in the twelfth card, is part of the arcane programme of the Wirth deck. The crossed legs of the hanging man are a further reference to the fourfold elements extended into space: the fact that this hanging man

le Bateleur ✠   le Pendu ♄

PERSONAL TAROT DESIGN

Two cards from the Oswald Wirth Tarot deck – the Juggler (*Le Bateleur*) and the Hanging Man (*Le Pendu*). With the Wirth designs we see arcane symbolism taken to its extreme: Wirth has refined and developed the symbolic potential of all the esoteric hints which may be perceived (imaginatively or otherwise) in the traditional Marseilles designs. Note, for example, how the paraphernalia on the Juggler's table has now become the symbols of the four elements, represented in the four suits of the minor arcana. After the contributions of Wirth, who took the traditional occult symbolism to its extreme, there was only one other esoteric development left for cartomancers – namely, for them to design their own, as Crowley and Harris did (*see page 78*).

has his arms tied behind his back is intended to ensure that the cross of the legs is affixed firmly on top of an inverted triangle. The "hidden" sigil formed from his painful position is actually one of the arcane sigils from alchemy, representative of Sulphur, the will force of the human being.

In contrast, the arms of the Juggler are opened into space-one (carrying the wand) points upwards, while the other, lightly touching the centre of the cross on the pentacle, points downwards. The Juggler wears on his head the curious lemniscate hat, which is said by Wirth to be symbolic of the meeting of the Sun and Moon. The secret structure and symbolism of the cards link each with arcane symbolism of the occult tradition, calling into play the whole gamut of cabbalism, alchemy, astrology, and so on. For all its complexity, Wirth's approach to the Tarot symbolism has its own meaning and utility, as it certainly deepens the autoscopic potential of the cards. The cartomancer who is well

THE ASTROLOGICAL TAROT

The finely designed Astrological Tarot of George Muchery. The image of a dog howling at the moon (above left) is the symbol for the third decanate of Scorpio, while the image of the winged horse, Pegasus (above right), is the symbol of the third decanate of Aquarius (Verseau, in French). The winged Pegasus of the constellations does hover above the star Sadalmelek, in the constellation of Aquarius, so there is a cosmological purpose behind the design of this card.

informed about the arcane symbolism of the forbidden sciences usually finds these arcana useful quarries for insights and ideas, and a rich source for divinatory imagery

The main value of the Wirth deck lay in the fact that its designer published, in 1927, a detailed commentary on his interpretation of the arcane symbolism in the design (which, in essence, followed the Marseilles tradition), and for the first time issued a correspondence between the twenty-two letters of the Hebrew alphabet and the twenty-two major arcana which had been suggested by the magician Eliphas Levi. Hand-coloured decks of the original (1889) Wirth designs are understandably rare, for printing was limited to one hundred copies: the set was published as the LIVRE DE THOT or BOOK OF THOTH.

A beautifully produced version of the Wirth major arcana, plus fifty-six newly created minor arcana, was printed in metallic colours in Switzerland by A.G. Muller, with the French nomenclature and the all-important Hebrew-letter equivalents. In 1976, a quality version of this deck was made available in the United States by the historian of TAROT-LORE, Stuart R. Kaplan.

In the past few decades there has been a proliferation of "Tarot designs", some of a highly personal nature and quite unrelated to the Tarot iconographic tradition. Among these are designs related to Celtic iconography, a modern mythology of feline lore (the TAROT OF THE CAT-PEOPLE), and several packs inexpertly linked with a pseudo-Egyptian mythology and Greek mythology (the MYTHIC TAROT DECK).

While some interesting images are found in these inventions, their value as Tarot cards is questionable. Undoubtedly, they are intended for divination purposes, but since they pertain to the cartomantic stream of occult designs, they should not be sold as Tarot. Their divinatory value appears to reside not in any arcane quality of the designs, so much as in the fact that the individual cards may work as AUTOSCOPES, providing useful associations, or channels for the individual psyches of the Tarot-user. Many Tarot purists refuse to use such designs, and insist on the more familiar Marseilles or Paris decks, the arcane symbolism of which may be related in a meaningful way to the occult tradition.

One interesting modern design which does use traditional occult images, yet remains outside the orthodox Tarot iconography, is the ASTROLOGICAL TAROT of the French occultist George Muchery, sometimes called the MUCHERY DECK (*left*). The major arcana of this set consists of forty-eight cards bearing images taken from zodiacal and planetary symbolism. Each of the twelve signs of the zodiac is presented in three different images, corresponding to the traditional DECANATES. A decanate is a division of a sign into ten degrees; in the astrological tradition such a division has been accorded a planetary ruler and an interpretation, used by certain modern astrologers, but far more popular in medieval times.

In addition to the thirty-six decan cards, there is the Ascendant card, figured as a Sphinx, a card dealing with the duality of the Dragon's Nodes (Head and Tail), the Part of Fortune (a winged disk), and nine planets (Pluto was not discovered until 1930, after the deck had been designed).

THE CONSTELLATION DECK

There have been many attempts to link the tradition of cartomancy with the astrological lore. A set of eighteenth-century cards, sometimes called a CONSTELLATION DECK, was designed around the imagery of the stars. Two of the cards are shown here. The first is the asterism, CAPRICORNUS (Steinbock); the second, the group CANIS MINOR (the Lesser Dog) and MONOCEROS (the Unicorn). It is clear that the cards were not designed for ordinary Tarot use, yet they might be used as autoscopes in order cartomancy.

RUNES

In contrast with the Tarot, the RUNES were used well over two thousand years ago for looking into futurity. The Roman writer Tacitus left us a passage in which he describes with some clarity how the priests operated the runes. Of course, Tacitus did not give particular examples of priestly interpretation – in those days such sacred activities would have been held in awe as MYSTERIES about which it would be wise not to speak. Many modern writers do not have the same sense of religious awe, however, and there is no shortage of recent books dealing with the divinatory value of the runes.

The names and forms of the traditional Nordic runes, and the meanings originally ascribed to them, are listed below:

RUNE-NAME	RUNE FORM	MEANING	RUNE-NAME	RUNE FORM	MEANING
Feoh		Property, wealth	Tir		Tree
Os		God	Ing		?
Gyfu		Gift	Daeg		Day
Nyd		Distress	Aesk		?
Eoh		?	Weord		Bait
Sigel		Sun	Gar		?
Eoh		?	Dorn		Thorn
Lagu		Water	Cen		?
Ac		?	Haegl		Hail
Ior		?	Yer		Year
Stan		?	Eolx		Elk
Ur		Drizzle	Beorc		Birch
Rad		Wheel, ride	Man		Man
Wynn		Pleasure	E(th)el		Property
Is		Ice	Ear		?
Peord		Horse	Calc		?

As with the Tarot, there are many different types of runes, though it is likely that they have a common ancestry. The secret writing seems to have been used only by initiates in the first instance, and was limited to divination, but by the middle of the first millennium of our era, runes began to appear on stones, especially in Scandinavian countries (*illustration, page 162, top*).

The runes offer an excellent illustration of the way an autoscope works, and by means of it we may consider the difference between the state of mental preparation of one who knows little about the runes, and one who has made a deep study. With this in mind, we may sense in what must be the simplest of all occult sigils, or secret symbols, the Is, which is a vertical line. Even someone who has only a little knowledge of these symbols will know that this vertical represents the ancient sigil for Ice, and it is therefore easy to sense in its meaning something of coldness, and to bear in mind its obvious opposition to Fire. This knowledge is already sufficient for one to use the autoscope of the rune to project into the archetypes.

Someone better prepared for treading among the archetypes will also know that Is represents the principle of upright stasis, which is human life itself, poised between heaven and earth. Such a person may even have studied what the esotericist Blavatsky has written about this upright (albeit not within the context of runes), and see that it touches upon morality – the true spirit strives to be the upright man, aware of his responsibility to the earth below, and to the cosmos above. Such a person may, without too much dislodging of iconographies, trace the upright "human being" in the figure of Robert Fludd's image (*page 52*) of ANIMA with the earth-monkey (what we might become if we give ourselves over to earthly appetites) and the symbol for God (which is the state man is designed to achieve in far distant ages).

To the initiate, the rune Is is also Ice in cosmic opposition to Fire, but the Ice is that which lies at the centre of Dante's *Inferno*, where the Devil is himself stuck in the ice flow of his own making (*illustration, page 57*). It is an Ice which will melt because everything in the world, even evil, is subject to the laws of change.

This Is, which points to the centre of the created world, is a symbol of gravity, of inertia, the non-creative, where the Devil himself has control of the soul.

The single upright stroke has been linked with the magical wand of the hierophant (an expounder of esoteric truths) – a wand which changes the world by invocations, yet remains unchanged itself. Static, it carries the power of creativity, and therefore (also) is phallic.

Perhaps it is no accident that the ancients would represent Scorpio as the ruler of the private parts in the ZODIAC MAN, or MELOTHESIC MAN (*illustration, page 13*), for this part of the body may also be a creative rod, and its associate zodiacal sign is linked with the Devil in exoteric (non-secret) astrology, and with karma in esoteric astrology.

RUNESTONE OF SKAANE

This fine example of Nordic runes in a banderolle is from an engraved stone at Skaane, in Sweden. The canine figure prancing above the boat is Fenrir, the terror-wolf of the Teutonic mythology.

KOSBABS RUNES

From a purely divinatory point of view, the most satisfactory modern runes system is that proposed by Werner Kosbab, in *Das Runen-Orakel*, 1982. Kosbab uses the eighteen Germanic runes with a further series of thirty-eight variations on runes, astrological sigils and one or two sigils which are derived from occult sources, such as astrology and alchemy.

The double meaning of the Is, its relation to creativity, to phallicism, and its sense of "oneness" and togetherness, associate it with the inner rituals which accompany the use of the Is-like sword in magical rituals – especially in those rituals where its graphic and symbolic opposite, the circle (for example, the orb of the full Moon) is involved (*photograph, page 103*). Some schools of magic recognize that it is useful to have an outer form – such as a sword, or even a crude drawing of an I, or Is rune – when seeking to establish an inner state which corresponds to that form. The sword echoes the inner quality of oneness, of separation from the outer world, of the severance of ties.

If the Is stroke is the magician's wand, and phallic as well, then it is also the stick used in the English Morris Dance, with its spermatic sense of life, where upright men celebrate the growth of the corn and the greening of the world. And just as the symbol of inertia implies the creative, on the grounds that an immovable force of spirit must beat against the immovable force of matter to create any new thing, or to allow the cosmos to descend into matter, so also does the Is carry within its form the completion of another rune. This is the Cen rune, itself Fire, the Fire which glows around the Ice at the diabolical centre of the earth, which is also the centre of the universe.

Thus it is impossible (or at least misleading) to consider a rune in isolation, for it is always turning into its opposite, in much the same way as the trigrams of the Chinese "I Ching" constantly change as their component yin and yang lines change in a special sequence.

Indeed the fact that a single line of the runes may be subjected to so many layers of interpretation should indicate just how complex are other divinatory arts – like the Chinese "I Ching", or Book of Changes.

THE BOOK OF CHANGES

One very important modern divinatory technique involves the use of a book known as the I CHING or BOOK OF CHANGES, or ORACLE OF CHANGE. The original Chinese text of the I Ching is from remote antiquity – it was one of the few books allowed to survive in 213 BC, when the greater part of ancient literature in China was destroyed on the orders of the Emperor, Hwang-Ti, who wished to eradicate all records of the past.

Because the ancient text is full of wisdom, the I Ching is sometimes used as a philosophical machine, rather than merely for answering personal questions about the past and the future. However, its most popular use is as a book of divination (*below*), in which the diviner manipulates a number of sticks or yarrow stalks, according to a complicated numerological system. It is reliably reported that the Chinese generals in charge of the Korean War used the I Ching to augment and determine their strategy. Normally, however, it is approached for less dramatic purposes, by those who seek to learn the outcome of certain relationships, the wisdom or folly of beginning certain undertakings, and so on.

Often, the response from the I Ching is more pertinent than one might expect. A young man who thought he might test the I Ching asked whether it would be wise for him to visit the United States (from London) in the next couple of months. In fact, he had no intention of going there during that period. The I Ching sublimely ignored the question, but dealt very succinctly with the reasons why the young man should find it necessary to lie in such a way.

Before we look at the way in which this remarkable book is used for divination, we must glance at its underlying philosophy. In its surviving form (at least two related commentaries have been lost) the book consists of a collection of pithy and sometimes gnomic philosophical statements, which may be used to answer questions. These statements are derived from the interaction of six lines, each consisting of either a broken YIN line, or an unbroken YANG line. In simple terms, a yin represents the dark, yielding feminine element

BOOK OF DIVINATION

Practising divination with the aid of sticks, according to the Book of Changes system. The book in front of the girl is a tenth-century printed copy of the I Ching. In the place of the conventional yarrow stalks, she is using Chinese fortune sticks.

in the world. This, by its very nature, is striving to become its opposite, the yang, which is light, unyielding and masculine. Just as the yin strives towards its opposite polarity, so the yang strives to become the feminine yin.

The result of this constant change in polarities gives rise to a number of conditions, which are expressed in sets of trigrams. A TRIGRAM is made up of three sets of lines (yin or yang) ranged one upon the other. By this arrangement, it is possible to obtain eight different figures. It is traditional for diagrams in the Chinese scholarly editions of I Ching to present the names of these eight in a series of diagrams, showing "How the One becomes Many" from the primal division into two, through the eight, to give the trigrams, and then by alternating in yin and yang, up to the sixty-four figures of the I Ching.

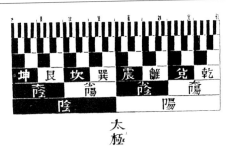

MAGICAL PROGRESSION

Ancient Chinese I Ching diagram, illustrating "How the One becomes Many". The One is not illustrated but is expressed by the two Chinese characters (T'ai Kih), which means "The Supreme Ultimate", and which includes not only the space around the diagram, but the page of the book, the person looking at the diagram, and the cosmos beyond.

Each of these figures has been associated with a large number of different earthly, psychic and spiritual associations. For example, the trigram called LI, which resembles an enclosed space is said to be like an Eye, with a central pupil,

and is therefore linked with Perception. Since the weak inner is protected by the outer yangs, it is a place of sensitivity, and will cling to more secure forms and energies. In the inner space, a Fire may burn, the flames protected from the wind. It is sometimes called the Fire Trigram, or CLINGING FIRE.

Its opposite is a weak trigram, with the yin lines on the outside insufficiently strong to protect the inner yang. This is an emblem of danger. It is a defile, a crossing which is not securely bridged, and (perhaps because it is the opposite of the perceptive Li) it tends to produce unforeseen circumstances and danger. This is the K'AN trigram.

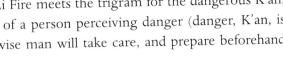

A set of eight trigrams may be united as pairs to make sixty-four figures, called HEXAGRAMS. Such a hexagram is quite different from the hexagram of European magic (*see page 138*). In some Chinese editions of the I Ching, the sequence of hexagrams is arranged in a diagrammatic rectangle, in others as a circle. The circle is by far the more satisfactory arrangement, for the cycles of changes are envisaged as continuing endlessly, without beginning or end.

The oldest texts of the I Ching deal with the natures of the changes and cycles revealed by this sequence, and are a set of statements concerning the image which arises from their interactions. When the trigram for the Li Fire meets the trigram for the dangerous K'an, with the latter above, the image is one of a person perceiving danger (danger, K'an, is ahead, watched by the eye of Li). The wise man will take care, and prepare beforehand against this danger. In the text of the I Ching, this meeting of K'an and Li is the KI TSI hexagram, No. 63 in the sequence.

KI TSI

It is part of the philosophy of the I Ching that the movement of the hexagram should be read upwards (a curious twist to Chinese lore, as the Chinese are accustomed to reading downwards). Thus, the Ki Hsi hexagram begins with a yang, and ends with a yin. This is one reason why, in the reading for this hexagram, the text advises that the situation may begin well, but may tend towards disorder.

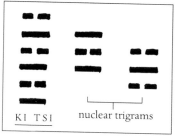

KI TSI   nuclear trigrams

The Chinese insist that the lower and upper lines do not play a significant part in the action, which really belongs to the innermost four lines. These are therefore subjected to a further analysis. The innermost four are viewed as being hidden trigrams, contributing to the force of the figure as a whole. The hidden trigrams are called the NUCLEAR TRIGRAMS. From the Ki Tsi hexagram, we obtain the two Nuclears Li (Fire) and K'an (Abyss), though this time in a relationship reversed to that found originally, in the primal figure.

The Chinese diviner may interpret a hexagram without reference to the text of the I Ching. The rules for interpretation, while complex, and deeply rooted in Chinese philosophy, are applicable to each figure, and some scholars maintain that the existing text of the Book of Changes is really nothing more than a collection of notes derived from particular interpretations – that is, a sort of case history for each figure.

The Western diviner, however, rarely has the knowledge required to interpret the figure without reference to the text of the I Ching. Since most of those who use the I Ching (and even many authors who publish European editions of the book) have little or no knowledge of Chinese, the majority of translations are of little value. The most widely used English text is actually translated from a German translation by Wilhelm; for all the fame of this, it is a highly imaginative view of the I Ching, a somewhat flowery and poetic version in which much of the Chinese spirit is lost.

Probably the best translation available in the West is YI JING by Dr. Wu Jing-Nuan, who has a profound knowledge of the Chinese system and of Chinese etymology. He is also a highly proficient painter, with the I Ching playing a leitmotif through his pictures (*page 167*). Dr. Wu Jing-Nuan's work, and the awakening interest in Chinese etymology and symbolism, have encouraged other artists and photographers to attempt very original work in illustrating the pictorial content of some of the hexagrams (*photograph, page 166*).

In Europe, there are two ways of consulting the I Ching. The most popular is frowned upon in China, because it is regarded as being disrespectful. It consists of deriving a hexagram for interpretation by means of coins, the COINS OF CHANGE. In China, the three coins are holed coins, with an ornate obverse and a blank reverse: in the fall of the coins,

THE KU HEXAGRAM

In modern times the dynamic philosophy behind the Chinese divination system of the "I Ching" is being appreciated by Western artists. As a result many painters and graphic designers are now influenced by the I Ching, and use its secret traditions as a basis for pictorial themes. This image is a photographic exploration of the dark sexual dynamism of the eighteenth hexagram of the Chinese text, which is called "Ku". This hexagram has intrigued many occultists (including the magus Crowley) because of the way its arcane associations – linked with vampirism, and other sexual matters – forge links with esoteric traditions of Western occultism. Unfortunately, the Ku hexagram has not been well transplanted by Western scholars, and its deeper implications are known only to esotericists or those familiar with Oriental arcane traditions.

two or more blank coins indicate a yin, while two or more ornate surfaces indicate a yang. The set of three coins is thrown six times in order to determine the nature of the six lines, building the figure upwards. It is popular in Europe because it is relatively quick and easy to perform.

The system favoured by the Chinese diviners demands considerable expertise and feeling for ritual. Each line is constructed in a series of numerologically determined move-ments with a set of sticks – ideally, yarrow stalks. The method itself is too complex to set down here, but details may be found in most of the better-quality translations of the I Ching.

The really significant thing is that while the majority of Western prac-titioners believe that the fall of the coins and the manipulation of the sticks is operated by chance – that the final hexagram is revealed "by accident" – the Chinese masters insist that both coins and yarrow sticks are manipulated by spirits. Their rituals are designed to propitiate such spirits, and it is main-tained that if the proper rituals are not observed, the inner spiritual energies of the diviner himself will deteriorate. This energy is called LI, and is a sort of inner spiritual power, related to the Clinging Fire of the perceptive trigram Li.

PAINTING THE I CHING

Dr. Wu Jing–Nuan of Washington, DC, specializes in Chinese herbal medicine and acupuncture. A highly gifted painter, he has chosen to explore the pictorial possibilities in the ancient Chinese lore of the I Ching, one or two cosmological themes of which may be seen on the painting behind him.

CRYSTAL-GAZING

CRYSTALLOMANCY, or CRYSTAL-GAZING, is the art of determining the future by means of images perceived in a CRYSTAL BALL. The word CRYSTAL is derived from *krystallos*, the Greek name for ice; crystals are frozen mineral substances, which have been formed over a quarter of a million years.

Although the occult tradition insists that beryl is the ideal crystal for looking into futurity, a large number of modern so-called crystal balls are made from glass (as revealed by the air-bubbles inside the globe). One of the characteristics of crystals is the rigid three-dimensional lattice of their structure: the molecules of glass have no such orderly lattice pattern. Glass definitely is not a crystal, so properly speaking crystallomancy should sometimes be VITRIOMANCY, or merely SHEW-GAZING (since a general name for crystals or glasses was shew-stones). In cases where a specific stone such as beryl is used, it could be called berylomancy – but see page 169.

One advantage in using cast-glass bowls (their comparative cheapness aside) is that they generally offer highly translucent surfaces which make them ideal for SCRYING. The scryer who gazes intently at the reflective surface of glass, or genuine crystal such as beryl, will claim to see images formed upon its surface. An American PSYCHOMANCER (someone who determines futurity by recourse to the spirits), Atkinson, writing in 1908, confessed that fixing the gaze upon a crystal ball is the best means of "bringing out the latent faculty of ASTRAL VISIONS".

Of course, it is a moot point whether such visions – astral or otherwise – are on the surface of the glass, or in the mind of the scryer. For all practical purposes, the source is unimportant, for most occultists insist that the crystal scryer is aided by spirits. Few modern crystal-readers are aware of this ancient occult tradition, which firmly anchors their art in the realm of DEMONOMANCY or ANGELOMANCY.

In her amusing and informative work *The Book of Sacred Stones*, Barbara Walker takes the less rigorous exponents of CRYSTAL-LORE to task. On sound scientific grounds, she debunks the New Age notion that gems and stones (other than those which are radioactive for one reason or another) emit radiations, or magnetic influences, however subtle or imperceptible.

With her tongue firmly in her cheek, Walker notes that, in 1985, Julia Lorusso and Joel Glick claimed that the beryl

CRYSTALLOMANCY

Woman crystal-gazing, using a crystal ball mounted upon a golden tripod, the supports of which are formed from images of the three Fates.

family was extra-terrestrial, having been "seeded" on the planet earth. This alien seeding might account for its popularity with clairvoyants, who, with less drama and more sense of history, insist that the power of the beryl is derived from the moon, and is firmly under the sway of this satellite. In the occult tradition, the BERYL was favoured as the ideal shew-stone, or SCRYING GLASS, and its use was advocated only during the time of the increasing Moon, or even during the one day or night when the Moon was full. The implication here is that the moon itself increases either the spiritual quality of the beryl, or the imaginative faculty of the scryer. Scientists (quite rightly) will have none of this notion of there being a celestial magnetism in stones.

The nineteenth-century German occultist Baron von Reichenbach, who was famous for his theory of ODIC FLUID (*below*), an etheric substance visible to clairvoyants, did maintain that there was such a thing as a magnetic EYE-BEAM, "an efflux of magnetism projected from the cerebellum [part of the brain]", which could be fixed upon a given point. This was a distinctly quasi-scientific theory of how the crystal invited a visionary state in the one who gazed into it.

One seventeenth-century amuletist had a similar spiritual power in mind when he called the beryl the PANZOON (the Greek for "All Life"). The beryl would perform certain amuletic deeds which depended upon the image engraved upon it; a picture of a frog would turn enemies into friends, while the image of a hoopoe (a type of bird) would invoke spirits.

Some scryers preferred a more Christian symbolism to disguise the activity of their spirits. One beryl shew-stone which came into the possession of the antiquary Aubrey was about two and a half centimetres (an inch) in diameter. It was set in a silver ring, on which were inscribed the names of the four archangels, Michael, Gabriel, Raphael and Uriel, surmounted by a holy cross. The handle, by which the scryer might examine the stone without touching it, was about twenty-five centimetres (ten inches) long, and of gilded metal.

The idea that one should not touch the stone (and thus remove its virtue) calls to mind one or two other rules behind practical crystal-gazing, culled from the nineteenth-century crystal-gazer Randolph. The scrying mirror must never be exposed to direct sunlight, which diminishes the virtue. The visions seen when the stone is supported in the left hand are real, while those in the right are symbolic. Clouds ascending in the glass mean "yes" in response to a question, while those descending mean

ODIC FLUID

This attempt to picture the emanation behind material forms – the luminous phenomena around magnets, plants, the human hand – was drawn from the personal vision of Anschutz, a German clairvoyant, and included in the nineteenth-century German occultist Baron von Reichenbach's book on magnetism. He called the phenomena the Odic Fluid, or the Odic Rays. From von Reichenbach, *Psycho-Physiological Researches on the Dynamics of Magnetism – [and] Vital Force*, 1851.

"no". The SCRYING CLOUDS which are famous for gathering in the crystal glass, and then clearing to reveal tiny visions, are explained as being "the magnetic field" collecting from the eyes of the scryer.

Strange notions concerning the occult powers of stones are not reserved for New Age visionaries. Writing in 1714, the German Valentinius explained the flight of an airship of 1709 as being motored by a CORAL-AGATE (silicon dioxide). The ship, invented by a Brazilian priest, obtained its energy from a series of large coral-agates, which were activated with a "magnetic charge" derived from the sun. These in turn activated a couple of powerful magnets, which lifted the ship. To judge from the woodcut, the raised ship was moved directionally by means of oar-feathers.

Certain medieval magical spells set out the rules for preparing shew-stones, and many emphasize that crystallomancy is the work of spirits (fairies and especially GNOMES), who work through mediums. One CRYSTAL-SPELL, preserved in the Ashmolean, at Oxford, recommends that the "crystall or Venice Glasse" be a rectangle measuring about eight by three inches. After washing and fumigation, the magician takes three hazel wands and peels them. On the white wood, which has been slivered so as to provide three flat strips, he writes the name of a fairy, three times. These wands are buried under a fairy hill on a Wednesday (the day of Mercury). On the following Friday (the day of Venus), at eight, three or ten o'clock, the magician, with face turned to the East, calls the named fairy. When she comes, obedient to the CALL, or magical summons, she is to be bound to the glass.

There is only a fine division between crystallomancy and scrying, since both depend upon reflective surfaces (or spirits, depending upon your occult persuasion) for their operation. Some magicians make simple scrying dishes by filling dark bowls with water, tracing their visions upon the reflective waters. Northcote Thomas, in his *Crystal Gazing* (1905), tells how medieval magicians would smear lamp-black on the palms of their hands, or even pour black ink into the cupped palm, and use these as scrying surfaces.

The CRYSTAL-GAZER, or scryer, will often recognize the importance of lighting in the construction of a working AUTOSCOPE (as scrying bowls are often described). Some clairvoyants like to work in a darkened room in which the crystal or glass has been lighted by a hidden source, or by a thin beam of light. Crystals (especially the hexagonal quartz crystals) have the wonderful facility of being able to throw exciting rainbow patterns of light, by transforming thin beams. Such home-made displays of auroras contribute to the sense of awe which is an aid to scrying.

Some clairvoyants insist that, just as important as the composition of the "crystal" and light-source in such attempts at scrying, is the nature of the support for the crystal balls. There are a number of such supports available today, ranging from the expensive tripod formed from gold-plated images of the three Fates (*photograph, page 168*), to the simple wooden frames. The Japanese and Chinese diviners appear to have favoured ornate supports made from DRAGONS (which are sacred beasts, guardians of spiritual energies, in

Oriental lore). Some clairvoyants make their own supports, and these range from the simple to the weird. In clairvoyance, one man's meat is often another man's poison, and the scryer is obliged to use whichever autoscopic paraphernalia brings out his or her talents to best advantage.

The most famous scrying device in the world – the SPECULUM of Dr. John Dee (now in the British Museum), sometimes called the DEVIL'S LOOKING GLASS – was not a crystal, nor was it made of black "kennel coal" as Dee himself thought. It was made of obsidian and was said to have been an AZTEC MIRROR. Modern research has confirmed this, showing that the occult-writer Lewis Spence was wrong when he claimed, in 1923, that the speculum was "an ancient Mexican scrying glass, or divinatory mirror" – it was merely a device used for everyday, mundane purposes.

Genuine crystal balls have always been highly regarded, and are very expensive indeed. One of the largest perfect spheres of true rock-crystal recorded by Kunz (the Victorian scholar and leading authority on the mystic lore of stones) has a diameter of just over fifteen centimetres (six inches). The GREEN VAULTS (Grune Gewolbe) crystal from Dresden was slightly larger and in 1780 it fetched 10,000 dollars. In 1653, a rock-crystal was found in the fifth-century tomb of Childeric, and is now in the Louvre, but this is only about four centimetres (one and a half inches) in diameter: by present-day prices, even this small crystal would fetch around half a million dollars.

Of a price beyond selling is the famous CURRAGHMORE CRYSTAL, which was brought back to Ireland from the Holy Land, where it had been liberated by the Crusader Godefroy de Bouillon in the twelfth century. About the size of an orange, it is set in an encircling silver ring, a reminder that in earlier times shew-stones were often suspended, rather than being balanced on stands as is the modern custom. Besides being used as a scrying ball, it is supposed to have the secret power to heal cattle of various illnesses. The healing is done by placing the crystal in a running stream or river, and driving the cattle into a ford below current, where they may bathe in its influence. This method of CRYSTAL-HEALING – using minute

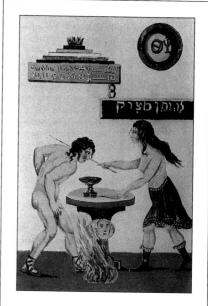

MAGIC MIRROR

A painted miniature from an arcane manuscript attributed to the Comte de Saint-Germain (c1710-1784), a Freemason and the most prominent occultist of his day, portrays a method of scrying by means of hydromancy similar to that used by Nostradamus. A woman is directing a naked man to look into a bowl filled with water, which acts as a MAGIC MIRROR. The flame burning on the floor is symbolic of the light of inspiration (the flambe exigue, as Nostradamus called it in the quatrain). Nostradamus mentions the wand he carries in his hand (La verge en main) – could this be the wand held by the topless woman in this strange picture? The arrow-head on the table is probably intended to point to the element of Air, for the four elements must meet in harmony for this divination to be effective. The other elements are traced in the Fire of the flames, the Water in the goblet and the Earth of the table, or the rod (which has grown from the earth).

doses as rarified as in homoeopathy – was practised with the Curraghmore Crystal late into the nineteenth century, and it was frequently borrowed by Irish farmers precisely for this purpose. With this crystal, which was undoubtedly designed as a shew-stone for looking into futurity, we move from crystallomancy proper into the realm of magical amulets (*see page 132*).

COSCINOMANCY is so closely related to crystal-gazing that it is as well to examine it here. This is the technique of scrying with the aid of mirrors, or reflective surfaces. Probably the most famous of all coscinomancers was Nostradamus (*right*), who, in 1555, published the first of a series of QUATRAINS (four lines of gnomic verse) relating to his vision of futurity. A lot of nonsense is written and believed about the CENTURIES, the title of the book in which the predictive quatrains were published. Nowadays many people believe that Nostradamus used astrology to look into the future, or that he used the medieval equivalent of CHANNELLING – acting as a conduit for the opinions or wisdom of higher spirits. Nothing could be further from the truth. In the opening of the *Centuries*, Nostradamus sets out his method very clearly: he would sit in front of a brass tripod on which was set a dish of water, used for scrying. A voice – almost certainly his inner voice – would speak and from this he would construct his texts.

This divinatory method falls under the general heading of HYDROMANCY, and has nothing to do with astrology or channelling. The source of this type of divination may be traced to a fourth century Neoplatonist, Iamblichus, whose book on the ancient mysteries had been published in Lyons, in 1547.

The PROPHECIES of Nostradamus are not easy to read, and are even more difficult to translate, as they are written in French with a Latin syntax, and incorporate Greek, Italian and English words, along with special terms from alchemical and Green Language sources. Further difficulties arise from the fact that the oldest editions of the books, which remain undated, were quickly followed by several counterfeits and forgeries, and there are a number of different versions of the texts. The first printed version came out in two parts, in 1555 and 1568.

While it is true that some of the prophecies of Nostradamus have been remarkably accurate when viewed in retrospect, it is also true to say that interpretations of them, in terms of coming events, have rarely been successful. Most interpreters suffer from what George Bernard Shaw called the "elation of contemporary success", and tend to interpret the quatrains with reference to their own situation. This is an understandable propensity, and we shall see it at work shortly – however, most interpretations of this kind are not based on what Nostradamus actually said. Social crises tend to renew the interest in prediction, and this probably explains why there are so many different editions of the *Centuries* – well over a hundred since the first publications. As the history of the modern world is essentially the history of crises, each generation sees its own body of self-appointed interpreters.

THE GREAT NOSTRADAMUS

Portrait of the great French savant, Michel de Nostradamus (1503–1566), whose famous collection of prophecies, *Les Centuries de Michel Nostradamus*, published in 1555, have proved time and time again to be both accurate and apposite in the use of references and terminologies unique to the events.

Examples of the use of arcane and obscure terms abound in the *Centuries*, but many of them reveal Nostradamus to have been a brilliant seer. He rarely gave accurate names for the personalities he foresaw playing important roles on the world stage, but in retrospect, the code-names he gave were incredibly accurate. For example, the three codes, PAU, NAY and LORON, which appear in various quatrains, are a simple anagram of the name Napoleon (NA PAU LON) leaving the three letters ROY. This last word is the French for King, so the entire anagram means King Napoleon, or Emperor Napoleon. The code is cunning, for until the name Napoleon was known, and until it was realized that he was likely to become "King", there was no possible way of interpreting the various prophecies until after the event. Similarly, the code name HISLER, referring to Hitler, was easy to interpret once this dictator had taken control of the Nazis.

The name DOUX is less easy to pierce: it appears in a line which says that the ROY-ROY will meet his death at the hand of DOUX. ROY-ROY means King-King, of course, and must refer to Henry III of France, who was first King of Poland, and then King of France – hence a twice-king. He was murdered by a monk called Jacques Clement in 1588. The word *doux* means "clement" in French.

For all the opacity of the quatrains, the book was an enormous success, and has remained so to this day. Within a century of the publication of the quatrains, a forged edition was published, dated back to 1568, intended to demote the unpopular Cardinal Mazarin. With more reason, the revolutionaries who stormed the Bastille, in 1789, recognized themselves in a couple of the opening quatrains. Apparently, a copy of the book was laid out, relevant quatrains to the view, on a table in the stormed prison, so that people could file by and see how they were present at the making of predicted history. During the last World War, the British Government authorized the forging and distribution of spurious quatrains attached to the name of Nostradamus, predicting the downfall of Nazi Germany.

One widespread belief in modern times is that Nostradamus predicted the END OF THE WORLD for the final years of this present century. This is simply not true. Generally speaking, these interpretations have been drawn by people unfamiliar with the complex astrological terminology which Nostradamus used (and even intentionally misused in the technique of the OCCULT BLIND – an intentional error put into a text by an occultist, in order to mislead the uninformed) in his quatrains. Only one quatrain – the Tenth century, 72nd quatrain – may be interpreted as relating to July of the year 1999. This has been interpreted as the date of the coming of the ANTICHRIST, but Nostradamus does not say this himself. He says that in this month will come from the sky a great King – possibly, a great King of terror.

L'an mil neuf cens nonante neuf sept mois, Du ciel viendra un grand Roi d'effraieur

Usually the predictions of Nostradamus are not so clearly expressed. Even so, one must question the popular translation of *Roi deffraieur* as meaning King of terror. In fact, the verb *defrayer* means "to amuse" or "to entertain". The interpreters choose to read the French *deffraieur* as relating to the transitive verb *effrayer* – possibly because a darker interpretation attracts more attention. It is unlikely that Nostradamus, intimately familiar with the millenarian literature of the preceding centuries, would have spoken of the Antichrist impersonally, as "a" great King – he would have been "the" great King. These objections are worth noting, for the tradition of translating the quatrain as relating to the Antichrist seems to be born more from millenaristic expectations than from any sound or undeniably accurate reading of Nostradamus.

DIVINATION METHODS

In 1619, the English occultist Robert Fludd published a diagram which sought to classify the range of DIVINATORY ARTS available to man. He named seven methods of divination – a shorter list than the twenty-eight (a figure linked with the Moon) proposed by the thirteenth-century Scottish magician Michael Scot. The diagram Fludd designed showed a monkey at the centre of the circle (*below*) – an indication, within Fludd's system of symbolism, that the lowest forms of divination were linked with what we would now call the unconscious realms, and what in medieval times would have been the realm of demons.

This simian is at the feet of the man, suggesting that mankind has some sort of control over it, some dominance or control over the lower forces. At his head is the radiant triad which denotes the Trinity, the source of all true illumination and spiritual insight. The two details suggest that the seven divinatory processes may be involved with either spiritual or demonic entities.

The seven divisions are interesting, for several of them would not appear to be linked with divination in the sense that the term is used nowadays. We do, however, recognize the hand of CHIROMANTIA as representative of palmistry, and the face above PHYSIOGNOMY as the art of reading the features of men and women (even though this appears to have little to do with divination, or fortune telling – *see page 193*). GEOMANTIA – with the shield device which shows how the eight figures obtained in response to a given question may be reduced, by three stages, to the single geomantic figure which answers the question – is the modern geomancy (*see page 191*). GENETHLIALOGIA, with its inset square horoscope diagram, and the man taking a reading of the stars, is meant to symbolize astrology.

Prophetia, or PROPHECY, as the inset engraving indicates, is the art of divination by

THE EIGHT DIVINATORY ARTS

The divinatory arts, according to the English esotericist Robert Fludd (1574–1637). While there appear to be seven divinatory arts, there are in fact eight, for Fludd regards man himself as the main source of the chief method of divination, DIVINE INFLUX. This is why the radiant triangle of the Godhead hovers over the man's head. At his feet is the monkey; no demonic simian, he is a symbol of NATURE'S APE – that is, man, who seeks to practise art, or to imitate the creative process of nature. From Book II of *Utriusque Cosmi Maioris*, 1617.

means of the influx of holy spirit, or by means of angels. This type of clairvoyance is the early form of what is now called CHANNELLING, the opening up of a spiritual contact with a disincarnate entity. Fludd's inset picture indicates that prophecy is linked with the higher realms, but it is an open question from which level certain levels of channelling proceed.

One of the most puzzling inclusions in the seven, ARS MEMORIA, or the Art of Memory, was not really linked with divination; it was a system of mnemonics, designed to help individuals memorize things. Could it be that Fludd saw a parallel in the notion of organizing the past and attempting to organize the future?

The remaining section, PYRAMIDUM SCIENTIA, is the great puzzle, for it points to a division of knowledge which has almost been forgotten in modern times. The simple diagram, with its interlocking triangles – one projecting the rays of the upper Sun, the other projecting the rays of a darkened semi-circle – recalls the adjacent image of man, with the Trinity above, and the simian below. This interesting division of the divinatory arts is the only one which has passed into modern experimental science – a concept entirely alien to Fludd and his contemporaries.

Although modern scientists will usually reject outright the notion of the occult divinatory arts, even so, they must work within systems which are involved with prediction and probabilities. In fact, every time we cross the road, or open a door, we must predict the future. If we did not predict what was going to happen within the next few minutes, we would not stay alive for very long.

Fludd's Pyramidum Scientia portrays the ladder of knowing which stretches between heaven and earth – it depicts the mathematical, geometrical and spiritual connections between the archetypes and their earthly counterparts. Fludd recognized that thinking is a spiritual and moral activity. In our thinking, we live in such a geometric structure, for we are aware of the archetypes, and we govern our intellectual, emotional and moral life according to our concept of them. Our life within this structure may be lived to advantage only if we are able accurately to predict. In contrast to the method of Prophetia, which balances this Pyramidum on the other side of man (and which works by the direct influx from heaven), the method of the Pyramidum depends upon human thinking.

Individual diviners, who had reputations for specialisms in certain areas, were usually proficient in other forms of divination. This was partly due to the fact that good diviners were anxious to satisfy the demands of their clients, and recognized that certain forms of divination were more suited than others for answering particular questions. A question as to whether an investment in a ship's cargo might prove to be satisfactory would probably be dealt with through horary astrology (in which the astrologer sets up a chart for the moment it is asked, to obtain the answer), whereas a question about the type of death a person might expect could be answered by reference to that person's hand (in other words, by the art of palmistry). Identification of a suspect in a crime was often determined by such simple methods as COSCINOMANCY (*see page 172*).

When the Emperor Valens wanted to know the name of the person who would succeed him in office, he used cock-divination, or ALECTROMANCY (often employed by magicians who wished to identify robbers). The cock, placed in a circle of grains of corn which had letters near by, pecked at the corn and spelled out a name, THEOD. According to the popular histories of the time, Valens proceeded to kill all those with the name Theodorus, on the grounds that they would rob him of his kingship. The moral is that, had Valens been a little more careful with his divination, he might have been more successful, for he was eventually succeeded by Theodosius.

The type of divination was suited to the question or questions in hand, which meant that most diviners would familiarize themselves with a wide variety of divinatory techniques. On page 148 we noted Cocles's fame as a chiromancer; however, he was multi-talented in the art of divination. In his day he was famous as an interpreter of dreams, and for his skill in GEOMANCY, originally an Arabic technique which depended upon interpreting figures derived from making marks in the sand or earth.

In his finest work, the *Anastasis*, Cocles lists several predictive techniques in such a way as to suggest that he had practical familiarity with them. He mentions that SPATULOMANCY is a means of divining by means of a recently slaughtered goat: since the word is properly reserved for the art of divining by means of

RITUAL LAMP

A good example of the demonic forms of so many objects used in divination rituals is this bronze demon head, mounted upon a bird's foot. The tongue is pierced to take a wick, which is fed with oil from the mouth. This object may be used for divination by means of flames (PYROMANCY) or by means of smoke issued from the burning wick. Bronze cast sculpture by Graham Fenn-Edwards. Private collection.

the shoulder-blades of sheep, it would seem that Cocles had indulged in the former art. Among the more far-out systems he lists in the book are LITTERAMANCY (divination from letters), NOMANCY (from names) and SOLMANCY (from the rays of the sun). The arts of VENAMANCY and UMBILICOMANCY are divinatory systems linked with childbirth, which he claims to have learned from his mother, a skilled midwife. This wide range of divinatory methods leads us into a realm of prediction which has a bewildering number of terminologies and methodologies.

The medieval commentators who listed the majority of these divinatory tools had no doubt that such methods were not given to mankind by God. They worked – if or when they worked – only because they were manipulated by demons. This is the main reason why, in former times, almost all the arts of divination were said to be a form of DEMONOMANCY, or prediction by means of the demons.

In the thirteenth century, the theologian Thomas Aquinas had sown the seeds for much of the witchhunting of the coming centuries when he insisted that the words, figures, sigils and characters of the magicians are the language favoured by the demons,

Portrait of the German occultist Henry Cornelius Agrippa of Nettesheim (1486–1535), whose influence on popular occultism has been inestimable. Coloured print from his *De Occulta Philosophia*, 1534.

and the magicians are nothing more than the dupes of the Devil. Even more sweeping is his view that the whole of the magical arts are "fallacies of the demons". The general belief that all divination is done at the behest of demons probably accounts for the reason that so many ritual objects which are intended for divination are in the form of demons. Many occultists tacitly agreed to this notion when they claimed that only pure men could be magicians, or see into the future, since it takes extraordinary purity of will, or great inner discipline, to compel the devious and unruly demons. Cornelius Agrippa (*left*), after giving instructions on how to use the suspended sieve (in the art of coscinomancy) as a method of discovering the name of a felon, concludes that it is "by the help of the demons" that one discovers in this way who committed a certain crime, theft or injury.

In his diagram of the eight divinatory arts (*page 175*), Robert Fludd was careful to portray the simian at the feet of the man – a symbol of the pure soul standing in triumph over the lower telluric (earthly) forces, dominating the chattering monkey-voice within. This notion, of the suborned demonic entities as the source of divinatory knowledge, crops up again and again in the literature dealing with the following popular methods of divination.

It is clear that there are several different ways of classifying divinatory methods. The most useful is that which accords each method a place on what is called the LADDER OF BEING. This is a spiritual ladder, which has its topmost rungs in heaven, and its lower rungs in the depths of hell. In the middle of this occult scale is mankind:

HEAVENLY THINGS
ELEMENTS OF FIRE
ELEMENTS OF AIR
ELEMENTS OF WATER
ELEMENTS OF EARTH
MANKIND
WORDS & LETTERS
ANIMALS
PLANTS
METALS & ROCKS
SPIRITS & DEMONS

When we examine the divinatory systems within the terms of this ladder, we shall find that there are many ambiguities. For example, within the element of Fire is a divinatory system which derives its meanings from the pattern of smoke left by the flames of a candle. To one occultist, this will be taken as an example of divination by Fire. Another occultist might argue that the patterns of smoke are not made by the flames, but by the currents of air, or even by the air-spirits (sylphs), and so would be convinced that divination by smoke makes use of spirits.

However, while there may be disagreement about details, the Ladder of Being does afford a useful way of approaching the wide diversity of different systems within the tradition of divination. Within the eleven divisions we find no fewer than 140 systems of looking into futurity.

DIVINATION BY MEANS OF HEAVENLY THINGS

Some occultists maintain that the only legitimate forms of divination are those which are practised with the aid of angels. All other forms, they claim, are a result of working hand in glove with the dark-angels, the demons.

Divination by means of the stars is called ASTROMANCY. In its most serious and intellectual phase this is a subdivision of the doyen of celestial divination, ASTROLOGY (*see page 181*), in which certain individual stars are taken into account in the study of personal horoscopes. In its less cerebral use, astromancy is restricted nowadays to such superstitious practices as estimating futurity from the chance sighting of "shooting stars", comets, and the like. METEOROMANCY was a specialist form, restricted from reading auguries into the movements of meteors.

Since it was once believed that dreams came to the sleeping human by way of the spiritual world (or, specifically from the rulers of the spiritual world, the ranks of angels), the art of such divination comes into this celestial category. ONIROMANCY is the

FEARSOME PHENOMENON

A great comet causing consternation in a medieval town. From a coloured German broadsheet of circa 1540. In the past, comets and meteors were interpreted in lurid terms, and were taken to presage the overthrow of kingdoms. Astromancy uses such sightings to predict future events.

INCUBUS

The incubus, pictured sitting on the breast of a sleeping woman, became a popular theme after the Swiss artist Henry Fuseli painted his famous "The Nightmare", of which many versions and copies exist. This coloured aquatint is dated circa 1870.

most generally used term which denotes divination by means of dreams. Nightmares also fall into this category, but the occult tradition maintains that nightmares come from demons – especially from the SUCCUBUS and INCUBUS, demonic creatures who attack sleeping humans sexually. The succubus is a female form, which attacks sleeping men, while the incubus is in male form, and attacks sleeping women (*left*).

The early DREAM-BOOKS suggest that we dream in images which are susceptible to interpretation as fixed symbols; for example, a dream of a snake is a prevision of a coming danger. The medieval dream-books – which claimed the authorship of such famous dreamers as the biblical dream-reader Joseph, who interpreted the dreams of Pharaoh's officers (Genesis 40:8–22) and the great Pharaoh (Genesis 41) – rarely stray from single-line interpretation ("To see in a dream one's own inside means secrets will be revealed").

Some of these crude books are so blasé that they do not bother even to deal with dreams. For example, some texts advise the reader to open a psalter at random, note the first letter on the left or right-hand page, and then refer to an alphabetical list in the dream-book, where the corresponding letter is interpreted – for example, B signifies victory in war. If the client had no intention of resorting to war at that point, then the interpretation may be toned down to refer to, say, a social quarrel. The lovely illustration (*right*) is a fold-out plate from a crude dream-book of the nineteenth century.

Modern DREAM-INTERPRETATION has been deeply influenced by the discoveries of psychoanalysis, and differs greatly from the medieval form. The general view nowadays is that while dreams do relate in many instances to the future of the dreamer, they must be interpreted with the aid of a psychological key relevant to that dreamer. No ascribed, fixed meaning of symbolic interpretation is regarded as being valid.

Occultists describe different types of dreams, not all of which are divinatory. Some dreams are more or less confused memories of astral experiences (*see page 24*) when the spirit is freed of the body, during sleep. Other dreams, according to the occultists, are definitely prophetic, and may be given to the dreamer through the agency of the angels.

An important form of celestial divination is that based on interpreting the Moon, called SELENOMANCY. This is not related to astrology, for it is restricted to reading augury in the appearance of the Moon, rather than from its position against the zodiac, or from its relation to the other planets. An ancient form of lunar divination is found in the crude

LUNARIA, or MOON-BOOKS. These list the thirty days of the month, and indicate which of these days will be favourable or unfavourable.

ASTROLOGY is by far the most complicated of all the methods of divination. Only a very experienced and competent astrologer can look at a horoscope with a view to determining the future of a client (often called the NATIVE, after the Latin word natus, meaning "birth", from which we have the English word, nativity).

Before we look at how a horoscope is used in divination, we must examine a few special terms. The HOROSCOPE, which once meant "the Ascendant degree at birth", is now used to denote the FIGURE (perhaps from "configuration"), or CHART, which represents the positions of the planets in the skies at a given moment. Usually, that moment is the time of birth. However, a horoscope may be "CAST", or calculated, for other reasons. For example, a figure may be ERECTED to determine an appropriate cosmic moment for such an event as the laying of a foundation stone for a building. A horoscope of the latter kind is called a FOUNDATION CHART. In the past, no important building was ever begun before a satisfactory foundation chart had been cast and approved by an astrologer. This was necessary because the architect wished his building to reflect the harmony of the cosmos, in both time and space.

The cosmos is symbolized in a fairly simple way. The astrologers' symbols take into account the ZODIAC, which is a band in the skies that defines the ECLIPTIC, or apparent movement of the Sun throughout the year. This zodiac is divided into twelve SIGNS, the zodiac signs, each of thirty degrees arc. By convention, the circle begins at Aries, and ends in Pisces.

A woodcut by Dürer (*page 182*), shows the SOUL OF THE WORLD, the ANIMA which is the source of life, holding a simple schema of the heavens. The circle in her hands is divided by two diameters, which form a cross: this is the CROSS OF MATTER, the fourfold Fire, Air, Earth and Water. At the centre of the cross is the globe of the earth. Around the earth is the broad band of the zodiac, divided into its compartments, each bearing a sigil (symbol) of the relevant zodiac sign. From the sections marked Taurus, Cancer and Virgo, the planets

DREAM INTERPRETATION

Fold-out sheet from the *Royal Book of Dreams*, a popular nineteenth-century (undated) dream-book. The outer circle contains signs of the zodiac, while the innermost circle contains thirty symbols closely resembling the geomantic sigils, save that these have five levels, rather than the orthodox four.

SCHEMA OF THE COSMOS

In this woodcut by Dürer, circa 1498, Anima, or the Soul of the World, is holding a schema of the cosmos. Rays, or radiations, pour down from the planets in the signs of the zodiac onto the earth, at the centre. The cross of matter is centred upon the earth.

project their influence lines, or RAYS, on to the earth.

This picture is a representation of the way the medieval world perceived the operation of the horoscope. The modern horoscope, which has survived from this medieval vision, places the zodiacal circle, as a broad concentric band, near the outer circle. The entire circle is divided into four segments, or quadrants, while the zodiac band is divided into twelve sections. At the centre of the quadrant is a smaller circle, which represents the earth, the birth-place of the native.

The newborn child is imagined to be at the very centre of the circle, born on the earth, and therefore enmeshed in the cross of matter. This is why astrologers divide the basic horoscope figure into four quadrants, giving each of the dividing lines a special name. The point which represents the East, and therefore the point of sunrise, is called the ASCENDANT. This symbolizes the ego of the native.

The point which represents the West, the point of sunset, is called the DESCENDANT. This symbolizes the native's relationship and attitude to others – the freeing of the ego, so to speak.

The point at the top, which represents the South, is called the MEDIUM COELI (shortened to MC), the "middle of the skies". This represents the point at which the native aims – his or her aspirations, career and ambitions.

The point at the bottom of the chart represents the North, and is the IMUM COELI (shortened to IC), the "bottom of the skies". This represents the source from whence the native comes. It symbolizes the home, the influence of the mother, and so on.

These four points are sometimes called the ANGLES. In the drawing (*page 184*), the Ascendant is in Cancer (the sigil for which is ♋). This means that the Descendant is in Capricorn (opposite to Cancer), the sigil for which is ♑. The MC is in Pisces (sigil ♓), and the IC is in Virgo (sigil ♍). Since the angles mark degrees, the precise degrees are marked – in this case, 22 degrees of Cancer, 22 degrees of Capricorn, 22 degrees of Pisces and 22 degrees of Virgo.

In astrology, the Sun, though a star, is called a PLANET. Similarly, the Moon, which is a satellite, is also regarded as being a planet. The ten planets recognized by most modern astrologers appear to move within the ecliptic band, or zodiac, and as they proceed from one sign to another, their energies appear to change. The horoscope is a record of the individual forces at work at any given moment.

The geometric relations which the planets hold to each other also influence the energies which they exude. When, for example, a planet is at 90 degrees to another, then the two are said to be in tension; technically, they are in SQUARE aspect to each other. When they are at 120 degrees, they are said to be in harmony; these are in TRINE aspect. The theory of ASPECTS is rooted in the theory of elements which underlies astrological symbolism. In theory, planets in trine are manifesting through the same element, while those in square are manifesting through conflicting elements. Thus, a Moon in the fire sign Sagittarius is in a harmonious elemental relationship (the trine aspect) with a Mercury in the fire sign Aries. Since it is the element which is important, rather than the strict geometry, aspects are allowed ORBS, arcs of variation in which they are still regarded as being operative. For example, in the drawing overleaf, the Moon (sigil ☾) is in 21 degrees of Sagittarius (♐), while Mercury (sigil ☿) is in 26 degrees of Aries (♈). These two are still in trine, although they are 5 degrees off the true aspect.

In fact, in this same chart, Jupiter (sigil ♃) is in 25 degrees of Sagittarius, which means that it is more precisely in trine with Mercury. What does this aspect mean? Since Jupiter rules the religious impulse, and the generosity of the native, and Mercury rules the mentality, creativity and general alertness, and (further) since the trine is expansive in operation, we may be sure that the native is deeply interested in religious issues, creative in some way, intellectually inquiring, and generous.

There are several other important issues which an astrologer must take into account when making a preliminary reading of a chart. Usually, the first task an astrologer undertakes is to cast and interpret the figure, without reference to the future indications which might be contained within it. Under normal circumstances, an astrologer can examine the way in which the planets are disposed within the horoscope, and from this determine something of the personality, life-expectations and energy-directions of the individual. All these factors do not in themselves create a future event, but they certainly help to forge the general drift of the native's future.

A planet has a different meaning, or energy, according to which sign it is in. For example, when Saturn is in Taurus, as in the sample chart, it suggests that the native might find the earth energies of this sign are threatened. He or she may feel very insecure, and in some way restricted in regard to resources; as they might say today, the native might find himself materially or financially challenged. A Saturn in Leo, on the other

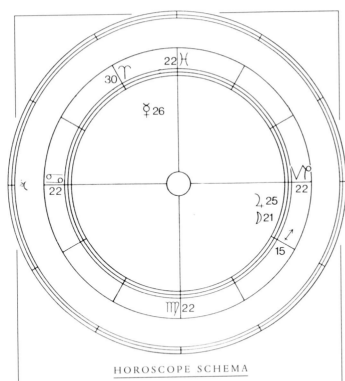

HOROSCOPE SCHEMA

The form consists of a circle of the zodiac belt, centred upon the earth (the place of birth), which is pinned to the zodiac by means of the cross of matter. The general schema is particularized – that is, it is pinned down into space and time – when the degrees of the zodiac are entered upon the four angles.

hand, may challenge the feeling of selfhood (an important leonine characteristic), and the person may have a deep-seated fear of mediocrity.

Having assessed the forces of the planets in the signs, the astrologer will begin to estimate the effects of the planets in the houses. Each of the twelve houses relates to an area of human endeavour, and the planets lend an energy force to the house in which each is located in a horoscope. Thus, the planet Mars, which is charged with energy, even with aggression, has a very distinctive effect when it is found on the Ascendant degree, in the most important part of the horoscope: such a person is go-getting, enthusiastic and even domineering. The same planet on the Tenth House, which is at the top of the horoscope, the southernmost part of the skies at birth, tends to direct this aggressive energy towards business, and to bring an emphasis on career. In the sample chart (*page 187*), Mars (♂) is not on the Ascendant. It is in the Twelfth House, in Gemini (♊). Since Gemini is the sign of communications, the energy of Mars will be poured into this realm of activity: the native will dedicate a great deal of his Martian power in attempting to communicate with people. Since the Twelfth House is sometimes called "The House of One's Own Undoing", the native may find considerable conflicts and difficulties in communicating his or her ideas.

Step by step, the astrologer will build up a general picture of the personality of his client, long before they begin to concern themselves with predicting the future. When, after several hours poring over a chart, an astrologer is convinced that a valid picture of the client has been established, then, and only then, he or she may begin to look into future tendencies.

There are several techniques involved with looking into the future, by means of a horoscope. In modern astrology, the most usual approach is for the astrologer to employ PROGRESSIONS. In their simplest form, progressions involve extending, or progressing, into the future the motions implicit in the birth chart angles and planets. The astrologer calculates how the planetary and zodiacal degrees unfold in time. This unfolding will reveal the potential in the chart at very definite times.

In fact, progressions are not quite so simple as this sounds, for there are a variety of symbolic systems which are based on the idea that the time of the cosmos is not precisely the same as the time of the human being. From this notion has arisen a technique of progressing the NATAL CHART (that is, the original birth chart) by a fixed rate of one degree for every year of life. Thus, in this technique, if an astrologer wishes to find out what will happen in the twenty-eighth year (usually a most important period in a human life), then he or she will project the chart to twenty-eight days after the birth, and examine the two charts together. In those twenty-eight days, some of the planets will have moved considerable distances, while others will have moved scarcely at all. The Sun, which appears to move one degree each year, will have progressed 28 degrees. The Moon, which is the most rapid-seeming of the planets, will have completed a circuit of the zodiac: twenty-eight days being almost a month. The astrologer studies the effects of these cycles, or part-cycles, estimating the planetary power at the beginning, the change of this power at the end, and the influences of those planets which may have been transited by the planets making these cycles.

The sample chart (*page 187*) is the natal chart of the artist Vincent Van Gogh. It is a good example of just how symbolic the astrological system is. To read this chart, one has to be familiar with the sigils for the planets, the zodiacal signs and the house-systems. The key below sets out what these sigils mean, in ordinary linguistic terms:

Ascendant in Cancer, Descendant in Capricorn.
Medium Coeli in Pisces, Imum Coeli in Virgo.

Sigils

Sun in Aries	☉	♈	Jupiter in Sagitarius	♃	♐
Moon in Sagittarius	☾	♐	Saturn in Taurus	♄	♉
Mercury in Aries	☿	♈	Uranus in Taurus	♅	♉
Venus in Pisces	♀	♓	Neptune in Pisces	♆	♓
Mars in Cancer	♂	♋	Pluto in Taurus	♇	♉

It is not enough to know what the sigils mean. The astrologer has to be able to interpret the significance of these placings. It is not sufficient to know that Mercury is in Aries – one has to know precisely what this means. There are other factors at play also. For example, the astrologer has to take into account the fact that this particular Mercury is in trine with Jupiter, for here is a potential which will unfold in the progressed chart. Van Gogh's profligacy, of finance and heart, is one reason for both the joys and frustrations in his life.

In contrast to this beneficial aspect, the same planet Jupiter is in a tension, a SQUARE aspect, with the planet Venus, which is in a Water sign. The fire of Sagittarius is not harmonious with the water of Pisces. This accounts for the difficulties which Van Gogh had with women in his life – love (Venus) and spiritual expansiveness (Jupiter) could not work in harmony.

If we calculate a progression of this same natal chart (according to the system of A DAY FOR A YEAR) for Van Gogh's 37th year, we would see some important changes in planetary positions. Each of these will reflect in the life of Van Gogh during that year. The most important of these changes, however, must be evident even to a non-astrologer. Since the Sun is the determinant of the earth's year, it is evident that, in 37 days, the Sun will appear to move 37 degrees. This means that the Sun of Van Gogh's chart will have moved from 10 degrees of Aries to 17 degrees of Taurus. Now, this same degree of Taurus happens to be occupied by the dark planet, Saturn.

In traditional astrology, Saturn was sometimes called the ANARETA, from a Greek word meaning approximately "destroyer", or "death-dealer". In that year, Van Gogh's 37th year, the life-enhancing power of the Sun must have been darkened and threatened by the dour life-denying planet Saturn. Not surprisingly, this was the year in which Van Gogh shot himself, on July 27th, 1890.

Of course, the progression of the Sun to the place of Saturn does not in itself imply the native will commit suicide. The Sun progresses Saturn in very many charts, and while it usually brings difficulties, these are by no means so dramatic. However, such a progression, combined with other adverse astrological factors, contributed to the inner darkness which troubled Van Gogh during the last year of his life.

Another method of astrological prediction, which was very popular in the past, is involved with assessing the meaning of the FIXED STARS on the life of the native. When a planet, or one of the angles of a horoscope, is exactly upon a fixed star, then it is inevitable that the influence of this fixed star will be manifest in the life of the native. In fact, it is often the presence of a fixed star which accounts for genius.

Not surprisingly, the horoscope of Van Gogh offers an excellent example of genius. His Ascendant, in 22 degrees of Cancer, was very close to the powerful fixed star, POLLUX, which, in 1853, when Van Gogh was born, was very close to this degree. This star is so important that it is actually marked on the horoscope (*right*).

In fact, there are several important stars in Van Gogh's horoscope. Proficient astrologers recognize that it is difficult to understand the pattern of his life, and the nature of his death, without these stars being taken into account.

As we have seen, Van Gogh's chart has an Ascendant in 22 degrees of Cancer, a Moon in 21 degrees of Sagittarius, and a Venus in 29 degrees of Pisces. In terms of astrological method, this means that, when he was born, the fixed stars Pollux, Rasalhague and Scheat were operative in his horoscope.

Astrologers depend greatly upon the Arabic astrological tradition for the lore of fixed stars. From this tradition, we learn that when Pollux is rising, it is sure to bring injuries to the face or head.

RASALHAGUE is said to bring misfortunes through women, perverted tastes and mental depravity. When the Moon is associated with it, then religious intensity develops.

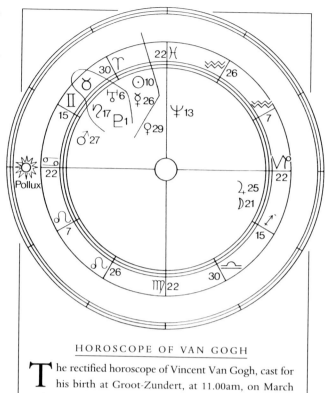

HOROSCOPE OF VAN GOGH

The rectified horoscope of Vincent Van Gogh, cast for his birth at Groot-Zundert, at 11.00am, on March 30th, 1853. A difference in birthtime of only two or three minutes would have meant that the fixed star POLLUX would not have been operative in his life.

SCHEAT is particularly associated with suicide and general misfortune. The Arabic astrologers also say that when this star is with Venus (as in the horoscope), the native will suffer through his own acts, and be subject to imprisonment or other restraints.

Van Gogh mutilated his own face, cutting off the lobe of his ear to send it as a present to a lady-friend. Details of his life reveal him as a supreme example of a person who constantly suffered from his own acts.

It is surely no accident that on the day Van Gogh killed himself, the Moon of his horoscope (loaded as this satellite was with the direful star Rasalhague) was located precisely upon his Sun, in ten degrees of Aries. This Sun had progressed to Saturn. In the symbolism of astrology, this solar-lunar Rasalhague was merging with the dark power of Saturn on the tragic day the artist died.

Already, it must be evident that the use of astrology to predict the future is a complex matter. Anyone who is anxious to have their chart examined for future trends is advised to seek out a proficient and practised astrologer. Only those with an intimate familiarity with the art are really in a position to make predictions from a personal horoscope.

Erroneous prediction may often be very dangerous. Few people have been better

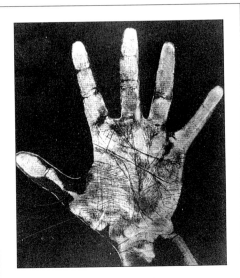

MADAME NORDICA'S HAND

The nineteenth-century palmist Cheiro, (whose real name was Count Louis Hamon) was usually prepared to predict the time and type of death of his clients. He does, however, seem to have made a mistake about the death of the spiritualist W.T. Stead, who foiled the predicted death by a horse kick when he went down in the *Titanic* in 1912. Many of Cheiro's predictions proved more accurate, and were widely attested by his contemporaries. This smoked-paper print – from Cheiro's extensive collection of palm prints – is of the well-known prima donna Madame Nordica, A gift of a silver cigarette case from this lady actually saved Cheiro's life. Several attempts had been made on the outspoken palmist's life in New York: after advising a young woman to break off a degrading relationship, the woman's lover attempted to stab Cheiro in the heart. The cigarette case, carried in the breast pocket, deflected the blow. From the 1897 edition of *Cheiro's Language of the Hand*.

placed to learn about the future than the editor of the influential *Pall Mall Gazette*, and champion of spiritualism, W.T. Stead. In his capacity as founder-editor of the spiritualist magazine *Borderland*, he attended a vast number of seances, and rubbed shoulders with most of the society clairvoyants of his day. Inevitably, he had his future told by mediums, crystal-gazers, palmists and astrologers on a large number of occasions: indeed, his palm print was even included in the published collection of famous hands by the society palmist CHEIRO (*left*). From these many consultations, he gleaned that he would die as a result of being kicked to death in a London street – presumably by a horse. This was the main reason Stead did not insure his own life. It was also why he laughed at the advice offered by a close friend – a very competent clairvoyant – who warned him against booking a cabin on the maiden voyage of the *SS Titanic*, in 1912. Had he listened, and been forewarned, he might have saved his life. The *Titanic* sank, and Stead was among those who perished.

DIVINATION BY MEANS OF THE ELEMENTS

In the Western occult tradition, there are FOUR ELEMENTS – Fire, Air, Water and Earth – each of which is associated with a particular group of spirits. The occult tradition maintains that the diviner who uses any or all of these four ELEMENTS can be successful only if he or she works with the elemental beings who control them. The salamanders control Fire, the sylphs control Air, the undines control Water, and the gnomes control Earth.

The prime methods of ELEMENTAL DIVINATION – divining by means of the four elements – are pyromancy (Fire), aeromancy (Air), hydromancy (Water) and geomancy (Earth). There are many different ways in which these four forms of divination are practised.

PYROMANCY, sometimes called PYROSCOPY, is divination by means of fire or flames. The diviner watches the flames, the movement of the flames and, if gifted with higher vision, the activities of the Fire elementals, the FIRE-SOULS (SALAMANDERS) which sport in the flames. However, the first-century magician Apollonius of Tyana seems to have associated pyromancy with divination from the Sun, the great cosmic fire. It is recorded in Philostratus's *Life of Apollonius* that he visited an Egyptian temple (then the centre of divination techniques), where he sacrificed an image of a bull made from frankincense. After this sacrifice, he told the priests that if they really understood pyromancy, then they would see many things revealed in the circle of the rising Sun. The story indicates that the true magicians were not inspecting the physical flames – the incandescent gases – but the entities (invisible to ordinary sight) which lay behind or beyond the mere appearance of things.

In another pyromantic system, the diviner throws objects (powdered dried peas, for example) into the flames, and makes divination from their manner of burning. Related to pyromancy is the art of LYCHNOSCOPY, practised with the aid of three candles arranged in a triangle. The diviner reads presages into the movements of the three flames.

LAMPADOMANCY, sometimes called LYCHNOMANCY, is the art of divination by means of the flames from lamps. Essentially the technique involves the interpretation of the movement of the flame, but in some cases the magician reads meaning into spots of carbon deposited on paper sheets held over the flame. Some mediums use lampadomancy as a means of "attracting spirits to the flames", in the hope of consulting them regarding future events. As we have seen, some magicians use specially designed lamps, which by their grotesque forms are believed to attract the spirits.

Properly speaking, divination from the inspection of smoke (as opposed to the flame from which the smoke arises) of incense burned during rituals is called LIBANOMANCY.

AEROMANCY is the name given to a general class of divination whereby aerial phenomena, such as clouds, lightning or thunder, are studied to reveal their hidden meanings. In its simplest form, this kind of divination may be seen in the interpretations which people make from the shapes made by the clouds moving across the sky.

The early books on occultism are less materialistic, however, for they define aeromancy as the art of foretelling the future by means of the activities of the SYLPHS, AERADI or AIR FAIRIES, which may be seen clairvoyantly. These creatures are supposed to makes signs by way of the Air elements which the magicians may interpret.

The reading of the significance of comets (*illustration, page 179*) was once an important branch of aeromancy, as was prediction by means of weather. ANEMOSCOPY, or divination by means of the winds, and NEPHOMANCY, by means of clouds, was also part of aeromancy, as was BRONTOSCOPY, or KERAUNOSCOPY, both methods of divining by means of thunder.

CAPNOMANCY, divination from the patterns of smoke carried into the air from a fire, is also a form of aeromancy, even though the flames might lead one to associate the method with pyromancy.

AERIAL CONFLICT

This hand-coloured woodprint broadsheet shows an aerial vision recorded by Samuel Coccius in Basle, Switzerland, on August 7th, 1566. On that day, many black globes moved before the sun at great speed, and seemed to be fighting. Some became fiery red, and faded away. In modern times, the plate has been taken by some ufologists (those who study UFOs) as referring to a medieval aerial conflict between spacecraft, but in the sixteenth century the strange phenomena were taken as signifying a divine warning of dreadful things to come – in a word, as predictive images.

The once-popular art of reading futurity from meteorological phenomena, or HYDATOSCOPY (literally, divination from water vapour in the air), is also a subdivision of this aeromancy, and must be distinguished from HYDROMANCY, or divination from water and from the rain. A popular form of aerial divination in times past was by means of the flight of an arrow. This was the art of BELOMANCY. The magician shoots arrows, which (it is believed) are directed by spirits of the Air (sylphs) to hit targets, or spaces in special formal patterns. The actual target reveals the future, or answers specific questions.

Another form of belomancy involves writing possible answers to questions concerning futurity on the shafts of a number of arrows, and then accepting as the solution that which is shot furthest.

Hydromancy is the art of divination from water or rain, and is sometimes called HYDRASCOPY. This is a general term for specialist forms of divination, such as CASTRONOMANCY, which involves looking into images on the surface of water in a glass or magical receptacle. If spring water is used in this method of divination, it is termed PEGOMANCY. Some castromancers prefer to colour their water with black ink in order to give a more reflective surface. Very often, the diviners choose a distinctive receptacle for the darkened water, on the grounds that the more they like the objects they use, the more accurate will be their divination.

A form of hydromancy is divination from the appearances of ripples on the surface of water. In former times, it was believed that elemental spirits (the undines) dwelled in water, and would aid those seeking knowledge of futurity. Interpretation could be made by methods as diverse as observing the movement of fish (persuaded into such meaningful movements by the water-sprites) or in studying the fall of pebbles cast into the waters. One specialist form of hydromancy is LECANOMANCY, a method of divination by interpreting the patterns and ripples left on the surface of water, when precious stones are dropped in.

Hydromancy covers divination by all forms of liquid, of which there are many varieties. Thus, for example, the specialist form OINOMANCY, divination by means of wine *(right)*, is similar to other forms of hydromancy, because the reflective surface of the liquid is used as a scrying glass.

CAFEDOMANCY is a method of looking into futurity from marks left in the cup, after the liquid coffee has been swilled out, leaving the grains to make seemingly chance patterns on the inside of the cup. The patterns are interpreted in terms of the images they appear to form. This is a variation of TEA-LEAF READING, but since it is mentioned as being in use in Florence, Italy, as early as the seventeenth century, it may be older than tea-leaf reading, at least in the West. In ancient times, a related form was SCYPHOMANCY, in which a drinking cup was filled to the brim, and then was poured as a libation to the gods: the empty cup was examined for signs of oracle.

As we have seen, CASTRONOMANCY is a form of water-divination by means of evoking images in the surface of water in a glass. The water acts as a sort of scrying surface (*see page 168*), and is somewhat similar to the catoptromantic method used by the seer Nostradamus, while preparing his famous quatrains, entitled CENTURIES. Nostradamus would look into a bowl of boiling water, wherein he would perceive his remarkable visions of future events (*see page 172*).

Properly speaking, CEROMANCY is divination by means of wax, yet its method places it in the realm of the element of Water. Several different forms of ceromancy have been recorded, but the most popular involves dropping hot candle wax into boiling water. When the water cools, figures of congealed wax may be "read" or "interpreted".

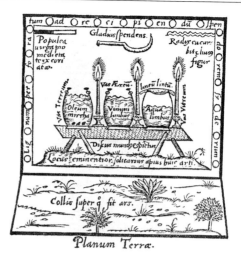

DIVINATION BY LIQUIDS

One interesting, if complicated, system of water-divination is the so-called VASES OF ARTEPHIUS, which is presented in many old books on divination. The method combines the magic mirror (hydromancy) with oinomancy (divination by means of wine). This eighteenth-century illustration shows a number of ritual instruments (poplar wood, a knife and a pumpkin root), though instructions for use are omitted from most manuscripts. The vase on the left contains oil of myrrh, the one in the centre wine, and the one on the right water. Three lighted candles separate the pots. All these instruments for searching futurity must be protected from the sun, and the weather must be very calm: peace and silence are required for this magical working, which is why this divination is practised in the countryside. The operator must be dressed in white, with his or her face covered with red silk or linen, so that only the eyes are visible. In the water, the diviner will see the shadow of the thing or event; in the oil, the appearance of the person involved; and in the wine, the thing or event itself. From *L'Art Magique d'Artephius*, undated but eighteenth century.

A related art is MOLYBDOMANCY, or divination by means of molten lead poured into hot water.

GEOMANCY, which is divination by means of earthly things, has become one of the most confusing of modern occult words. It is from the Greek roots, *geo* (earth) and *manteia* (divination) and relates to a system of looking into the future by interpreting

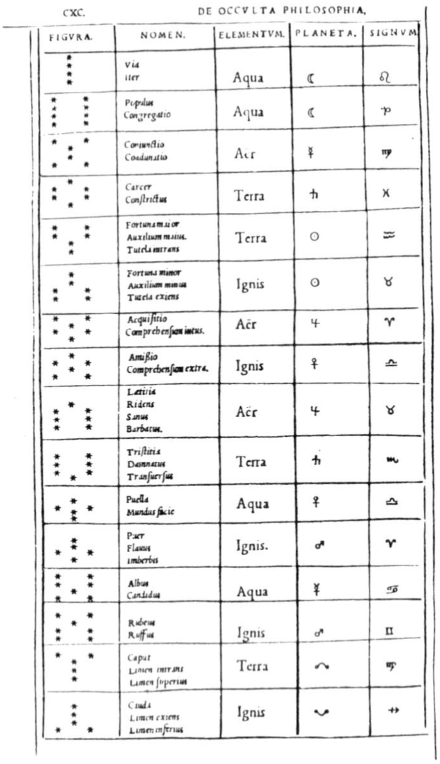

CXC. DE OCCVLTA PHILOSOPHIA.

FIGVRA.	NOMEN.	ELEMENTVM.	PLANETA.	SIGNVM.
	Via iter	Aqua	☾	♌
	Populus Congregatio	Aqua	☾	♑
	Coniunctio Coadunatio	Aer	☿	♍
	Carcer Constrictus	Terra	♄	♓
	Fortuna maior Auxilium maius. Tutela intrans	Terra	☉	♒
	Fortuna minor Auxilium minus Tutela exiens	Ignis	☉	♉
	Acquisitio Comprehensum intus.	Aër	♃	♈
	Amißio Comprehensum extra.	Ignis	♀	♎
	Lætitia Ridens Sanus Barbatus.	Aër	♃	♉
	Tristitia Damnatus Transuersus	Terra	♄	♏
	Puella Mundus facie	Aqua	♀	♎
	Puer Flauus imberbis	Ignis.	♂	♈
	Albus Candidus	Aqua	☿	♋
	Rubeus Ruffus	Ignis	♂	♊
	Caput Limen intrans Limen superius	Terra	☊	♍
	Cauda Limen exiens Limen inferius	Ignis	☋	♐

GEOMANTIC SCHEMA

The basic figure, or formal pattern, used by the geomancer is made up of a combination of sixteen figures, each with specialized names and associations with the elements, planets and signs of the zodiac. Sometimes the interpretation of the figure follows some of the rules of reading the horoscope. The names and forms of these basic GEOMANTIC CHARACTERS, as recorded in the sixteenth century by Agrippa, are set out in this geomantic table, showing the sixteen four-level figures with their names, related elements, planets and zodiacal signs. From Agrippa's *De Occulta Philosophia*, 1534.

figures which have originated in the random throw of stones, pebbles, shells, etc., onto the earth, or by the random markings made by the diviner on the earth.

Unfortunately, certain modern writers on the occult, ignorant of this accurate use of the term, have attempted to use it to denote the study of earth currents, leys and geo-energies, quite unrelated to divination. Thus, the term is often used in popular occult texts to denote the European equivalent of the Chinese system of FENG SHUI, which studies the spiritual energies on the surface of the earth and makes use of these for the benefit of man, to determine the most suitable places to live, and the most satisfactory places for burial. The French writer on magic Grillot de Givry says that geomancy is called the ART OF LITTLE DOTS. Almost all treatments of the art unashamedly link this divination from the earth with the skies, enriching it with astrological, zodiacal and planetary imagery. For example, in the DREAM-BOOK plate (*page 181*), the geomantic symbols are linked with the twelve signs of the zodiac.

HALOMANCY is closely related to geomancy, being divination by salt.

ASTRAGALOMANCY is the art of divining the future by means of small bones. The bones are thrown, and form patterns upon a formal pattern or grid: the diviner reads futurity from these patterns. In some respects, this method is linked with geomancy. Since dice were once made from bones, the word is used nowadays to denote divination by means of dice. Another form of astragalomancy involved throwing bones marked with letters of the alphabet. Dice, were sometimes used in popular prediction by means of Pythagorean Spheres (*see spheromancy, page 196*).

LITHOBOLY involves reading the future from patterns left from a random fall of thrown stones.

Closely related to astragalomancy is CLEROMANCY, divination by means of casting lots with the aid of specially marked stones, bones, or slips of paper.

VITRIOMANCY is divination by sand – though quite unlike geomancy. The querent places a thin layer of sand on a sheet of glass, and then, keeping the glass steady, draws a violin bow along one edge. The resultant vibrations form strange patterns in the surface of the sand, which are interpreted as being prophetic.

Closely related to divination by Fire, yet clearly pertaining to the element of Earth, is SPODOMANCY, the art of divination from an examination of ashes left by a fire. In ancient times, this was an important form of augury, but it was restricted to reading the ashes left over from sacrificial fires.

LITHOMANCY is the art of reading the future by means of the inspection of the form of stones, selected at random. Usually only stones with known magical qualities are used. The related MARGARITOMANCY (*see page 209*), or divination by means of pearls, does not concern itself with the appearance of the pearl, but with its surface, using the smooth glassy surface as an autoscopic SCRYING device (*see page 168*).

While dealing with divination by Earth, we should glance at the word NIGROMANCY. This really means "divination by means of black", and is often wrongly used to denote various forms of predicting the future by means of black-magical practices. However, the occult tradition has attempted to reserve the word nigromancy for the art of seeking out lost objects (those lost in "black darkness", especially in the darkness of the earth and in caves), such as hidden objects or treasures buried in mines. Some modern dictionaries confuse the issue by claiming that the word is merely an alternative form of necromancy, which is very far from the truth – even though the word "nigromancy" is often wrongly used in this sense.

DIVINATION BY MEANS OF MANKIND

The most popular form of divination is that which we practise almost unconsciously, whenever we meet someone for the first time. It is said that we all have the innate faculty of being able to sum up the personality of another individual within a millisecond, merely from their outer appearance.

PHYSIOGNOMY is sometimes defined as "divination by means of the face", but is more usually confined to reading character by the face. This is often supported by the notion that certain facial characteristics have had associations with animals (*illustration, page 194*). As an art, it is often included in early magical books, and is an early form of the invented science of PHRENOLOGY, or character reading from the skull-shape.

An important branch of physiognomy was based on the idea that there were seven facial types, linked with the seven planets. The nearest Cocles got to making specific predictions was in connection with the saturnine face, which predisposed the gloomy individual to accidents and a violent death. However, a few cases of divination by physiognomy have been recorded. For example, in 1556 a diviner named Robert Harris impressed the people of Maidstone, Kent, by revealing futurity merely by staring intently into his clients' faces. In the early seventeenth century, John Traske had among his many "novel fancyes" (as a contemporary called Traske's theories) the belief that he could determine whether a man was damned or saved by examining his face.

METOPOSCOPY is the art of divination (and character reading) from the shape and lines upon the forehead. It is really a sub-division of phrenology (*see page 193*), though the latter rarely makes a pretence of divining the future, and is more involved with character-reading.

Man is a complex subject, and a whole battery of divinatory systems have been constructed around his physical body, as around his psyche. Among the most obvious methods are PALMISTRY (*see page 146*) and PSYCHOMANCY. Related to palmistry is ONYCHOMANCY, which is one of the scrying arts, in which the diviner examines the sunlight falling on the nails of the hand, and interprets the images seen therein.

CHIROLOGY is distantly related to palmistry, for it is a form of divination (and character reading) from the hand. This is not merely a branch of palmistry, but something more, for the art emphasizes the study of hand gestures as a useful index of temperament. The seventeenth-century savant John Bulwer used the word to describe the "natural language of the hand", which he had discovered for conveying knowledge to the deaf and dumb by means of hand-gestures. He called the "art of manuall rhetoricke" CHIRONOMIA. Bulwer is also noteworthy for being the first person to observe the capacity which certain deaf people have for "hearing" music through the medium of their teeth.

PALMOMANCY has nothing to do with palmistry, as one might think, but involves the use of a person's palm as a sort of scrying surface (*see catoptromancy, page 207*). The palm is first liberally inked, to produce a richly textured surface which acts as a kind of living Rorschach test. The method is related to ENCROMANCY (a hybrid word of French origin), or divination by means of stains of ink.

PHYSIOGNOMY

The belief in the link between character and the facial features is supported by the idea that some physiognomical types resemble animals. The bovine rustic and the porcine stupid man are illustrated in this lithographic print, based on Delaporta's series of theriomorphic types, from an edition of Collin de Plancy's *Dictionnaire Infernal*, 1875.

SIXTEENTH-CENTURY PHYSIOGNOMY

One of the most important books on physiognomy, which gathered together much of the medieval lore, was *Physiognomia*, written in 1532 by the Italian palmist Barthelemy Cocles. All the numerous woodcut illustrations deal with character interpretation, rather than with futurity. The two women exhibit distinctive noses – the one to the left is revealed as fickle, the one to the right as vain and untruthful. The two men are said to have distinctive eyes – the one to the left is crafty in mien; the other, simple-minded.

ANTHROPOMANCY is perhaps the most bestial of all divinatory practices, and the reverse of necromancy. In this method, a magician will put to death, in the most cruel way imaginable, a man or woman, in order to learn from their freed spirit what they perceived of the future, at the moment of death. This method is closely related to SACRIFICIAL MAGIC, in which pagan priests would kill a human being to propitiate and raise a demonic spirit; the spirit was believed to be possessed of the knowledge of futurity, and would impart it in return for the sacrifice.

Divinations obtained by those in a deep sleep, or in a hypnotic state are called CAROMANCY. In most cases, pronouncements made by mediums while in a state of trance are a form of caromancy. The notion is that when a person sleeps, he or she is astrally free, and may have converse with spirits who, in turn, have access to future events. If the spirit gives information to the sleeper, then this may be transmitted while he or she is still asleep.

CLEPTOMANCY is a misnomer: it is not really a form of divination, but any type of divination by which it is possible to determine the identity of a thief. The method does not predict a future theft, but deals with the past only.

DIVINATION BY MEANS
OF LETTERS AND WORDS

A once-popular form of divination by means of letters and numbers is SPHEROMANCY. Usually, this indicates a form of divination by means of magical spheres, or wheels – sometimes known as CYCLOMANCY. The so-called PYTHAGOREAN SPHERES sometimes called PLATONIC SPHERES, were a method of divination "according to Pythagoras", which was little more than a game of chance. The aim was to establish a number, which would then be referred to a fixed interpretation allegedly relating to the future of the client.

The simplest of such WHEELS OF FORTUNE, as they are sometimes called, is divided into compartments where different numbers are grouped under the heading of Life or Death. The relevant number is determined in a variety of ways – usually by adding together the numerical equivalents of the letters of the person's name, and adding to this the number of the day of the Moon, and other "related" factors. The resultant number is then found in the Wheel, and interpretation of Life or Death is assured. This method was widely used in ancient times to determine the fates of the contestants in gladiatorial combats. It was not because of any real concern for these unfortunates, but because it was usual to place bets on the outcomes of the fights.

By means of these concentrics the magician made calculations from the letters in the name of a person (sometimes considering also the date of birth, etc.) to derive corresponding numbers. The sum of these letters and numerical equivalents would lead, in turn, to short-text reading into futurity. Sometimes, the texts were in the central concentrics, and at other times, they were keyed into pages attached to the wheels. In essence, the method was not far removed from the modern fairground games of hazard, the Wheels of Chance, in which the pull of a lever moves a wheel, which finally comes to rest with a pertinent, or impertinent, dictum regarding the player's personality or destiny. Some of the PYTHAGOREAN WHEELS of popular fortune-telling were consulted by means of the throw of dice. In medieval times, when these volvelles were very popular, it was widely believed that diviners could predict death by interpreting a name. For this reason, some Wheels were sometimes called "wheels of Life and Death". Many famous occultists and philosophers were associated with

SPHEROMANCY

The more sophisticated Wheels of Fortune were drawn on paper and consisted of a series of concentric circles, with the outer concentric marked with letters or numbers, and the inner concentrics carrying simple predictions. In elaborate wheels, in place of fixed concentrics, VOLVELLES (movable circles of paper on a central pivot) were used. One circle bore letters of the alphabet, and the other bore numbers. These chance numbers gave rise to random letters, which in turn spelled out oracles. This method of prediction is still popular.

such wheels, with the result that in medieval times there were spheres associated with such famous men as Petosiris, Apuleius, Plato, Ptolemy, and Democritus.

Some spheres were linked with the power of the Christian saints, rather than with the old magi, or magicians. For example, a Sphere of St. DONATUS has survived from medieval times, and is designed to challenge the whole basis of astrology. This it does by pretending it is possible to determine the sign of the zodiac under which a person was born not by observation of the stars, but by collating the numerical differences between the personal name and the name of his or her mother.

ARITHMOMANCY is the art of divining by means of numbers. This art includes the popular methods by which names are given corresponding numerical values (*see page 46*). Words thus manipulated have arithmetical values, which may be used for establishing correspondences between things (of similar number), and for predicting the outcome of events.

WORKING THE OUIJA

Séance in which the Ouija board is being consulted. The planchette is little more than a board, mounted upon free-running wheels, designed to move in any direction. This is the most popular form of grammatomancy, divination by means of letters.

GRAMMATOMANCY is divination by means of letters. The OUIJA board is the most popular form of grammatomancy, in which a PLANCHETTE, sometimes a BAGUETTE DIVINATOIRE, or diving stick, is used by a medium to spell out messages by means of an alphabet (*above*). Another method is called GYROMANCY, in which a person arranges the letters of the alphabet around himself, and then turns (eyes closed), and moves out at random to choose a letter. Some accounts of the method say that the diviner must fall down, from sheer dizzy exhaustion, to reveal the letter. By whichever means the letter is chosen, it is taken as an oracular response to a question.

This is related to the DIVINATORY CUP, which is a bowl or cup with letters of the alphabet imprinted on the inside. The magician swings a ring on the end of a piece of string inside the bowl, and notes the letters which the ring touches in its circuit. In this way a message is spelled out, and taken as being oracular.

ONOMANCY is a form of divination by means of letters, the numerical equivalents of letters and word-groups.

In former times, BIBLIOMANCY was a very popular form of divination. A person would take a book (usually the Bible, or a breviary) and open it at random. The first sentence upon which the eye fell (or the first complete sentence on the left-hand page) was taken as a response to a given question. This method is sometimes called VIRGILIAN SORTS – since the book used in classical times was by the Roman poet Virgil.

RHAPSODOMANCY is bibliomancy in which books or poetry are used, rather than classical or holy works.

STOICHOMANCY, the art of divining by means of a pin, is really a subdivision of bibliomancy, in which the blindfolded querent or magician, sticks a pin in a text (sometimes, the Bible) opened at random. The marked word relates, as gnomic response, to the question posed. There are many variants of this method.

DIVINATION BY MEANS OF ANIMALS

Within the occult tradition are found an enormous number of divinatory methods based upon the interpretation of the movement, actions and habits of animals. Among these, APANTOMANCY is a method of omen-reading based on the chance meeting with animals, objects, or natural phenomena. In Roman times, the sight of an eagle in flight was regarded as being a sign of good fortune. In medieval Europe, the chance meeting with a hare was interpreted as a sign of ill fortune, as witches were frequently disguised as hares.

The seemingly random movements of animals and birds are also used as a basis for interpreting the future. For example, ALECTROMANCY is the art of predicting the future, or answering questions, by means of a cock. In some methods, a cock is placed in a circle of piles of grain. The pile he first begins to eat is the significator of the response.

In ancient times there was an entire battery of predictive techniques based on the interpretation of the movements of wild animals, called THERIOMANCY. The Romans and Celts were fond of interpreting futurity by observing the direction and manner in which a liberated hare ran. ZOOMANCY was predictions drawn from the appearance of imaginary or psychic animals, such as unicorns, sea-monsters, or salamanders (fire-souls, sometimes called AETNICI).

Divination or augury by means of the flight of birds is ORNITHOMANCY.

Within the category of "random movements" lies the art of MYOMANCY, divination by means of rats or mice. Some magicians interpret by their noises, but the most popular form involves allowing a caged mouse its freedom, and reading futurity in the direction and manner in which it escapes. Others

EVIL OMEN

A ghostly dog runs over Bodmin Tor in the South-west of England. In the popular form of apantomancy, it was regarded as presaging evil to meet such animals, even in the wilds. At one time, it was widely believed that any running hare was a disguised witch, running to the sabbat.

place the mouse or rat in a specially construc-ted maze, and read auguries, or answer questions, according to the escape route the creature takes (*right*).

ICHTHYOMANCY was divination from the movement of fishes. An ancient form of divination involved watching how fish reacted to small pieces of meat thrown into their water; it is possible that Nero was practising this form of divination when he fed the flesh of slaves to his carp. Less kind to fish (but kinder on the slaves) is ichthyomancy by means of the inspection of the entrails of a sacrificed fish.

Some animal-divination verges almost on black magic. For example, CEPHALOMANCY, the art of divining by means of the severed head of an animal, if not black magical, is at least inaesthetic. The head is roasted, and the jaws

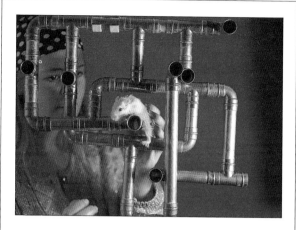

MYOMANCY

MYOMANCY involves divination with the aid of mice or rats. Clearly, a hamster will do just as well as a mouse, for this young lady is placing the creature into the pipe maze, and will draw divinatory conclusions according to the exit chosen by the hamster.

may (or may not) move in response to questions. In the Tchou *Encyclopedie de la Divination*, it is pointed out that in antiquity the heads of humans, as well as of simulacra (images of them), were used in this kind of divination. This may explain the frequency with which masks are used in magical procedures, and the curious stone heads, so erroneously called CELTIC HEADS, which must have been used in amuletic or divinatory rituals.

CHELONIOMANCY is divination by means of the cracks which appear on the surface of a heated, scorched or burned tortoise-shell. This method of divination is believed to have been the precursor of the ancient Chinese system of the I Ching (*see page 163*).

CLAVICULOMANCY, or divination by means of wish-bones of birds, is so popular nowadays that it is scarcely regarded as belonging to the occult tradition. The most popular form is that in which two people pull at a wishbone, which they each hold in a little finger (this is an important part of the ritual, for the little finger is ruled by Mercury, the messenger of spiritual knowledge). The wishbone will break, and the person who holds the larger portion will have good fortune, or should be used to seek futurity by means of a divinatory technique.

On the whole, the ancient colleges of diviners were not interested in animal welfare, and they evolved several forms of divination which involved the sacrifice, or even torture, of animals. For example, HARUSCOPY was divination by means of the entrails and livers of sacrificial victims. This ancient art form has many names, including HIEROMANCY (that is, the "sacred divination"), HEPATOSCOPY, SPLANCHNOMANCY, THYOSCOPY and BOMOSCOPY. The

MACABRE RITUAL

This dramatic woodcut of 1542 shows a magician holding in one hand a skull, in the other an astronomical device, standing in a magical circle. To his right a slaughtered animal, probably a goat, is having its entrails removed, in a hideous display of haruscopy. The entrails will be examined for predictive purposes. Woodcut from Petrarch's *De Remedius Utriusque Fortunae*, 1542.

importance of this form of divination in ancient times is still hinted at in an occult term: one who tells the fortune from omens is called an ARIOLATER, a word which is probably from the Sanskrit hira, which means "entrails". The discovery, in ancient Babylonian cities, of metallic and clay models of livers, with specific areas marked in sacred magical text, indicates that this is one of the oldest divinatory techniques. In Roman times the art of haruscopy was practised only by a chief priest, the HARUSPEX, who is said to have followed a tradition established by the magicians of the ancient Etruscans.

Divination by means of bird's eggs, of which many forms exist, is usually called OOMANCY. In some spell-books we find magicians advised to use only the eggs from a black hen, and, prior to using it for divination, to offer over the egg a large number of spells and orisons (prayers). In some systems, the egg white is used, and, when placed in a suitable receptacle, is employed as a scrying surface. Another method is to place the glair, or egg white, in a jar of water with a pinch of salt. The congealed figure which is formed during the next few hours is then interpreted, in the light of the question posed of the diviner. A version of this is the boiling together of yolk and glair, and the interpretation of the figure which is formed (by chance) when these are turned from the pan onto a plate.

Divination by means of the movement of serpents is OPHIMANCY. The ancient Greek oracle at Delphi was probably the most famous of all ophimantic centres (*right*). Some voodoo cults use snakes in their trance states, by which it is possible to obtain valid predictions, usually of a personal nature.

TERATOMANCY is the art of divining by means of prodigies and monsters, a subdivision of the occult science of PERATOSCOPY, which is divination from strange or unexpected phenomena. This is an art which is rarely practised, but in former times, strange events, the so-called FORTEAN PHENOMENA (such as a rain of frogs or fishes, or strange armies in the skies) were always taken as presage of some future event.

THE DELPHIC ORACLE

The pythoness at Delphi in a mantic fury, (the trancelike state associated with certain forms of divination), clasping at the snakes from which her power was derived. Snakes have been used from very ancient times for their power to confirm divinatory insights, as well as for incubatory sleep-healing, in the ancient Greek and Roman hospitals (incubatory sleep-healing, the main form of healing in ancient times, involved putting the patient to sleep, and then working magically upon his or her free astral and etheric bodies)

DIVINATION BY MEANS OF PLANTS

Divination by means of flour, or cereal grains, is called ALEUROMANCY. One form involves mixing flour with water (not as a dough) in a bowl, and then swilling away the water, to leave random patterns of wet flour, which are interpreted by the diviner. A related form of so-called divination is ALPHITOMANCY in which a suspect is fed with a specially prepared barley loaf: indigestion denotes guilt. This is scarcely divination, however, but a form of ordeal. The method known as CRITOMANCY is an ancient system in which the future is divined from the meal of barley corn, strewn over the bodies of sacrificial animals.

TWO HOMESPUN METHODS OF DIVINATION

Most traditional forms of divination involve the simplest and most readily available of objects – in these two images, flowers and bread are used. (*Top*) Among the most interesting methods of aleuromancy is that recorded in Brittany, France. When the location of a drowned body is sought in the water, the locals place a loaf of bread on the surface, in which a lighted candle or taper has been inserted. The bread is said to float to the place where the body will be found. (*Bottom*) The most frequently used method of floromancy, or prediction with the aid of flowers, is that by which a question is answered (yes or no) by pulling petals from the flower head. "She loves me, she loves me not ... " is the simplest form of this divination.

A popular form of divination is CROMNIOMANCY, a technique based on answering a question by means of onions. The diviner writes certain names on the skins of onions and places these on a church altar on Christmas Day. The onion bulbs are planted in the earth and closely monitored; the first one to sprout gives response in terms of the skins still preserved, revealing the name relating to the question posed.

FLOROMANCY is divination by means of flowers (*left*). Among the many methods used is the simple technique of plucking the petals of a flower, starting with a "yes" for the first petal, a "no" for the next, in the same sequence until the last petal is plucked. This final response is the answer to the question posed. Linked with floromancy is PHYLLOMANCY, divination by leaves – from their movement, and by the smoke patterns left by their burning.

RHABDOMANCY (*right*) is divination by means of sticks, the latter of which are sometimes called after the French term, *baguettes*. In fact, rhabdomancy really has nothing to do with divination, but is an occult means of seeking out hidden things. The term DOWSING is now more accurately used in place of rhabdomancy for those practices which are not concerned with predicting the future. In medieval times, rhabdomancy was widely used as a reliable means of searching for water or for underground seams of silver. Dowsing may be done with sticks or with pendulums, though the use of the latter is sometimes called RADIESTHESIA. In modern times a wide range of different pendulums have been

THE DOWSER, AYMAR

The famous seventeenth-century French dowser Jacques Aymar, who could trace murderers over long distances with his "baguette", merely from a sample of their blood. His extraordinary success lifted the art of rhabdomancy, or dowsing, to a different plane. From Pierre de la Lorrain's *La Physique Occult*, 1693.

designed for specialist radiesthesic work, including the so-called WITNESS PENDULUMS. These have a special bowl inside their metal bodies, wherein tiny samples of the thing sought may be placed, to aid the diviner in his or her search.

In the art of SIDEROMANCY, or divination by straws, the diviner throws a number of straws upon red-hot irons, and divination is made from the straws' movements and undulations as they burn.

DIVINATION BY SPIRITS AND DEMONS

In former times, it was widely argued that all divination was governed by demons, through the art of DEMONOMANCY. (For the names of certain individual demons who are associated with demonomancy, *see page 206*.) It was argued, for example, that the seemingly random fall of the dice was not accidental, but manipulated by demons. When statues were made to speak, then it was neither the power of the magicians, nor the artifice of the priests, but the workings of the demons which gave forth the raucous sounds that were translated as relating to futurity.

In those cases where the activities of humans were used as a basis for divination, there was much argument as to whether the good spirits or the bad were involved. For example, epilepsy, which was often used for making predictions about the future, was widely regarded as a holy illness, in which the fortunate sufferer was used as a dwelling by the gods. However, Constantinus Africanus records that the general populace called epilepsy and insanity DIVINATIO (the divining art) and accounted for them as possession by demons.

Some of the Chinese texts are insistent that the I CHING or Book of Changes, is the only method of divination which is protected from the operation of the demons – all other methods may be used by the inferior or infernal beings to their own ends.

A fascinating book on magic, the PIXATRIX (which claims that it deals with the very roots of the magical art, "the secrets of the ancient sages"), tells us that it was CARAPHREBIM who invented the magical arts, including the art of divination. The *Pixatrix* recognizes the importance of invocation in all the magical arts in which spirits (of whatever spiritual persuasion) are invited to participate.

The rituals for such invocations are complicated. To evoke one spirit, for example, the ritual must be conducted when the Moon is in the first degree of Aries – which effectively leaves a window of only two hours in any given month for what proves to be a complicated ritual. Another magical ritual, involved with drawing down the power of the Moon (though nothing to do with the ritual of DRAWING DOWN THE MOON of modern wicca – *see page 104*) involves the beheading of a cock with a sharp athame, or ritual knife, made from bone. As culmination of this lunar ritual, a man of good aspect appears as from nowhere, and will answer questions put to him. There is little doubt that this gentleman is from the lower regions.

Properly speaking, NECROMANCY should be divination by means of the dead. While some magicians have resorted to digging up cadavers to use as instruments for their art, in general the word is misused to denote "divination by means of the shades or souls of the dead" (*right*). One recorded example of this is the case of the English politician Goodwin Wharton, who was at one time Lord of the Admiralty. Wharton spent a great deal of his

SCIOMANCY

Conjuring the shade of a newly dead person. This engraving of 1812 illustrates the sciomancy practised by the Elizabethan magician Edward Kelly, and his assistant Paul Waring, in Walton-le-Dale (Lancashire) churchyard. The purpose behind resurrecting the soul of the departed was to learn from him the whereabouts of his lost riches. From Ebenezer Sibly's *The Science of Astrology, or Complete Illustration of the Occult Sciences*, 1812.

life hunting for hidden treasure, using almost any means at his disposal. On one occasion, he and a friend, John Wildman, used the spirit of an executed felon to help in a search through the government building Somerset House in London and its extensive grounds for treasure. Using the same discarnate spirit, they hunted specifically for the lost magical breastplate of the Jewish High Priest of the Temple. Their necromancy was in vain: perhaps their spirit, named George, was an unwilling partner.

This type of divination is really SCIOMANCY, divination by means of shades of the dead, or PSYCHOMANCY (*see page 194*), and versions of it seem to exist in virtually every culture. In reality, it is a form of black magic, and most of those who seek to raise "spirits", in the belief that these are the spirits of the dead, may really be practising demonomancy.

One of the greatest of all clairvoyants, the American seer Andrew Jackson Davis, warned of the deceptive belief that the spirits raised in seances are actually the personages (or ex-personages) they claim to be. Davis invented a special name for such

THE DEMON GOMORY

Gomory is one of the few demons to appear in a relatively pleasing form, when first commanded. This demon manifests as a lovely female, riding a camel, and is conjured by demonologists because she will grant knowledge concerning the future and past – and also because she has the ability to grant power over women. Wood engraving from Collin de Plancy's *Dictionnaire Infernal*, 1864.

invading usurpers from the spiritual space, calling them DIAKKAS, who preyed on the life-forces of their "earthly victims" – those who conduct seances without the requisite knowledge.

The ancient grimoires, or black DEVIL-BOOKS, include lists of demons who are especially adept at predicting the future. For scrying, the demon FLORIGET is recommended. Certain demons have the reputation for revealing all secrets of the divinatory arts. FURCAS, who appears in the form of a man riding a pale horse, teaches specific divinatory arts, such as chiromancy and pyromancy. CAIM, who appears disconcertingly in bird-form, is generally prepared to give information about future events. VINE, who has the terrible appearance of a lion riding a black horse, with a viper in his hand, will tell of "things present, past, and to come". GOMORY, one of the rare demons who appears in a pleasant form, as a woman riding a camel (*above*), answers "well and truelie of things present, past and to come". The demon FLAUROS, who appears in a leopard form, has a deserved reputation for lying, yet conjurers still raise him in order to gain knowledge of futurity. Most grimoires hedge their bets, even with the more "reliable" demons, by insisting that the words of the fallen angels cannot be trusted, so their predictions may well be false.

The use of the especially attuned psyche to read into futurity is sometimes called PSYCHOMANCY. Since most diviners and mediums use their psyche in this way, it is probably true to say that virtually all forms of divination are rooted in psychomancy. Properly speaking, the term should be limited to divination by means of communication with the SOULS of the dead – those in a psychic condition.

PSYCHOMETRY, which originally meant measuring the soul, now relates to divination by means of the examination of physical objects, with the aim of contacting the psychic aura of things or people who have been in contact with those objects. Some psychometers will offer to read the history of a room from the PSYCHIC MEMORY of a stone in a wall of that room. Again, a sensitive may read the life-history of an individual who has written a letter, merely from touching that letter. Psychometry is not so much concerned with futurity, however, since it involves prying into the hidden past.

DIVINATION BY MEANS OF METALS AND ROCKS

The art of seeing future events, visions and images (which may also relate to the past and present) in reflective surfaces is called SCRYING. The most popular form of scrying is crystallomancy (*see page 168*), but dark polished surfaces, called SHEW-STONES, or SCRYING GLASSES, are used in a similar manner. As we have seen, some magicians manufacture small bowls, which they fill with black ink, and use as the equivalent of shew-stones, claiming to see visions in the reflective surface of the liquid. These bowls are sometimes called SHEW-BOWLS, or SCRYING BOWLS, and are often manufactured in bizarre designs.

Related to the use of shew-stones or scrying is CATOPTROMANCY, divination by means of mirrors. The "mirror" may be artificially manufactured – such as a sheet of water, in a vase – as in castronomancy. The MAGIC MIRRORS of the medieval magicians were really catoptromantic devices. The word NECTROMANCY is a more modern equivalent term, in the practice of which the psychic images are called FLAGAE.

The medieval text on magic entitled the PIXATRIX gives a complicated recipe for making a reliable magic mirror for scrying, involving the use of seven (the magical seven, which appears in so many magical spells) rejects from the human body – blood, tears,

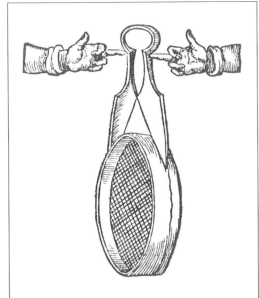

TURNING THE SIEVE

Coscinomancy is divination by means of a round wooden sieve, held in the air by two participants by means of pairs of metal shears or scissors. At the mention of a guilty name, or a particular name important to the question in hand, the sieve will begin to turn. Responses to questions may be established in this way. This appears to have been a favourite technique for determining the identity of a thief in medieval times (*see* Cleptomancy, *page 195*). The French, who sometimes use the term coscinomancy, often refer to it as *tourner le sas*, or "turning the sieve". The diagram is from the posthumously published writings of the great Agrippa, who was convinced that the sieve turned at the command of demons. Not all occultists agree as to how the sieve should be balanced, or even how it works.

earwax, spittle, sperm, urine and excrement. These items are burned, and the fumes are allowed to play over the surface of the mirror, to infuse it with magical virtue. Presumably, this is an attempt to form a magical connection, a sympathy, between the mirror and the diviner – yet the ritual could also be a throwback to an ancient sacrificial rite, in which the smoke of sacrificial victims was used in a special type of divination.

The thirteenth-century savant Michael Scot recommended water, ice and mirrors as suitable surfaces for scrying, but tended to see these as falling under the heading of hydromancy (*see page 190*). Just like the English magus (or magician), Dr. John Dee, Scot maintained that scrying should be done in a secret place, and that the visions should be seen by a young child ("a virgin of five or seven years old"), who would describe to the magician what he or she had seen. A particularly distasteful element in Scot's instructions is that the divinatory session should begin with a conjuration over human blood or bones, with a mumbo-jumbo conjuration intended to attract the divining spirit Floriget.

A different form of divining by means of metals is ACUTOMANCY, or divination by means of sharp or pointed objects, such as needles. In some methods, the diviner allows a number of needles (usually about seven) to fall onto a table, and reads from the pattern they make, taking these as a response to a given question. A related form of divination is stoichomancy (*see page 198*).

Divination by means of an axe is called AXINOMANCY. It is not practised nowadays, but in the past several different techniques existed, among which the most interesting was that in which a magician chopped the head of an axe deeply into wood, and then read futurity from the vibrations which followed. Yet another method, practised in ancient Greece, was to place an agate stone on the face of a red-hot axehead. The motion of the stone was interpreted as relating to the future.

CLEIDOMANCY is the art of divining by means of a key. The key is suspended from the nail of a girl's third finger, and will revolve in response to questions. A related divinatory art is DACTYLIOMANCY, divination with the aid of rings, hung from threads. The word is from the Greek *dactylios*, for "finger ring". Usually the ring is hung over the top of a basin, around the interior of which have been placed letters of the alphabet. The ring will swing in the hand, and from time to time tap against a letter, eventually spelling out a message "from the spirit world" in response to a question. This is an ancient equivalent of the more popular OUIJA board (*see page 197*).

IDOLOMANCY, which we have already discussed, is a form of metal – or stone-divination, involving the use of idols or images for the purpose of divining the future. In ancient times, when the temple priests were trained in the art of making AUTOMATA, huge metal or stone statues were made to come to life, and make utterances about the future. Besides the evidence of such man–made oracles, there was a widespread belief that spirits could be made to dwell in statues, and that these could be made to reveal secrets of futurity. A closely related term is AGALMATOMANCY,

IDOLOMANCY

It is believed that performing a ritual before a statue will in some cases cause it to either speak or move, to give response to questions. In other cases, it is believed that the statue, when informed of the wishes of the diviner, will invisibly cause an answer to be given.

divination by means of statues. The word is from the Greek *agalma*, meaning "figure".

On a smaller scale, there is MARGARITOMANCY, divination by means of a pearl. According to the French judge Pierre de Ancre, who boasted of burning over six hundred witches, the pearl must first be enchanted (perhaps dedicated to a fairy or a demon), and shut up inside an earthenware pot. When the name of a thief is pronounced (even by chance), the pearl will leap around, and strike against the sides of its container. In fact, de Ancre is too specific, for there are many different forms of pearl-divining, including the use of the pearl as a scrying instrument (*see page 193*).

MOLYBDOMANCY is divination by means of melted lead. Some say that the diviner reads from the patterns formed by the lead as it drops into water, and congeals. Others say that the diviner makes pronouncements from the hissings the lead makes as it drops through the water.

KEY WORD INDEX